THE ESSENTIAL
HUMPHREY BOGART

THE ESSENTIAL HUMPHREY BOGART

Constantine Santas

ROWMAN & LITTLEFIELD
Lanham • Boulder • New York • London

Published by Rowman & Littlefield
A wholly owned subsidiary of The Rowman & Littlefield Publishing Group, Inc.
4501 Forbes Boulevard, Suite 200, Lanham, Maryland 20706
www.rowman.com

Unit A, Whitacre Mews, 26-34 Stannary Street, London SE11 4AB

British Library Cataloguing in Publication Information Available

Library of Congress Cataloging-in-Publication Data

Santas, Constantine.
 The essential Humphrey Bogart / Constantine Santas.
   pages cm
 Includes bibliographical references and index.
 ISBN 978-1-4422-6093-1 (hardback : alk. paper) — ISBN 978-1-4422-6094-8
(ebook) 1. Bogart, Humphrey, 1899-1957—Criticism and interpretation. I. Title.
 PN2287.B48S34 2016
 791.4302'8092—dc23

                                                              2015034030

Printed in the United States of America

To my brother, Gerasimos

CONTENTS

ACKNOWLEDGMENTS

I would like to express my gratitude to Professor Gerasimos Santas of the University of California, Irvine, for reading large sections of the book and offering useful suggestions on the readability of the text. Also thanks to Professor James M. Wilson for allowing me to teach films of Bogart in his classes and to test ideas from the book in classroom discussions. Also thanks to Joseph M. Dmohowski, librarian at Whittier College, for providing me a list of potential reviewers, and Harikleia Sirmans, from Valdosta Public Library, for compiling the index.

INTRODUCTION

The countless books, articles, reviews, and online comments that have been written about Humphrey Bogart's life and work testify to his longevity and legacy in the cinema of the last sixty-plus years since his death in 1957. But most of these works center on the great classics—*The Maltese Falcon, Casablanca, The Treasure of Sierra Madre, The African Queen*, and a handful of others. The purpose of this book is to broaden the scope of the study of Bogart's work by offering a close analysis of a good number of others, including several from his early period in the 1930s and others from the 1940s and 1950s, films by and large left behind either because of sheer neglect or lack of availability. Such films as *Dead End, The Enforcer*, and *Battle Circus*, to mention a few, were not available on DVD until 2012, and even Blu-ray versions of classic films were late in coming. The Warner Bros. Archives Collection has brought to the surface forgotten movies of merit (*The Left Hand of God* is a notable example), allowing today's viewer to broaden his or her knowledge of the Bogart oeuvre. Streaming in outlets such as Netflix, Google, and Amazon also offers the viewer a chance to study Bogart's work with the aid of commentaries by film historians, critics, moviemakers, and online reviewers. Of the grand opus of Bogart's eighty-one movies (including shorts), thirty-eight are included here. Only ten of those come from the 1930s period, but a substantial number of his 1940s and 1950s movies are included, with none of the classics left out.

This is not a biography of Bogart. That task has been compellingly achieved by several biographers, including his wife, Lauren Bacall, in *Lauren Bacall by Myself*; his son, Stephen Humphrey Bogart, in *Bogart: In Search of My Father*; Nathaniel Benchley, in *Humphrey Bogart*; and A. E. Sperber and

Eric Lax, in the monumental *Bogart*—to mention some of the most important sources used for this book. The aim of *The Essential Humphrey Bogart* is to evaluate the work of Humphrey Bogart as an actor by a close examination of his most significant movies during the most productive years of his career. The films selected for this task include all his major works, mostly those of the decade between 1941 and 1951, along with many others less famous but nevertheless essential in showing Bogart's evolution as an actor. Bogart's screen persona evolved through the decades, from the juvenile roles he played in the early 1930s; to the gangsters, killers, and hoods he was forced to play when under contract to Warner Bros. until the end of that decade; to the sharp turn his movie career took in the early 1940s, when he became the superstar with classic works such as *The Maltese Falcon*, *Casablanca*, and many others to follow. The path that Bogart followed shows his versatility as an actor, his ability to adjust and refine his screen image as it progressed from that of a hood to lover, patriot, sharp-eyed detective, writer, lawyer, prospector, and even priest. No matter what the mask, Bogart showed he could handle any role, revealing his total mastery of the art of acting. He took his art with utter seriousness, was proud to be an actor, and followed his motto "to keep working," which eventually brought him recognition and continued esteem among his fans and peers. The selected films here are meant to show how Bogart's art progressed and matured with nearly every film he attempted to the very end.

Bogart's work continues to attract audiences today, something that can be ascribed, at least partly, to the digital age, which has enabled contemporary viewers to rediscover both Bogart's classics and his second-tier but still viewable works. Since 1997, when the original version of *The Big Sleep* (1945) was released, scores of as-yet-unknown-to-the-public Bogart works—among theme *In a Lonely Place* (1950), *The Enforcer* (1951), *Battle Circus* (1953), *The Left Hand of God* (1955), and *The Harder They Fall* (1956)—have been issued on DVD and subsequently on Blu-ray. The increasing availability of Bogart films on DVD and Blu-ray, streaming on various outlets such as Netflix and Amazon, and through the release of older classics from Warner Bros. Archive Collections has brought about what one might call a Bogart renaissance.

In this discussion of Bogart's classics and other significant movies, every entry examines important film highlights and draws relevant biographical materials from the aforementioned biographical sources and other materials, such as critical appraisals and DVD/Blu-ray commentaries. Though Bogart's life is connected to his movie career and is an essential part of it, it is the movies themselves that above all still attract audiences and continue his legacy as one of the legendary actors of Hollywood. Aside from a biographical sketch and a description of the characteristics of his movie persona, our discussions will center on the movies that demonstrate these characteristics. The book has a full Bogart filmography, related documentations citing sources, and a selected bibliography.

A BIOGRAPHICAL NOTE

Humphrey DeForest Bogart was born on Christmas Day in 1899 and died on January 14, 1957, a relatively short span of an extremely eventful life, during which he rose to be one of the greatest stars in American cinema. His father, Belmont DeForest Bogart, was an affluent physician, and his mother, Maud Bogart, was a renowned painter and an illustrator of children's books. The family lived in New York City, where Dr. Bogart practiced, but moved to their summer residence in Canandaigua Lake, in west New York State, where young Humphrey and his two younger sisters, Frances and Catherine, mixed and played with other children of the elite neighborhood of Seneca Point. Bogart attended Trinity School in New York City and later transferred to the Andover Academy in Massachusetts, one of the oldest and most distinguished prep schools in the country. He was dismissed for lack of discipline, and at the age of eighteen, he joined the US Navy, when the First World War was nearly over. When he was released, at the age of nineteen, he returned to New York, aimless and without work. His family's fortune had nearly vanished due to his father's poor investments and declining health, and young Bogart found himself in diminished social status. He still had no clue as to what his future would be.

After several failed attempts to enter the business world, Bogart found employment as a stage manager and gradually advanced to acting roles on Broadway, where he established a stage career that lasted until the end of the decade. His good looks—he was called a young Valentino—and his work ethic helped him gain steady employment, and he gradually found a place for himself on the New York stage, usually in juvenile roles. Bogart also enjoyed the high life of the Jazz Age and tasted its many pleasures, especially as a visitor in the speakeasies, where he and his friends drank through the night. This started his addiction to alcohol, a habit that dogged him throughout his life and led, along with heavy smoking, to his early death. Bogart's successes on Broadway were at best ephemeral, and his career as a screen actor was late in coming. But he was a hard worker, highly motivated, ambitious, and resilient. He developed qualities for himself that aided his career in unexpected ways: for example, playing chess for a living at the height of the Depression sharpened his wits, helping him appear strategic on the screen, as in the opening shots of *Casablanca* where he is seen playing a game by himself. He was a voracious reader of good books, could cite passages from Plato and Shakespeare, and his socializing with writers gave him an intuitive knack for quality screenplays. Laconic by nature, Bogart could develop a point without lapses of logic, and this is evident when, often without the aid of a script, he could improvise on the set (though he made no habit of this) or remember lines even after a severe bout of drinking.

His transition to Hollywood was slow, and it took many years before it materialized into a successful career. Bogart shuffled back and forth between New York and Hollywood from 1930 to 1935, making a few forgettable movies, until a big break came when, on the insistence of Leslie Howard, Warner Bros. signed him up to play the role of Duke Mantee in Robert E. Sherwood's *The Petrified Forest*, which had been a smash hit on Broadway. The solid success of the play and the ensuing rave reviews brought him a long-term contract with Warners, where he was to be tied to for the next decade. Warner Bros. was a studio known for its quality gangster movies but also for its production-line B quickies, to which Bogart was relegated for the first six years of his contract there. He was almost always given second or third billing to the established stars in that flourishing genre—James Cagney, Edward G. Robinson, George Raft, and Paul Muni—who had priority over him. Those were hard years for Bogart. His father died of addiction to morphine and left debts behind, which Bogart undertook to honor. He also had the heavy burden of supporting his mother, who by that time had lost the glamor of her elite status as an artist, and his two sisters, Catherine (Kay), who died of alcoholism in her thirties, and Frances (Pat), who had been hospitalized with a mental illness and was taken care of by her brother to the end of her life. Bogart undertook to honor these additional family burdens at a time when his income as an actor was still minimal.

While on Broadway, Bogart had married actress Helen Mencken in 1926, but they divorced a year and a half later. His second wife was Mary Philips, a distinguished Broadway actress who had trouble staying with him once he moved to the West Coast and was frequently absent. Finally, they were divorced, and Bogart married Mayo Methot, an able and successful screen actress, but that marriage also proved a disaster, as Methot's career began to decline at the time while Bogart's was beginning to take off. After his third divorce, in 1945, Bogart finally found his match in Lauren Bacall, after they fell in love during the making of Howard Hawks's *To Have and*

Have Not. Bacall gave him two children, Stephen and Leslie, and the happy married life for which he had yearned for many years. Born in a Victorian era, Bogart was brought up to believe a husband ought to support his wife, and though Bacall rose to stardom almost immediately, Bogart had by that time gained both precedence and fame, and he and Bacall were deeply in love and proved compatible.

Bogart's second big break came when Bogart was assigned to play Roy Earle, in W. R. Burnett's *High Sierra*, a role that both Paul Muni and George Raft had turned down. The screenplay was written by John Huston, who liked Bogart, and the two men started a close collaboration and a friendship that continued for many years. Though Bogart received second billing to Ida Lupino, this was the first time that he appeared in the leading credits in a major movie. A string of successes followed, starting with *The Maltese Falcon* (1941), directed and adapted from the Dashiell Hammett novel by John Huston, who also directed several other movies with Bogart in later years. After *Casablanca* (1942) had catapulted Bogart to superstardom, a succession of major movies, including *The Big Sleep* (1946) and *The Treasure of Sierra Madre* (1948), made Bogart the highest paid star in Hollywood by the end of the decade.

The decade of the 1940s was not free from trouble, however. Bogart, who was an ardent follower of Franklin D. Roosevelt, was disturbed by the sudden turn of the country to the right and the tensions that resulted from the emergence of the Soviet Union as a super power and the consequent fear of communism penetrating the social fabric in America. As many screen writers had been members of the Communist Party before the war, Hollywood was regarded as the seat of subversive forces, especially among the writers and directors. Many of them were brought to testify before HUAC (House Un-American Activities Committee) and were blacklisted and banned from active service; ten of these screenwriters also served prison sentences. Movies made during the war, when America and the Soviet Union were allies, were looked upon with suspicion—for instance, *Mission to Moscow* (1942), which gave praise to Soviet fighters and which Jack L. Warner, a Roosevelt supporter, had to denounce.

Bogart, a Roosevelt liberal although not politically active, felt, as did many others, that these investigations were an infringement on free speech, joined the Committee for the First Amendment (CFA), and, with a group of other Hollywood celebrities—among them Paul Henreid, June Havoc, Richard Conte, Danny Kaye, and his wife, Lauren Bacall—marched to Washington in protest in October 1947. Though crowds were impressed by the presence of the actor who had played Sam Spade, Philp Marlowe, and

Rick Blaine, the CFA quickly disbanded under increasing pressure from HUAC, and Bogart, to save his career, made a declaration that he was not a communist and that his actions had been "a mistake."

Bogart continued to make movies. *Key Largo* (1948) and *The Treasure of Sierra Madre* (1948) were followed by seven produced by his own company, Santana Productions: five with him in the lead—*Knock on Any Door* (1949), *Tokyo Joe* (1949), the distinguished *In a Lonely Place* (1950), *Sirocco* (1951), and *Beat the Devil* (1954)—and two others, *And the Party Makes Three* (1949) and *The Family Secret* (1951), without him in the cast. Subsequently, he made movies for several other studios, some of which became classics: *The African Queen* (1951), which brought him his only Oscar for Best Actor, and *The Caine Mutiny* (1954), which gave him a third nomination, although he lost to Marlon Brando in *On the Waterfront*.

During these productive years, however, Bogart was battered by personal tragedies—the deaths of his father, mother, and his sister Catherine; the permanent disabilities of his sister Frances; and three painful divorces—and his unrelenting smoking and drinking also took their toll. His health had been rapidly deteriorating, and he died of cancer of the esophagus on January 14, 1957.

BOGART'S SCREEN PERSONA

The screen image of Bogart will be examined in detail in the discussions of his movies (see the complete list in the contents), but some of the general characteristics of his screen persona are outlined here.

Tough Guy

Bogart was a tough guy, and his screen image is built around that concept. Whether as hero or villain, Bogart looked like a man who would not go down easily, physically or otherwise. In *The Maltese Falcon*, when Barton MacLane, a much larger man playing a cop, hits him, Bogart (as Sam Spade) steps backward, but he does not fall. A similar scene is repeated in *The Big Sleep*—when Lundgren punches him, Marlowe withstands the blow, dares Lundgren to pick up his gun, and then kicks him in the mouth, knocking him unconscious. Had Marlowe fallen backward, he would have given a huge advantage to his opponent. The toughness is mental, but it is reflected in his characters' faces and bodily movements. Bogart's face, handsome in his early career, is gradually lined; his eyebrows grow thicker;

his forehead becomes wrinkled; his voice, despite his famous lisp, quite resonant. Though not athletic looking, he could dish out a punch, and better yet, he could fire a gun at an opponent with steely precision; for example, as Frank McCloud he dispatches Edward G. Robinson's character, Johnny Rocco, with several shots after luring him out of a boat cabin in *Key Largo*. (The opposite happens in *Bullets or Ballots* when after being shot first, Robinson, as Johnny Blake, retaliates with a string of bullets, making sure Bogart's character is finished before he himself expires.) But as Raymond Chandler once observed, Bogart "could be tough without a gun." As a detective licensed to carry a weapon, in both *The Maltese Falcon* and *The Big Sleep*, Bogart's character doesn't. In both these movies he is seen easily taking guns away from characters like Joe Brody, Joel Cairo, and the "gunsel," a hood played by Elisa Cook Jr. But when compelled to exchange shots, he rarely misses.

A Loner

With the exception of a few movies, Bogart appears as a man without family connections of any specific social class. He can do both if needed (in *Black Legion* his character has a wife and child; in *Sabrina*, he is a high-class tycoon), but in his major movies he seems to be unconnected, his past a blank or vague. As detectives Sam Spade (*The Maltese Falcon*) and Philip Marlowe (*The Big Sleep*), nothing is said of his past, except for a laconic response to General Sternwood—"Nothing much to say: I'm thirty-eight, some college, I can still speak English when my job demands it." In *Casablanca* we only know that Bogart's character is an expatriate for vague reasons, and we are only told that he ran guns to Spanish rebels and to Ethiopia, always to the losing side. In *Sahara*, a war movie, when asked where he is from, his character says, "No place. Just the army." Occasionally, Bogart will get the girl at the end—especially in the four movies he made with his wife, Lauren Bacall—but on the whole he enters and exits a loner figure. He seems unconnected to the point of abstraction, like an ancient deity that visits the world on his own terms only, and then exits when a task is accomplished. Bogart appears self-centered, yet he often evolves, taking up a cause and shedding his neutrality when pressed by circumstances. "I stick my neck out for nobody" is the phrase in *Casablanca*, but this aloof mask drops when he does. That happens mostly in his major films, for these better scripts allow him to develop, moving in either direction—from indifference to heroism, as in *Casablanca*, *To Have and Have Not*, and *Key Largo*, or from ordinariness to self-destruction, as in *Black*

Legion, In a Lonely Place, The Treasure of Sierra Madre, The Caine Mutiny, or *The Desperate Hours.*

Professional Code

This code applies both to Bogart's work ethic in real life and to his screen characters. During his early years at Warners, Bogart was cast in second-string roles that consigned him to hood or heavy, yet he adhered to his work ethic "to keep working," slowly building a screen persona that would enable him to branch out to bigger roles. His screen characters were sometimes compared to those of Hemingway, especially that of Harry Morgan in Hemingway's *To Have and Have Not,* which became the basis for the movie. Bogart's actual live persona, however, and often that of his movie characters, was a far cry from that of Hemingway. The latter was expansive, gregarious, an avid adventurer seen in the bullrings in Pamplona, Spain, or as a big-game hunter in Africa; a fisherman; and a traveler. Bogart, on the other hand, traveled mostly when professional obligations demanded, and mainly in the United States, and his usual hangouts were spots where he imbibed profusely with close friends, for the most part writers whom he admired. His screen code, however, assumed the motto of Hemingway's heroes—"grace under pressure." Bogart's characters were often in a tight spot, where principle demanded that they act in a certain way. An example is *The Maltese Falcon,* where the character's professional code demands that he turn in the killer of his partner, the woman he loves.

Getting Out of a Predicament

The Bogart character was known for his ability to get out of a tight spot unharmed. He had a nimble mind that enabled him to slip out of predicaments in a way that might have doomed others. Consider *The Maltese Falcon,* where Gutman's gang had Bogart (as Sam Spade) cornered—in his own apartment, no less—and he holds his own knowing that he had what they wanted, the falcon. In that movie, Gutman (Sidney Greenstreet) aptly calls him "a man of many resources," envying his abilities, which his cohorts lacked. Something similar happens in *Across the Pacific,* when the same Greenstreet tries to entice him into treasonous activity by offering him money and fake sympathy. Getting Laszlo and Ilsa out of Casablanca puts Bogart (as Rick Blaine) and others in extreme peril, yet Blaine manages to stay cool and play out his game, moving the pawns as the expert chess player that Bogart was. In *Key Largo,* trapped by a storm and forced by Rocco and his gang to take them to Cuba, McCloud knows that his chances of getting out alive are minimal—one against five. Yet after he lulls them into a sense of safety, he masterminds their demise and his own escape. Many more examples of this are offered in the discussion of movies in this book.

Patriotism

A distinction needs to be made between Bogart's patriotism in real life and his screen persona. In real life, Bogart served in the navy during World War I and volunteered to serve in the Coast Guard in Los Angeles as soon as the United States entered World War II after Pearl Harbor. For several weeks in November 1943, he toured war locations in Italy and North and West Africa, including the actual Casablanca, entertaining the troops along with his then wife Mayo Methot and a few friends. On-screen, Bogart appeared in a string of patriotic movies during and several years after the war, among them *All Though the Night* (a movie made just before *Casablanca*), in which Nazis and Fifth Columnists threaten to sink a warship in New York Harbor; *Across the Pacific*, in which his character singled-handedly razes a platoon of Japanese soldiers; *To Have and Have Not*, where his character sides with the cause of the French underground resistance; *Sahara*, in North Africa, in which his character commandeers a tank and its crew through German lines; *Key Largo*, as a war hero who finally acts like one to defend a hotel owner and his daughter from a gang of hoods; and *Tokyo Joe*, in which his character risks his life to save an innocent life and in the process uncovers a conspiracy to foment a rising in American-occupied postwar Japan.

Screen Charisma

In star power, Bogart matches the four or five superstars of his era: Clark Gable, Jimmy Stewart, Cary Grant, and Henry Fonda, to mention some of the most prominent. While the aforementioned were usually open-minded, gregarious, and talkative, and had the good looks to match, Bogart was small in size, introverted, and later in his career he looked worn down and in poor health—as indeed he was. For the most part, he remained reticent, speaking only when he had to, but he was listened to when he spoke. His foremost ability as an actor was to be convincing in the role he played—good or bad guy. In *Conflict*, Bogart played a deranged wife killer, and his costar Rose Hobart, his screen wife, notes that, "When we shot the thing where he *did* kill me, he was scary—he really was. I screamed bloody murder."[1] In *In a Lonely Place* as Dixon Steele, he nearly stones to death a driver who protested the damage done to his car, and in *The Caine Mutiny*, Bogart is unforgettable as the neurotic Captain Queeg breaking down in court as he rolls steel balls through his fingers. In *The African Queen*, he is a river tramp, stupefied by drink but gradually settling into commonsense and even heroic status, after Katharine Hepburn throws the bottles with booze away. And as Rick Blaine, he made female hearts palpitate and males fantasize that they, too, could be loved by the celestial Ilsa.

Versatility

Film historian David Thomson calls Bogart "a limited actor, not quite honest with himself."[2] Leaving aside the vagueness of this statement, the word *limited* does not truly apply to Bogart. The facts speak for themselves. For the first six years at Warners, Bogart did not really have a choice over the roles he played—hoods, villains, heavies of all kinds, and generally unappealing characters. Yet with all these varieties of characters, Bogart did not seem to be compromised. He was a trained stage actor, and as is seen in his first significant film *The Petrified Forest*, he had honed the character of Duke Mantee in its Broadway stage production before he was called to repeat it on the screen. He was a hard worker and a conscientious actor who took advantage of his lengthy servitude to second or third (or fifth) billing to develop his skills and his unique stage presence. Among others, he played a blue-collar worker (*Black Legion*), a lawyer (*Marked Woman, Knock on Any Door*), a prize-fighter trainer (*Kid Galahad*), a cowboy (*The Oklahoma Kid*), an Irish horse trainer (*Dark Victory*), a truck driver (*They Drive by Night*). When he became a big star in the 1940s and '50s, his versatility expanded: his known roles as a detective, which somehow stereotyped him, as Sam Spade (*The Maltese Falcon*) and Philip Marlowe (*The Big Sleep*); a café owner Rick Blaine (*Casablanca*); the owner of a fish boat (*To Have and Have Not*); a Hollywood writer, twice (*In a Lonely Place, The Barefoot Contessa*); a gold prospector (*The Treasure of Sierra Madre*); a navy captain (*The Caine Mutiny*); a warrior and tank commander (*Sahara*); a tycoon (*Sabrina*); and even a priest (*The Left Hand of God*). That leaves out quite a few other roles, but the point is that Bogart from beginning to end worked hard to play all these parts in his unique style, capable of metamorphosis, as any good actor would, but underneath each role was the same Bogart, tough to bring down, capable of enduring hardship, owning to his own inner force, almost incapable of hamming up any role for the sake of playing it, and always coming out true to himself, even as the costumes changed. Bogart accommodated himself to any role, even one he didn't want (and there were many of those) out of professional pride. Hal Wallis, a producer at Warners, said that "whether he played killers or detectives, Bogart was to remain Bogart."[3] And he kept honing his skills, whatever the scripts or directors, to the very end.

Ambiguity

In their biography of Bogart, Sperber and Lax speak of Bogart's "moral ambiguity" as a character, and they entertain the notion that Bogart's early roles as a heavy enabled him to remain ambiguous when he started playing heroes.[4] Their example is *The Maltese Falcon*. There, as Sam Spade, Bogart first appears as an amoral character running a detective firm, but he is having an affair with his partner's wife. When Spade is dealing with seductress Brigid O'Shaughnessy, we are never certain whether he has real feelings for her or wants to pursue the search for the falcon for personal gain. Those notions are cleared at the end, when he says to her, "I am not as crooked as I seem to be," and then later makes a short and emphatic speech that he has to do something after his partner is killed. He sends her to the gallows, but not before he has said, "I'm not going to be the sap for you." That means his motives had not been fully explained: justice, yes, but me first, too. Bogart, in real life and on the screen, was a survivor, and the "kill or be killed" motto he had practiced for years before his ascent to stardom had conditioned him to tiptoe the fine line between life and death.

Another example may be the most obvious one: in *Casablanca*, Rick Blaine is generally described as a patriot who sacrificed love for a higher purpose. But what are the facts? When Rick first sees Ilsa in his establishment with a tall European aristocrat at her side, he is shocked, pained, and above all, jealous. After a flashback showing their affair in Paris, Rick is seen drowning his sorrow in gin when Ilsa comes to his apartment and tries to explain what happened, and he is downright vicious with her, asking her sarcastically whether it was only Laszlo "or were there others in-between?" Disgusted, she leaves him, and when Rick tries to apologize the next morning, Isla turns down his apologies, telling him he is not the man she knew in Paris. Attempts by her and Laszlo to gain the letters of transit all fail to have an effect on him, turning him even more vicious, as when he tells the puzzled Laszlo, who offers him 100,000 francs for the letters, "to ask his wife" why he doesn't. Rick is not only exacting a high price for the letters, which are altogether useless to him, but making the point that he is bitter and jealous. There is no patriotism or higher thoughts there. But when Isla breaks down in his office and tells him that in spite of everything she still loves him, and she explains the situation and they make up, his change is immediate. That is what he wanted to hear. From that point on, he takes over, plans their escape to his own extreme danger, and even kills Strasser for her. His ego has been soothed, and safe now in the knowledge that the woman he loved still loves him, he becomes "noble," though he says he is not good at it. We are still in the dark as to who the real Rick Blaine is. He settles for what he can get, before he vanishes into the mist. Another, more remote, example is found in *The Left Hand of God*, when Bogart's character is forced to play a fake priest. Though his motive is just to survive, he turns into a friend to the tribe, a man troubled by love, and eventually performs the duties of a real priest. It is fun to watch Bogart treading this fine line of good and evil, though the outcome is not always predictable.

Sex Appeal

This was late in coming in Bogart's career, if one tabulates his successes with leading ladies chronologically. In Hollywood, one had to be a big star to gain the lady of his heart. Errol Flynn, a contractual property of Warners, had been a hot lover from the start, and he had the heart of Ms. Olivia De Havilland brought to him on a platter in his first roles—*Captain Blood* (1935), *The Charge of the Light Brigade* (1936), and *Adventures of Robin Hood* (1938)—and also starred with several other leading ladies. Big stars like Clark Gable, Jimmy Stewart, William Holden, and many others of that stature had an easier time being glamorized as lovers in Hollywood. Warners generally had tough guys under contract—Cagney, Paul Muni, Edward G. Robinson—who were good as leads in gangster roles but not particularly as sex symbols. By disposition, Bogart was not "a lady's man," as John Huston, who worked with him for several projects, attests. That of course does not mean that he was entirely "clean," as starlets, especially after the release of *The Maltese Falcon*, clustered around him. But his coin value as a lover skyrocketed when he attained star status as a romantic lover when he costarred with Ingrid Bergman in *Casablanca*, and after that, ladies of distinction were attached to his name on the marquee—as his to theirs—Lauren Bacall (four times), Barbara Stanwyck, Ann Sheridan, Alexis Smith, Lizbeth Scott, Gloria Grahame, Katharine Hepburn, June Allison, Jennifer Jones, Audrey Hepburn, Ava Gardner, and Jean Tierney, to mention the most recognizable names. Generally, however, Bogart remained loyal to his craft and respectful of his female costars, becoming an utterly loyal and faithful husband after his marriage to Bacall.

Bogart: The Professional Artist

Nathaniel Benchley, Bogart biographer, defines a professional as "someone who is paid for doing whatever it is he does, but in the narrower sense a professional is a man who respects his trade, tries as hard to perfect his work, and realizes that one failure is not necessarily the end of the world."[5] This indeed defines Bogart's attitude toward his work to perfection. Despite setbacks, in a career that had its ups and downs, going from stage to screen and back in the early 1930s, and languishing in the minor leagues for six years at Warners in the latter part of that decade before moving up to the majors, Bogart fielded humiliation and second-class status with dignity, loyally going to the set on time, knowing his lines, and, ultimately, believing in himself. When he finally got the big breaks with *High Sierra*, *The Maltese Falcon*, and *Casablanca*, all his accumulated experience and professionalism paid off. But instead of relaxing and resting on his laurels, he intensified his efforts, made sure that he stayed on top, and despite battles with the studio and illness, he gave his all to any movie for whatever its worth.

KEY

This book examines the screen image of Humphrey Bogart for the two-plus decades that he worked in Hollywood, mostly for Warner Bros., from 1936 until 1957, the time of his death. The ratings for Bogart's films are as follows:

Five stars (★★★★★): A classic, not only as a Bogart film but as a film overall; a film that has stood the test of time and is still celebrated as such (*Casablanca, The Big Sleep, The African Queen*)

Four stars (★★★★): A great or near great film that has the essential Bogart qualities in it and is still attracting audiences (*To Have and Have Not, The Caine Mutiny, Sabrina*)

Three stars (★★★): A good film, especially one that had a great Bogart performance in it (*Black Legion, Across the Pacific, Dead Reckoning, The Desperate Hours*)

Two stars (★★): An average or below-average film that still has some value because of Bogart's presence in it (*Love Affair, San Quentin, You Can't Get Away with Murder, Chain Lightning*)

One star (★): A dud; a film that may still have some value because of Bogart's presence in it (*Body and Soul, A Holy Terror, Midnight*)

The majority of films discussed in the main text of this book are rated at least three stars. All of Bogart's films are rated in the filmography.

THE PETRIFIED FOREST

(Warner Bros., 1936)

★ ★ ★ ★

Director: Archie Mayo
Screenplay: Charles Kenyon, Delmer Daves, adapted from a play by Robert E. Sherwood
Producer: Hal B. Wallis. Cinematography: Sol Polito. Music Score: Bernhard Kaun. Editor: Owen Marks
Cast: Leslie Howard (Alan Squier), Bette Davis (Gabrielle Maple), Humphrey Bogart (Duke Mantee), Genevieve Tobin (Mrs. Edith Chisholm), Dick Foran (Boze Hertzlinger), Porter Hall (Jason Maple), Charley Grapewin (Gramp Maple), Paul Harvey (Mr. Chisholm), Slim Thomson (Slim), Joseph Sawyer (Jackie), Adrian Morris (Ruby), Nina Campana (Paula), John Alexander (Joseph)
Released: February 1936
Specs: 82 minutes; black and white
Availability: DVD and Blu-ray (Warner Home Video); streaming (Amazon)

The Petrified Forest was Bogart's first big break in Hollywood, coming at a time when he was languishing in New York, in the middle of the Depression, practically without a job, aimless and ignored. His marriage to Mary Philips, his second wife, was crumbling, and his father died leaving him a huge debt of over $10,000, which took Bogart years to repay. Luck brought him to the stage again, when he was given the role of Duke Mantee in the Robert E. Sherwood play *The Petrified Forest*, which was a big hit in New York. But when Warners bought the property, the role of Duke Mantee was assigned to Edward G. Robinson, who had made as big splash as a gangster in *Little Caesar* (1930) and continued to be a proven star at the time. It was only through the insistence of Leslie Howard, Bogart's partner in the stage play and a big start himself, that Bogart was given the part of Duke Mantee, his first big break in Hollywood. When the film turned out to be a big hit with both audiences and critics, Warners signed Bogart to a contract for the next five years, although he was relegated to playing gangsters and killers, most often ending up dead on the screen in the sixth or seventh reel. But the big leap from an unknown entity to having a contract with a steady job ahead had been made.

The movie also established the screen image of Bogart as a character who was tough, laconic, tense, behaving as if an inner rage dominated his actions. As Duke Mantee, he looked menacing, dangerous, close to being deranged, but always acting if society had done him harm and he was repaying. Nathaniel Benchley, Bogart's biographer, describes his onstage (and subsequently his on-screen) appearance as follows:

> When Humphrey Bogart walked onstage as Duke Mantee there was a stir in the audience, an inaudible intake of breath. He *was* a criminal; he walked with a convict's shuffling gait, and his hands dangled in front of him as though held there by the memory of manacles.[1]

Benchley also mentions that Bogart's Mantee "bore an eerie resemblance to John Dillinger,"[2] a notorious outlaw and bank robber of the times who was shot and killed in a confrontation with the police in 1934 and was in the news almost daily. *The Petrified Forest* established Bogart's career for the duration, though it would take Bogart more than six years to outgrow the image of a heavy and become the likable Rick Blaine of *Casablanca*—and a mostly sympathetic character after that. But Bogart always remained enigmatic. His screen persona was never completely revealed to the audience, and he later became an existential icon, essentially that of an antihero who would strike out only when pressed, and never gratuitously.

The film begins with a man walking on the dusty landscape of the Petrified Forest in Arizona, holding a cane, a backpack hanging from his shoulders. This establishing shot is the only one that was made on location, as the prohibitive cost of shooting in the desert obliged Warner Bros. to shoot the rest at the studio, on a simple set, showing a roadside gas station, with a sign hanging on the front of the Mantle Barbecue, the neon lights outside spelled BAR-B-Q. The first scene inside the café shows two men stopping to supply their car with gas and momentarily go inside, where an effusive old man tells them of his confrontation with Billy the Kid, who missed him twice. Gramp Maple (Charley Grapewin) provides color, and some histori-

Flanked by Jackie (Joe Sawyer) and Ruby (Adrian Morris), Duke Mantee (Bogart)—looking like a man still wearing manacles—first appears at the roadside café. *Warner Bros. Pictures/Photofest* © *Warner Bros.*

cal perspective, in a bleak environment meant for exiles from humanity. A husky young man named Boze (Dick Foran) is seen playing with a football and a bit later talking with the waitress Gabrielle (Davis), whose father, Jason Maple (Porter Hall), a war veteran, soon dons his uniform and with other vigilantes goes out to a meeting of the Black Horse Committee, designed to protect natives from the bandits. Boze courts Gabrielle, or Gabby, who is busy reading a book of poems, which turns out to be a collection of poems by the French poet François Villon, which shows her refinement of character.

Soon, the man who was seen walking on the dusty road appears, entering the roadside café, where he draws the attention of the chatty Gramp Maple, who seems starving to talk to anyone about the outlaws of yesteryear. Gabrielle notices the handsome stranger coming into her father's remote establishment and offers to feed him, and as he eats his soup, they get to chatting and becoming fast friends. She finds out the his name is Alan Squier, and she tells him that she dreams of going to Borges, France, where her mother lives, and becoming an artist. Alan sees she is reading Villon, and when Gabrielle shows him her paintings, he is so impressed—or seems to be—that he encourages her to go to France to develop her talents. Gabby spots him at once as an intelligent man and is curious to probe into his past, but he tells little of himself, except that he is a failed writer, actually giving up on civilization—at least the intelligentsia—and thinks man should return to nature. Though disillusioned, Alan does not seem bitter and accepts reality and his poverty stoically, but he is evidently attracted to Gabby, a good-natured girl, and an oasis in the desert. She gives him a dollar coin before he leaves the establishment, getting a ride from Mr. and Mrs. Chisholm and their black chauffer, Joseph, in their luxury sedan.

The scene shifts to Mantee and his gang—Jackie (Joseph Sawyer), Ruby (Adrian Morris), and Slim (Slim Thompson), a black man as hard-boiled as the other two. As their own shabby vehicle has broken down in the desert, the four men hijack Chisholm's shiny coupé, expel its three occupants—Mr. and Mrs. Chisholm and their black chauffer—take their car, and soon appear at the Maple Barbecue. Squier is seen walking back to the café, as he had not waited for the Chisholms' chauffer to fix the gang's vehicle. Mantee and his gang are escapees and running for the border, but on the radio they hear that a swarm of policemen and various troopers is after them. They enter the café and take over, waiting for Mantee's girl, Doris, and some men to join them there. Soon, Squier comes back in, and the Chisholms and their chauffer also join the group, having repaired Mantee's car.

The expanded group remain in the café, entirely under the control of Mantee and his gang. The only person who is happy about all this is Gramp Maple, who after decades of waiting sees real killers and outlaws invade their little establishment, and sees his wish come true. He is a relic of the old West, where killers and gunslingers were the folk heroes and filled the Arizona deserts with their legendary feats. When Boze says that these men are gangsters, Mantee counters that gangsters are "foreigners": Mantee, a throwback to Billy the Kid, is "an American." This is probably the most astute, if casual, remark in the entire movie. In *Little Caesar* (1930), Edward G. Robinson was embodying Al Capone, of the Chicago gangland and the Mafia generations that followed—the Johnny Rocco of *Key Largo* (1948) and, much later, Vito Corleone of *The Godfather* (1972). That was the classic American gangland of the East. The West had different heroes: Bonnie and Clyde, Billy the Kid, and Bogart's contemporary, John Dillinger. Bogart has the latter's appearance and reputation, Gramp Maple's idea of a "real killer." Gramp gloated in saying that the Kid had missed no man, except him, twice, and that was because the Kid was drunk. The Kid's boldness and contempt for death (the Mafiosi were protected by a shield of hired thugs) matched the West's openness of space, where outlaws could hide or run across the border. If it came to confrontations, they rarely missed, fought for themselves, and died bravely. That's what life was about in the exciting world of western outlaws, in the old man's imagination, and that is what excited him. Mantee's hesitant step, hunched shoulders, frowning forehead, and shining black eyes give the impression of a man who knows he is doomed, and yet is defiant, not begging for mercy.

But Mantee is also stuck with a group of nervous captives, who outnumber the four outlaws; the latter have to keep an eye on the former and also watch out for police and troopers, as the radio announces the massive manhunt to capture Mantee and his gang. The only person who seems to be unaffected is Squier, who continues to prattle, theorizing that he has similarities with Mantee: both are an extinct species—Mantee, the last of the great outlaws who filled the deserts, and he, one of the last intellectuals/artists—and both belong there to be buried in the Petrified Forest, Arizona's fossil-filled, dust-and-rock natural monument. Mantee, irritated when Squier stands up, bluntly tells him to sit down. But when Squier unfolds his plan to pass on his life insurance of $5,000 to Gabrielle if Mantee promises to kill him before he leaves the premises, Mantee's stunned look reveals his admiration for the babbling Englishman, who possesses astonishing courage, something that Mantee himself does not lack. Mantee is surprised only once—when Squier asks him to kill him. He could tell a doomed man and accords him the respect of doing what he is asked, though only when he is pressed. The two doomed men meet halfway, not without a dose of admiration for each other. Both are relics of the past, though in quite different ways: one is a dying intellectual and writer, a species of human that Squier thinks is extinct; the other a gunman, a hero in folk legend, one of those for whom old Gramp yearns. Regardless of the ethics, or the reality of such a parallel, that is the impression one gets when Mantee looks at the mad intellectual with mixed admiration. When surrounded and forced to leave the establishment, Mantee shoots Squier when the latter blocks the door and then leaves him there to die in Gabby's arms. News soon arrives on the phone that Mantee has been captured.

The tensions created between Mantee and Squier are indeed what keep *The Petrified Forest* alive as a movie, despite the clichéd trivia in the rest of its plot. Boze wants Gabby, but he is just a muscled fool who childishly dabbles in football practice and who has no clue as to what is passing between Gabby and Alan. Gabby's father, who brings back two fellows from the vigilante meeting he attended, is just a cartoon character and is immediately disarmed. Only two other characters are truly up to the task: Mrs. Chisholm and Gramps Maple. Mrs. Chisholm cheers Squier's plan and signs the insurance documents as a witness; she sits next to her robotic husband, who thinks the government is not good enough to protect its citizens, though he too signs the insurance papers. The Petrified Forest has been a part of nature, left to its natural devices; unused, it will decay and die, fossils and all, and its denizens will be washed away in its dusty storms. Gramp Maple has lost his sense of reality living in the desert, now a dusty and windy wasteland since its heroes/outlaws are gone and there is nothing worth noting in it. Oddly, he is the only one who provides the key to the continuation of the species in the desert: he holds the singed document that will allow Gabrielle to go away and fulfill her dream, and he remains behind to tell that he witnessed the demise of Mantee, a man whose legend no dust can quite blow away.

②

BULLETS OR BALLOTS

(First National/Warner Bros., 1936)

★ ★ ★

Director: William Keighley
Screenplay: Seton I. Miller, adapted from a story by Martin Mooney and Seton I.
  Miller
Executive Producer: Jack L. Warner. *Associate Producer:* Louis F. Edelman.
  Cinematographer: Hal Mohr. *Music Score:* Heinz Roemheld. *Editor:* Jack
  Killifer
Cast: Edward G. Robinson (Johnny Blake), Humphrey Bogart (Nick "Bugs"
  Fenner), Joan Blondell (Lee Morgan), Barton MacLane (Al Kruger),
  Henry O'Neill (Ward Bryant), Joseph King (Captain Dan McLaren),
  Frank McHugh (Herman), Richard Purcell (Driscoll), Joseph Crehan
  (Grand Jury Spokesman), Gilbert Emery (Thorndyke)
Released: June 6, 1936
Specs: 82 minutes; black and white
Availability: DVD (Warner Bros., with running commentary by film historian
  Dana Polan); streaming (Amazon)

Bullets of Ballots followed on the heels of *The Petrified Forest* (1936) in
which Bogart had been an unforgettable presence as Duke Mantee and had
established him as a significant screen asset at Warners. But he was not yet
big enough to challenge the precedence of Edward G. Robinson, who was
then at the height of his career—and continued to be for many years after
his *Little Caesar* debut five years earlier. But as the climate was changing
with the more strict enforcement of the Hays Code, which compelled studios to rethink the glorification of the gangster in the big gangster movies
of the early thirties, the tables turned. While the gangster movie continued

to thrive for several more years, it was now the gangster who died in infamy
and the cops or detectives who got the credit or moral victory. Eventually,
the start of World War II would put an end to the thirties gangster era, the
focus of action movies shifting to war adventures with patriotic themes. Both
Bogart's and Robinson's careers were affected by those trends—Bogart's
swinging upward, while Robinson's gradually settling into secondary parts.

In *Bullets or Ballots*, Robinson played Johnny Blake, a good policeman,
while, conveniently (for the studio), Bogart continued to ride the tracks
he had established in *The Petrified Forest* as a bad guy. But here he was
more vicious, totally unlikeable, and as bad as they come—worse even than
Barton MacLane, who was to be his nemesis in several more movies. As
Nick "Bugs" Fenner, Bogart was a cunning and vengeful killer, any trace
of conscience totally wiped out of him; he was also as smart as he was ruthless, a man who could have become a top dog in a powerful syndicate—a
godfather of sorts—had the morality play in which he was starring allowed
him to. But that idea of a rising gangster who survives and thrives at the end
had to wait for a few more decades, when Michael Corleone wipes out his
enemies and becomes the new godfather in *The Godfather* (1972).

After Prohibition was repealed in 1933,[1] mafia syndicates were taken
over by top men who tried to run corrupt businesses in various parts of New
York, Harlem, and the Bronx. These businesses branched out individually,
and each connected to smaller units that supervised individual businesses,
collecting profits and storing them in secret hideouts in huge stacks of cash,
which they preferred in order to avoid traceable bank accounts. The syndicate resembled a pyramid scheme, where invisible, highly placed mobsters
ran units, which in turn had subunits, down to the last man on the street,
who sold the goods, kept order with threats or blackmail, and stacked up
the profits, which were channeled back to the men at the top.

Fenner and Al Kruger (Barton MacLane) are components of one of the
syndicates, Kruger being the chief who knows the three top men, receiving
calls from a phone hidden in his desk drawer, and doing as he is told. He
and Fenner, Kruger's underling in the chain of command, are first seen
going into a movie theater, where they watch a newsreel, while focusing
their attention on one Ward Bryant, a well-known publicist and a crusader
for justice, after a known gangster was acquitted by a compliant jury, despite Bryant's protestations. Such corrupt practices were typical of the time
gangsters were arrested, brought to a grand jury or to trial, and then let
go. In this syndicate, three powerful men remain behind the scenes and
are totally unknown to anyone except their chief operators, who also are
unknown to each other. Kruger, one of those operators, runs into trouble

after an overeager Fenner shoots Bryant, causing a big stir in the press and a new resolve by the police force. Kruger receives a phone call as he is reprimanding Fenner, and he is seen driving to a bank, the Oceanic Bank and Trust Company, where the three syndicate heads warn him that the shooting of Bryant was a mistake and that if he makes another mistake he will be through. "'Through' meaning what?" asks Kruger. "'Through' has only one meaning," one of them tells him.

Things turn around quickly, as Captain Dan McLaren is appointed commissioner to combat the syndicate more efficiently, and his first move is to fire Johnny Blake, to the surprise of everyone, as Blake is one of the ablest detectives in the force. Blake is visited by his girlfriend, Lee Morgan (Joan Blondell), who runs a nightclub and a pinball machine business in Harlem and who offers Blake a job. But Blake refuses, as he has other plans. After Blake makes a public spectacle by punching McLaren during a boxing match, Kruger, who is also attending the match, approaches Blake and asks him if he would like to join his organization. Blake does, to the surprise of everyone except Fenner, who suspects that the whole thing is a setup. But as the new commissioner is causing the syndicate serious trouble with constant raids, Kruger seems to have no option but to hire Blake, as he considers Fenner too volatile and unreliable. But when Blake gets arrested after a brawl with the police and is taken to jail, McLaren is waiting for him there, and it becomes apparent that this is a sting operation.

That changes the configuration of the story entirely. Blake has to stay above suspicion, and to do so he confronts Fenner and his group, saying he has new ideas for running things: the syndicate, he states, does not have to try to stop McLaren. While the latter is wreaking havoc, they can use new ideas, such as playing the "numbers" game, which meant that by betting at colossal odds at horse races—1,000 to 1, for instance—they were able to draw more customers, thus being able to accumulate large sums of money in no time. Kruger is impressed by Blake's bold ideas, and he accepts the deal and makes Blake the chief of the operation. But Fenner, resentful and more suspicious than ever, shoots Kruger, expecting to get his top status within the syndicate. But this plan backfires, and Blake gets the job, which means he now can find out who the three bosses are. They are all respectable bankers and seemingly upstanding citizens. Fenner asks an innocent Lee to reveal where Blake has gone, and she, unsuspecting, gives him Blake's hideout. Meanwhile, Blake is on his way to meet the three bosses with a bag of evidence he has collected. As he starts down the stairs, Fenner appears at the door and puts two bullets into him. Blake, seriously wounded, does not fall, but pulls out his gun and fires five times, making sure Fenner is dead. He steps over Fenner, gets into a taxi, goes to the address of the three, and shows them the bag, which in reality is proof against them. Then he staggers out, gets out of the building by crawling to the doors, and falls on the steps. A raid is on, and the three big shots are arrested. A grateful McLaren offers to take Blake to the hospital, but it is too late.

This movie is well paced and action packed, and makes its points quickly and effectively. But without the presence of Bogart and Robinson, it would have been just another gangster-era movie without any particular message aside from the fact that good guys win. But Robinson displays his amazing knack for imitating anybody. He is short but svelte, and mounts a punch that can fell a giant. His character has disdain for the thugs he faces, though he has to hide it for most of the movie, knowing he has entered a lion's den and must constantly watch his step at every moment. Though MacLane's Kruger is tall, tough, and seasoned in a life a crime, he falls for Blake's snares and proves a rather easy target for Blake. But Blake can't fool Fenner, who suspects him from the start and who eventually catches up with him.

As for Bogart, the best thing one can say about him is that his Fenner is no fool. He catches on to Kruger's weak spots; he knows Kruger's time is up and that he would be next in the line of succession. His gangster mentality does not eliminate his sharp mind. But he is doomed to a fall as he has failed to understand that the times have changed. Like Duke Mantee in *The Petrified Forest*, Fenner is an anachronism. Mantee was a throwback to the hero-criminals of the West, folk heroes like Billy the Kid, and he also reminded audiences of John Dillinger, a notorious killer of the thirties. Fenner could not get used to the idea the gangster days of the Prohibition had ended, when quick and vengeful action was the orders of the day, and that the syndicate was settling into violence-free, businesslike operations that could bring in the cash profits without blood and shootouts with the police. The top three syndicate heads were bankers and businessmen, seemingly upstanding citizens who were gathering the spoils through corruption, payoffs, jury intimidation, and legitimate entertainment clubs, rather than relying on the speakeasies of the past decade. Still, Fenner sees reality as it is, outsmarting the dull-headed Kruger, and not for one moment doubting the real identity of Blake. He has ambitions of getting to the top, but his one flaw—being too impulsive and quick with his trigger—finally dooms him. It takes five bullets to silence him for good—but that, again, is part of the script.

Bogart kept working for another two decades, reaching far beyond in his status as a star than Robinson ever did (Robinson never won an Oscar and was not even nominated[2]), and he had a chance, in *Key Largo* (1948) to repay the favor of being shot, doing it in a more measured way. In that movie, on top of a boat, wounded himself, Bogart's McCloud fires three bullets at Robinson's Rocco, spacing them out: one after Rocco emerges from the boat cabin door; another when he makes a move to draw his own gun; a third to seal Rocco's doom.

Incidentally, the title *Bullets or Ballots* acquired a new meaning over the span of a decade. Ballots would not do the job in the gangster era; bullets took the day. But after the gangster era and the Second World War, with FDR's three successive victories at the polls and a victorious America, ballots were the order of the day. But at the time *Bullets or Ballots* was made, no one could have foreseen that.

3

BLACK LEGION

(Warner Bros., 1937)

★ ★ ★

Director: Archie Mayo
Screenplay: Albert Finkel, William Wister Haines, adapted from a story by
    Robert Lord
Producer: Robert Lord. Executive Producer: Hal B. Wallis. Cinematographer:
    George Barnes. Music Score: Bernhard Kaun. Editor: Owen Marks
Cast: Humphrey Bogart (Frank Taylor), Dick Foran (Ed Jackson), Erin
    O'Brien-Moore (Ruth Taylor), Ann Sheridan (Betty Grogan), Robert
    Barrat (Brown), Helen Flint (Pearl Davis), Joseph Sawyer (Cliff Moore),
    Henry Brandon (Joe Dombrowski), Samuel S. Hinds (Judge)
Released: January 30, 1937
Specs: 83 minutes; black and white
Availability: DVD (Warner Home Video); streaming (Amazon)

Bogart plays Frank Taylor, a man employed at a machine factory who, out of resentment for being overlooked for a promotion in favor of a man of foreign origin, Joe Dombrowski (Henry Brandon), joins the Black Legion, a white supremacist group whose mission is to hound foreigners who get jobs at the expense of white Americans. The secret society closely resembles the activities of the KKK, as it presents the same hate motto—"America for 100% Americans"—but here the title Black Legion masks its intentions, as no black man is persecuted or mentioned in the story, only whites who take away jobs or get social advancement at the expense of the native born.

This was the eighth movie that Bogart made for Warner Bros., and/or First National–Warner Brothers, and one where he plays a leading role, though his name appears below the title. For him the usual fare, before and after this movie, until 1941, was to play hoods and gangsters, shot or sent to jail before the movie was over. In *Black Legion* Bogart plays the leading character, happily married to a good wife and earning his income by honest work, until he is enticed to join the Black Legion. He is not a bad man, but weak and easily drawn into illegal activity when the vigilantes, comprised of leading members of the community, see to it that he becomes one of them. When Taylor takes the oath of allegiance, a gun to his head, he becomes aware that those are terrible conditions that he is submitting to and that he will not be able to exit once he joins, but by the time he fully realizes he is entrapped, it is too late to retract. Once he is in, he participates in acts of arson, expulsion, and floggings; then his best friend, Ed Jackson (Dick Foran), is taken out of his home to an isolated spot and when he tries to escape, Taylor shoots him to death. When he realizes what he has done, Taylor stays at the spot while the others flee. He is picked up by police when he stops at a road café to ask for water.

Taylor's trial becomes the most dramatic part of the movie. His wife, Ruth (Erin O'Brien-Moore), had left him, taking their young son with her, but she returns and is present at the trial, as is Jackson's fiancée, Betty Grogan, a minor role played by Ann Sheridan. When Taylor is placed on the stand, where the Legion expects him to lie since he had received threats against his family if he didn't, he explodes and tells the truth to a stunned courtroom, which included top members of the Legion. They are arrested and a new trial ensues, during which the Black Legion members are all condemned to life in prison, including Taylor. As he leaves the court, he looks at his wife, whose face is the last shot of the film. It is full of horror, despair, and incredulity at what she learned about her husband and the crimes he has committed.

This is a film rare in the Bogart canon before 1941, his breakthrough year. It is one of the few movies where he does not appear as a rootless loner, but he has a family—a wife and a child to support. He is a regular guy, a blue-collar worker employed in a machine factory in Michigan, mixing with the guys and horsing around with them during breaks; he is not a drinker, earns his daily bread with hard work, and goes home to his family and dinner. The trouble begins when he hears an inflammatory tirade in a radio broadcast from someone who claims that Americans lose jobs to "multitudes that have swarmed our shores" and who "openly plot to seize control of our government." There is a call to defend "our beloved Stars and Stripes [that] wave over a united nation of free, white, and one hundred percent Americans." Almost overnight, Taylor changes from a harmless ordinary citizen to a vindictive, surly avenger who spends his first night with the conspirators setting fire to a coworker's house and barn, and then thrusting the two men, father and son, onto the platform of a freight train, acting out their fantasies of "united America." Taylor gets drunk before he returns home, and when he arrives, his wife sees his change with horror and wonders what happened to the nice man she knew.

Taylor becomes a foreman and buys a new car for himself and a vacuum cleaner for his wife, but his good fortune does not last. As the Legion wants more power, each of the members is ordered to recruit two more members. Taylor now begins to become conscious that his promotion has come with a price. His nightly absences and his drinking make his wife suspicious, and when she confronts him and calls him a coward, he slaps her hard on the face. He is finally brought to his senses by the death of his friend, the pressure from the Legion to perjure himself, and the presence in the court of those who destroyed him, and he decides to take those people down along with himself.

Bogart here appears much younger and not the seasoned actor he became later; nevertheless, he shows that he can handle this heavy stuff with ease, for his stage experience had allowed him to hone his craft and pave the way to his career as an actor of the screen. He is neither a hero nor entirely a villain, but a man caught in the trap of jealousy and resentment, blindly plunging into a world of haters bent on destroying those opposing them, for the leaders of the Legion were profiteers, carefully setting their sights on those who would stand in their way. Taylor's indignant outburst and confession at the trial shows him as a man who came to his senses, but too late to be allowed back to society and the happy life he had enjoyed since then.

It has been noted that it took an act of courage on the part of Warners to make a movie with such a serious subject, as underground supremacist groups existed in large numbers in small-town America. The movie gained serious attention and was praised for Bogart's performance, which the *New York Post* described as "dynamic and stirring."[1] This was still early in Bogart's later meteoric career, and it was a step in the right direction, pointing to the triumphs he was later to achieve as a man disintegrating under pressure, in such megahits as *The Treasure of Sierra Madre* (1948), *In a Lonely Place* (1950), and *The Caine Mutiny* (1954). At the time, the *New York Times* called *Black Legion* "cinema at its best,"[2] and in our days Leonard Maltin describes it as "powerful still relevant social drama."[3] Although its xenophobic theme is the main subject of the story, there is no doubt of its disguised racial overtones, a theme timely in the 1930s and just as timely today. And for Bogart fans, it shows that their beloved actor possessed his unique talents at that point in time, displayed and honed later on a much larger canvas.

4

MARKED WOMAN

(First National/ Warner Bros., 1937)

★ ★ ★

Director: Lloyd Bacon
Screenplay: Robert Rossen, Abem Finkel
Associate Producer: Hal B. Wallis. *Cinematography:* George Barnes. *Music Score:*
    Bernhard Kaun, Heinz Roemheld. *Editor:* Jack Killifer
Cast: Bette Davis (Mary Dwight Strauber), Humphrey Bogart (David
    Graham), Eduardo Cianelli (Johnny Vanning), Lola Lane (Gabby), Isabel
    Jewell (Emmy Lou), Rosalind Marquis (Florrie), Mayo Methot (Estelle),
    Jane Bryan (Betty), Allen Jenkins (Louie), John Litel (Gordon), Ben
    Welden (Charlie), Damian O'Flynn (Ralph Krawford), Henry O'Neill
    (Sheldon)
Released: April 10, 1937
Specs: 96 minutes; black and white
Availability: DVD (Warner Home Video); streaming (Amazon)

Following his success with *The Petrified Forest*, Bogart signed a long-term
contract with Warner Bros., and in contrast to the hoods and killers Bogart
played in his first two years at Warners, here he is a hero and a good man
with a mission. He plays David Graham, a prosecutor and a crusader for
justice who tries to rid the town of a notorious mobster who operates a
gambling joint and prostitution ring. But Bogart gets second billing to Bette
Davis, who at the time was trying to patch up problems with Warners and
was also looking for a good script. She got it and with it a juicy part as Mary
Strauber, a spirited young woman who shines as a "nightclub hostess" (read
prostitute), doing slave labor for Johnny Vanning, a mobster known for his

harsh retributions to disloyal underlings. Edwardo Gianelli, who played Vanning, bore an uncanny resemblance to Charles "Lucky" Luciano, a real-life notorious racketeer in those days.

This was the end of the Prohibition era, and as speakeasies had closed, mobsters changed routes, masquerading as businessmen who ran nightclubs that were fronts for prostitution, gambling, and other illegal activities. These men hired high-caliber lawyers who posted bail for anyone in the ranks arrested and jailed, and they employed an army of goons and killers who stayed out of sight and did the dirty work for them. These mobsters were the scum of the earth and the scourge of big towns. They were power-hungry but crude men who displayed their ignorance when opportunity offered; for example, when Vanning buys a club named Valentine, he asks what the word means. One of his goons explains that it means "intimate." Vanning gives orders to rename his club Intimate and remove all the elegant décor items in the club, including an artwork chandelier, and replace them with plainer furniture reminiscent of the speakeasy days. Intimate is the club where most of the action in the movie takes place.

In the opening scene of the book, Mary (Davis), who worked for the previous owner, is flanked by four other young women, the older among them being Estelle Porter, played by Bogart's future wife, Mayo Methot (she and Bogart were married a year later). Estelle is about to be dismissed as "too old" by Vanning, but is kept on the job due to Mary's intervention. Mary dares to talk back to Vanning, resisting his attempts to get her to spend a night with him. The other women are Dorothy "Gabby" Marvin (Lola Lane), Emmy Lou Eagan (Isabelle Jewell), and Florrie Liggett (Rosalind Marquis). When a group of young men comes into the club, all five women are asked to go to their table. Mary escorts a young man, Ralph Krawford (Damian O'Flynn) to the gambling table, where he loses large sums of money. He has no money and offers to pay by check, but the head of the speakeasy refuses. When Mary goes with him in the cab he hires to go to his hotel, he confesses he is penniless (she even lends him money to pay the cab). Mary saw someone following them, and she warns Krawford that he'd better get out of town quickly. But as he tries to go, two men, whom Mary recognizes, haul him hurriedly into their car. The following morning he is found dead in the river.

This is the time in the movie that Bogart, as prosecutor David Graham, comes in and takes over the investigation, despite warnings at the DA's office that it is futile to go against a mobster of Vanning's status. As David Graham, Bogart looks youngish, reminding audiences of his juvenile image projected earlier in his career on the stage and screen, and he even sounds a bit unpolished—compared to his seasoned image in his roles of the next decade. But his character is forceful and defiant, taking up a case against a top mobster who had never lost a case in court. When Mary's sister Betty (Jane Bryan) visits her, she is appalled to learn what her sister is doing, and after a breakup, she visits the nightclub, thinking she could be a hostess without the "extra" services required of her. So when an older man makes his intentions clear as to what he expects, Betty resists; an enraged Vanning pushes her downstairs, and she is killed.

In the ensuing trial, Mary testifies against Vanning, but under relentless questioning by Vanning's lawyer (Raymond Hatton), she is easily proven an unreliable witness. Betty's death is ruled an accident, and Vanning is let go. Because Mary dared to testify against him, though, Vanning has his men beat her and gash her face with a knife. A scar with visible stitches will be left there for life. That is Vanning's standard punishment for mutinous women. Mary now decides to take decisive action; she tells Graham that this time she will tell "everything" and does so when on the stand, as Vanning and his entourage are being accused of both murders—Krawford's and her sister's. The scar on Mary's face is visual evidence, but her unleashed tongue does the rest. Graham simply has to connect the dots and does so quite adeptly, but this is Davis's big scene. She is an actress who can be shrill, vindictive, and righteous at the same time. Vanning and his gang members get between thirty and fifty years in jail, putting an end to his career as top mobster in the city.

As the five women walk out of the courtroom, Graham approaches Mary and asks her if he can see her again, but she says she has to go, and the five women walk away in the foggy night. Warners and the script writers do not give Bogart the big prize. Up to that point, Bette Davis had proven to be a star, a big one who could make demands and see them fulfilled. But Bogart was not a big lover yet. He had to play some more bad guys in the coming years before he could match the fiery Davis with his own entirely different screen image. He crossed paths with Davis again, but each developed in a different direction, perhaps to the benefit of both. For the time being, Bogart had to content himself with marrying Mayo Methot, a falling star but as rambunctious a connubial partner as anyone offscreen. He and Mayo never appeared again in the same movie, but the town heard enough about their dysfunctional union.[1]

5

KID GALAHAD

(Warner Bros., 1937)

★ ★ ★

Directed: Michael Curtiz
Screenplay: Seton I. Miller, adapted from a story by Francis Wallace
Executive Producers: Jack L. Warner, Hal B. Wallis. *Cinematographer:* Tony
    Gaudio. *Music Score:* Heinz Roemheld, Max Steiner. *Editor:* George Amy
Cast: Edward G. Robinson (Nick Donati), Bette Davis (Louise "Fluff"
    Phillips), Humphrey Bogart (Turkey Morgan), Wayne Morris (Ward
    Guisenberry), Jane Bryan (Marie Donati), Harry Carey (Silver Jackson),
    William Haade (Chuck McGraw), Soledad Jimenez (Mrs. Donati), Joe
    Cunningham (Joe Taylor), Ben Welden (Buzz Barett)
Released: May 26, 1937
Specs: 102 minutes; black and white
Availability: DVD (Warner Home Video); streaming (Amazon)

This movie features one of the many confrontations between characters
played by Edward G. Robinson and Humphrey Bogart, something that had
already started with *Bullets or Ballots* (1936) and would be repeated a year
later in *The Amazing Dr. Clitterhouse* and many years later in *Key Largo*.
Personally they were good friends, but on the screen Bogart is bedeviled—
and killed—before he eventually pays Robinson back in the aforementioned *Key Largo*. At this time, 1937, Robinson was a proven quantity at
Warners, but it would take years for Bogart to reach that status and eventually go far beyond Robinson or any of Robinson's contemporaries—James
Cagney, Paul Muni, and George Raft, all valuable Warners properties, with
high salaries, priority billings, and a name (usually a billing determined an
actor's salary). For the time being, Bogart was consigned to a secondary

role, mostly that of a hood with a repulsive name, way down in billing and salary. So he is in this movie.

Here, both Robinson and Bogart play lowlifes, but Bogart's character gets the lower marks. Called Turkey Morgan, he is a prize-fighter promoter, a gang leader, and a natural hood; he has no redeeming qualities whatsoever, and he is a gangster with a morose disposition and a mean temperament. Robinson, on the other hand, plays Nick Donati, of Italian extraction, on the surface a gentleman (he played those enough times, projecting an outside polish) who has a mama living on a farm not far from the city, a young sweet sister called Marie (Jane Bryan), and a girlfriend going by the name of Fluff (a.k.a. Louise Phillips) played by a vivacious, youthful, and beautiful Bette Davis.

Into this group comes a fourth principal, a blond, tall youngster who grew up on a farm and came to New York to make his fortune, intending, after making enough dough, to go back and buy a farm of his own, marry, and live in peace. He is bellboy at a New York hotel who answers to the awkward name of Ward Guisenberry and becomes the laughingstock of patrons there, who include Donati and Turkey and his gang, one of whom tears off the boy's pants as a joke. He is one of the known prize fighters of the day, and when he verbally insults Guisenberry, the latter floors him with a right punch. The amazed bystanders gape at him, but Donati sees an opening—why not train the youngster to compete at the ring? Fluff, meanwhile, has met Guisenberry and learned that he has never smoked nor drunk, though he is past twenty, and she says, "I didn't know your kind still exists." Without realizing it at first, Fluff falls in love with him; she sees through his innocence and takes him under her wing.

Guisenberry easily floors opponents and progresses through the ranks, despite the fact that Turkey is jealous of Donati's lucky find and tries to intimidate the youngster with veiled or direct threats. But Guisenberry smacks him with a right, leaving him out cold on the pavement. Incidentally, the young boxer's trainer is Silver Jackson, played by Harry Carey, who differs from his boss, Donati, who is exploitative, manipulative, and concerned more with his feud with Turkey than upholding his honor.

Guisenberry is allowed to take a break on Donati's farm, where he is welcomed by Mama Donati and young Marie, who falls in love with him. He loves her, too, but before they can get too far, they have a rough exchange and he leaves for town, where he continues to ascend in the boxing business. Donati is jealous when Fluff tells him that she is leaving him because she is angry that Kid Galahad, as Guisenberry is now called, makes a deal with Turkey, rushing Galahad into a premature match with world champion Chuck

McGraw (William Haade) in a fifteen-round match. Turkey takes over from Silver, who sees through Donati's actions, and guessing the fraudulent bet, he instructs Galahad to come out punching. The Kid is nearly murdered by McGraw, but he withstands several knockdowns and is still fighting at round 9. Fluff and Marie, both in the stands, implore Donati to change tactics. He complies, and he now instructs Kid to retreat instead of fight, until McGraw is punched out. Subsequently, Galahad knocks McGraw out. Turkey tries to kill Donati, and they are both wounded in a gunfire exchange. Turkey dies instantly, but Donati lives long enough to express his regret and give his blessing to Guisenberry and his sister and apologize to Fluff.

The ending is not quite tragic but satisfactorily concludes a good, fast-paced melodrama, where Robinson once more displays his histrionic talent as a hood with some semblance of a heart. Bette Davis shines as an honest gal who is heartbroken but who understands and works hard to restore Donati's sense of honor and make room for Marie for the heart of Kid Galahad. Overall, though not a notable Bogart vehicle, the movie might be interesting to those who relish in watching Bogart as a bad guy, with no heart or conscience; just a tough guy who does not always manage to outsmart or outgun his opponents. By the way, this is a good opening for Bette Davis, who was then approaching the peak of her career and who often crossed paths with Bogart, but never romantically. In the forties, when both were in top form, their paths diverged and a romantic link was never fated for them, perhaps to the benefit of both.

DEAD END

(United Artists/Samuel Goldwyn, 1937)

★ ★ ★

Director: William Wyler
Screenplay: Lilian Hellman, based on the play by Sidney Kingsley
Producer: Samuel Goldwyn. *Cinematographer:* Gregg Toland. *Editor:* Daniel
   Mandell. *Music Score:* Alfred Newman. *Art Direction:* Richard Day
Cast: Humphrey Bogart (Baby Face Martin), Joel McCrea (Dave Connell),
   Sylvia Sidney (Drina Gordon), Wendy Barrie (Kay Burton), Claire
   Trevor (Francey), Allen Jenkins (Hunk), Marjorie Main (Mrs. Martin),
   Billy Halop (Tommy), Huntz Hall (Dippy), Bobby Jordan (Angel), Leo
   Gorcey (Spit), Gabriel Dell (TB), Bernard Punsley (Milty)
Released: August 27, 1937
Specs: 93 minutes; black and white
Availability: DVD (HBO Home Video); streaming (Amazon Instant Video)

Bogart made this movie on a loan to Samuel Goldwyn, after hard negotiations with Jack Warner, who was hesitant to part with his money-making, though underpaid, workhorse. The movie was shot at the Goldwyn Studios, with sets carefully designed to simulate the East River slums and the expensive riverside homes that bordered them. It was based on the successful Broadway play by Sidney Kingsley, adapted for the screen by Lillian Hellman, photographed by Gregg Toland (who photographed *Citizen Kane* a few years later), and directed by William Wyler. Much attention was paid to detail, art direction, speech, and costumes, and the group of youngsters who played the Dead End Kids[1] featured in the Broadway play were imported from New York to give credence to the street action. Overall, this was a high-value production that improved Bogart's status as an actor, though this was not reflected in his paycheck. The movie was a success and was nominated for Best Picture (Samuel Goldwyn Productions), Best Actress in a Supporting Role (Claire Trevor), Best Cinematography (Gregg Toland), and Best Art Direction (Richard Day).

Here Bogart plays Baby Face Martin, a hood who had left his slums neighborhood years before, gone into a life of crime, risen in the ranks, and had plastic surgery on his face (hence, his nickname) to evade detection. He is first seen watching the Dead End Kids playing along the pier, making cracks about the poverty of the neighbors he had left behind, and bragging about his new status to his fellow hood, Hunk (Allan Jenkins). Martin had returned to his old haunts in grand style to reconnect with his mother, still living there. He is also on the lookout for his former girlfriend, Francey (Claire Trevor), intending to marry her and settle down now that he has made a fortune out of a life of crime. But his mother, bitter and angry that her criminal son has ruined her family's reputation, denounces him, slapping his face and telling him to get out of there. When he sees Francey approaching him, Martin is repelled by the fact that she is sick (she has VD, not mentioned in the code-sensitive script) and her shabby appearance, and he turns her away, giving her a few bucks. Depressed and angry, he plans to kidnap a rich youngster living in the neighborhood, ignoring the advice of Hunk, who tells him to lick his wounds and go back west, where he can find "plenty of willing dames."

The movie follows another story line—that of a former friend, the dreamy architect Dave Connell (Joel McCrea), who is unemployed and dejected by the conditions of the slum, which he would have liked to tear down and rebuild. Connell has developed a lukewarm relationship with a young woman, Kay Burton (Wendy Barrie), who lives at plush apartment next door. His real love, though, turns out to be Drina Gordon (Sylvia Sidney), a respectable but poor young woman who tries hard to keep her younger brother Tommy away from the gang of brawling kids in the neighborhood. But Tommy gets into trouble when he tries to help a rich boy who lives next door and who is beaten and abused by the gang of young hoods. But as the boy's father intervenes and tries to seize Tommy, not knowing who is doing what, Tommy stabs him in the arm with his pocket knife. Drina hides her brother, trying to keep him from going to jail, but finally the boy is seized and sent away—from the doomed gang and self-destruction.

When Martin is ready to put into action his plan of kidnapping the rich boy, Connell confronts him and tries to dissuade him from doing so. When Connell turns his back and walks away, however, Martin tosses a knife at

Baby Face Martin (Bogart) and the Dead End Kids (Bowery Boys, clockwise from left: Bagriel Dell, Huntz Hall, Billy Halop, Bernard Punsly, Bobby Jordan, and Leo Gorcey). *United Artists/ Photofest © United Artists*

him and hits him in the back. Hunk kicks Connell into the river, thinking that they had finished him. But Connell climbs back up at the pier, knocks Hunk down, grabs his gun, and goes after Martin, who has climbed up to a roof to escape the gathering policemen. In the ensuing shootout, Connell wounds Martin, who falls on the pavement from where he attempts to shoot a number of police. But, outgunned, he is riddled with bullets and dies. Soon he is identified, and $20,000 is found on him. Meanwhile, Connell collects the $4,800 award. Drina pleads with the judge who lives next door to save her brother from jail, and he promises that her brother will be treated fairly by the justice system. Connell confronts Kay, who plans to elope with him and spend his award for a year, but Connell is no longer interested in her. Soon, he tells Drina that she is the one he loves, and the couple look forward to a happy future.

The movie would have been a conventional melodrama, had it not been for the presence of Bogart as Martin. Connell plays hero and gets the reward and the right girl in the end. He is a good example of a Dead End Kid who stayed around in the place that bred him, dreamed of a better world, and stuck to his principles. Martin, on the other hand, chose to get out and take the easiest path to riches—crime. After he makes it big, he returns—along with his notoriety—to the place he came from to brag, show what he can do, marry, and let bygones be bygones. It doesn't work that way, as the past haunts him and destroys him, right in the neighborhood that bred him. Bogart has no problem playing Martin exactly as he should be played, giving him some extra dimension. There is a glint of anger in his eyes at being rejected by his mother, an anger that is fed by his revulsion at the sight of his sick girl. There is also a short glimpse of bitterness and recognition, perhaps because he has gained some knowledge that crime doesn't pay. He never says that, and his last resort is to take revenge—kidnap a rich boy and reap the rewards. This is the road to hell, and his friend Hunk tells him, but Martin has no other choice. There is no exit. Bogart, under the guiding hand of William Wyler, captures the subtleties of a troubled mind. Yes, he was the product of the appalling slum, but also the product of his poor choices. He came to a "dead end," a roadblock telling him he had run out of options.

7

THE AMAZING DR. CLITTERHOUSE

(First National/Warner Bros., 1938)

★ ★ ★

Director: Anatole Litvak
Screenplay: John Wexley, John Huston, adapted from a play by Barré Lyndon
Producer: Gilbert Miller. *Cinematographer:* Tony Gaudio. *Music Score:* Max
    Steiner. *Editor:* Warren Low
Cast: Edward G. Robinson (Dr. Clitterhouse), Claire Trevor (Jo Kelly),
    Humphrey Bogart (Rocks Valentine), Allen Jenkins (Okay), Donald
    Crisp (Inspector Lane), Gale Page (Nurse Randolph), Henry O'Neill
    (Judge), Thurston Hall (Attorney Grant), John Litel (Prosecuting
    Attorney), Ward Bond (Tug), Maxie Rosenbloom (Butch), Bert Hanlon
    (Pat)
Released: July 30, 1938
Specs: 87 minutes; black and white
Availability: DVD (Warner Home Video: *TCM Greatest Gangster Films
    Collection*)

This movie is mixture of farce, crime story, and a showcase for the amazing
Edward G. Robinson, who steals his own show. Bogart is there as well, and
doing a good job as second banana to Robinson, along with Claire Trevor
and several other minor operatives, including Ward Bond. Bogart had little
respect for the movie, and in fact he often referred to it as "Dr. Clitoris."
He regarded it as demeaning to him, once more portraying him as a hood
and a fool—and he had had enough of that in his pre-*Casablanca* days—but
the movie is so unusual in his canon and so entertaining that it is worth a
fleeting glance.

Robinson plays Dr. Clitterhouse, a high-class physician, impeccably dressed, well spoken, and captivatingly mannered, a persona that reminds one of none of the hoods and criminals he played in his previous years. His patients include rich folk who like to invite him to their soirées and other evening gatherings, where most of them display their jewelry, some of which goes missing, as the good doctor steals it himself. During one of these heists, as Clitterhouse appears to be snooping around in the dark in a room where jewels are stored, he runs across two thieves, one of whom is Rocks Valentine (Bogart), who has a glimpse of Clitterhouse. A bit later, in the doctor's office, his secretary, looking in his bag for one of his instruments, finds the stolen jewels. Clitterhouse coolly explains to her that he stole the jewels as an experiment he is conducting on himself in order to study the mind of the criminal, a process that can be accomplished if the researcher plays the criminal himself. He is not a real thief, he explains to her while maintaining his aplomb, and she believes him. She is astonished by the very idea, but he is so slick with words and so convincing that she promises to keep silent. He, of course, as he explains, keeps meticulous notes on his own reactions as an active thief, and the notes are recorded in a large notebook, which will become the subject of a book that will improve the understanding of the criminal mind.

But his secret is soon shared by a gang of actual jewelry thieves who are not conducting research but doing this for real. The group is headed by Jo Kelly, played archly by Claire Trevor, a woman who understands the street thief's mind better than the doctor. Clitterhouse has heard of her gang and wants to improve his knowledge of crime; hence, he visits her at the hotel where she is staying. There, a scene unfolds that shows Robinson as a supreme comedian, among his other talents. The place is raided by a policeman, Lieutenant Johnson, who suspects the group of criminal activity. When he asks Dr. Clitterhouse to produce his identity, the latter cleverly dodges any direct answer by invoking his right not to do so unless he is suspected of something. He even hints that he would report Johnson to his superiors for violating citizens' rights, and Johnson leaves the matter for another day and departs. Clitterhouse's deft dodges impress the group, and they ask the doctor to join their gang. He takes over, accomplishing a double goal: he is now experimenting with actual criminals, and he has not revealed his identity to them; they simply call him "the professor."

Clitterhouse goes along, but one of the gang members happens to be Rocks Valentine, who soon catches on to the doctor's schemes—though not understanding, or caring to understand, his reasons—and finds out who he really is. After a successful heist, led by Clitterhouse, Rocks shuts him into a freezer and turns the temperature down, sure the doctor will be frozen in minutes. But one of the doctor's pals, Butch (Maxie Rosenbloom), bores a hole on the door with a torchlight and saves Clitterhouse, who appears in the next gathering, telling Rocks that he should be sure to finish a job when he starts it. Then Clitterhouse pays generous shares to his partners, and bids farewell to the group, telling Jo, who is a bit smitten with the mannerly doctor/thief, that he has to stop at this point before he gets to like, really like, this business. His research is complete (he doesn't tell her that).

But the story is far from over. Rocks traces Clitterhouse's phone number, calls his house, and finds out who he is. When Clitterhouse returns home from a "vacation" in Europe, Rocks is there, and soon Jo Kelly arrives. Rocks holds a gun and threatens to expose the doctor if he does not cooperate. He demands that Clitterhouse's establishment work as a "front" of which he, Rocks, would be the real boss, while Jo Kelly would remain his other connection with her gang. Clitterhouse, cornered, "accepts" and offers Rocks a drink to celebrate the deal. He mixes poison into the drink, and soon Rocks feels the effects, collapses on a couch, and has enough time to become aware of what has happened to him: the good doctor had warned him not to start a job he couldn't finish.

To cap the madness, when Clitterhouse is arrested for murder and then tried, he confesses the truth to his friend, defense attorney Grant, and asks Grant to defend him on the plea of insanity. However, the trial becomes a farce when the jury is unable to decide whether the doctor is sane or insane, especially when Clitterhouse, to the consternation of Grant, insists that he is sane. He does that fearing that his book—which he has been writing in note form, recording all his observations—will not be taken seriously if the court decides that it was written by an insane man. The jury then finds him not guilty on the grounds that only an insane man could plead sane. (This reminds one of *Catch-22*, before its time.) The jury foreman faints after he pronounces the verdict, and someone shouts, "Is there a doctor in the house?" "Amazing," cries Clitterhouse, stunned by the turn of events. He has become a celebrity, but we do not know whether his book will be an insane book written by a sane man, or a sane book written by an insane man. It is to be understood that Jo Kelly will marry him in either case. We don't know what happens to his secretary or whether he will practice again.

8

THE ROARING TWENTIES

(Warner Bros., 1939)

★ ★ ★

Director: Raoul Walsh
Screenplay: Jerry Wald, Richard Macaulay, Robert Rossen, adapted from a
    story by Mark Hellinger
Executive Producer: Hal B. Wallis. *Cinematographer:* Ernest Haller. *Music Score:*
    Heinz Roemheld, Ray Heindorf. *Editor:* Jack Killifer
Cast: James Cagney (Eddie Bartlett), Priscilla Lane (Jean Sherman), Humphrey
    Bogart (George Hally), Gladys George (Panama Smith), Jeffrey Lynn
    (Lloyd Hart), Frank McHugh (Danny Green), Paul Kelly (Nick Brown),
    Elizabeth Risdon (Mrs. Sherman), Edward Keane (Pete Henderson)
Released: October 23, 1939
Specs: 106 minutes; black and white
Availability: DVD (Warner Home Video; featurettes by historians Lincoln
    Hurst and Leonard Maltin); streaming (Amazon)

In this celebrated gangster movie that jumps back a decade, Bogart plays a
totally evil character without any redeeming qualities whatsoever. Though
not the lead, which belongs to Jimmy Cagney, Bogart's character is a part
of a trio of World War I veterans who come back to the States after they
are released and go in different directions. Cagney is Eddie Bartlett, Bogart plays George Hally, and Jeffrey Lynn is Lloyd Hart, who, like Bogart,
takes second billing to Cagney. The movie has interest as a reflection of
the bootlegger era, with Cagney reigning supreme as the top gun, while
Bogart seems to have been minimized in stature. For Bogart, that was a
career status soon to be ended, but for the time being, Bogart was still not

only playing a second or third banana to Cagney and Robinson and Raft, but also playing a worthless fellow, and a coward to boot, and perhaps some of his fans might want to forget him in *The Roaring Twenties*. Still, this is a film worth watching, because it is nothing short of an impassionate tale, as well as a clinical analysis of social ills that destroyed a bygone era. There are plenty of ironies in it, one being that Cagney's character is forced into a life of crime by necessity, while Bogart's character seems to be born into it. Though a Cagney vehicle, the movie has enough of Bogart in it to show how easily he could switch screen personalities at will, before and after he became a major star.

The three companions in arms, with a few others who also appear later in the movie, are first seen at the trenches, about the time the armistice is going to put an end to the war. Bogart, playing George Hally, shows his colors immediately when he shoots a fifteen-year-old boy, saying afterward, "He will not grow to be sixteen." When the men are back home, the story shifts entirely to Eddie Bartlett (Cagney), who seeks his old job at a garage, but he is told that the job is taken by someone else. He meets his old friend Danny Green (Frank McHugh), who is driving a cab, and they share duties. At that time, the Volstead Act (Eighteenth Amendment) went into effect and started the Prohibition era; Bartlett unknowingly delivers a package that contains liquor and is arrested as a bootlegger. One step leads to another, and before long, Bartlett rises in the ranks of the bootlegging business.

Meanwhile, two women come into his life. One is Panama Smith (Gladys George), the owner of a speakeasy who also has a crush on him. But he seems to be oblivious to her feelings, and instead, he has turned his attention to a young dancer, Jean Sherman (Priscilla Lane), a girl he had fantasized about while still in the army, having seen a picture of her that was sent to fighting men during the war. When Bartlett meets her again in a dancing hall, he envisions a singing career for her and helps her to get hired as a singer in Panama's establishment. But Jean shows a strong attachment to Lloyd Hart (Jeffrey Lynn), the third member of the original group. He has chosen a career as a lawyer, and as things turn out, he is employed by Eddie Bartlett.

Well into the film, Bogart's character, Hally, reappears. He, too, is in the bootlegging business—entirely by intention, not because he could not find a job—and he is working for a rival to Bartlett, Nick Brown (Paul Kelly), with whom he joins forces. But Hally discovers during one of their raids to steal alcohol that one of the guards is an ex-sergeant he didn't like and kills him ruthlessly.

The 1929 crash comes, and Bartlett loses everything and turns back to taxi driving. During one of his rounds, he sees the very girl he once loved, Jean, now in furs, having married Jeffrey Lynn, who has risen to the rank of district attorney. Jean recognizes Bartlett and tries to help him, but he readily rejects her offer. George Hally has also prospered in the gangland. When they meet, Bartlett proudly rejects Hally's fake pity, and in a scuffle, Bartlett shoots him dead. Pursued by Hally's goons, Bartlett is shot and dies on the steps of a public building. Horrified, Panama witnesses Bartlett's last steps as he staggers to his death.

While Cagney's character is well intentioned and tries in vain to gain lawful employment after the war, George Hally shows his colors from the start. Bartlett would have been a decent man, a hardworking fellow earning his daily living honestly and perhaps being a family man, had circumstances been favorable. Hally is bad from beginning to end, and as in most of his movies before 1940s, he is shot dead well before the movie ends. A commentator on the DVD, Lincoln Hurst, opines that here Bogart is as bad as he is in *The Treasure of Sierra Madre* (1948), but one could counter that the later movie shows a man—Fred C. Dobbs, a drifter and panhandler in Mexico—who is not particularly vicious or dangerous. He seeks honest work, and when he finds it, he works hard, and after he is cheated and turns to prospecting, he turns vicious and selfish, driven by greed. Dobbs is a far more complex character than George Hally, who is presented as a foil to Bartlett, who could have been fine, had circumstances allowed him. In *The Roaring Twenties*, Bogart is a workhorse for Warners; he takes what he is given—an ugly image—and turns it into a chilling one. He applies his own motto: keep working, and if you do, things might turn your way. In less than two years, they did.

9

IT ALL CAME TRUE

(Warner Bros./First National, 1940)

★ ★ ★

Director: Lewis Seiler
Screenplay: Michael Fessier, Lawrence Kimble, adapted from Louis Bromfield's
    short story, "Better Than Life"
Producers: Jack L. Warner, Hal B. Wallis. *Associate Producer:* Mark Hellinger.
    Cinematographer: Ernest Haller. *Music Score:* Heinz Roemheld. *Editor:*
    Thomas Richards
Cast: Humphrey Bogart (Chips Maguire/Grasselli), Ann Sheridan (Sarah
    Jane Ryan), Jeffrey Lynn (Tommy Taylor). Zasu Pitts (Miss Flint), Una
    O'Connor (Maggie Ryan), Jessie Busley (Norah Taylor), John Litel (Mr.
    Roberts), Grant Mitchell (Mr. Salmon), Felix Bressart (Boldini), Charles
    Judels (Henri Pepi de Bordeaux), Brandon Tynan (Mr. Van Diver).
    Herbert Vigran (Monks), Howard Hickman (Mr. Prendergast)
Released: April 6, 1940
Specs: 97 minutes; black and white
Availability: DVD (Warner Archive Collection)

Put Bogart in a comedy, and he can be comic without being a comedian. Make him a gangster, and then an impresario of a musical show, and he will impersonate both, no sweat. Make him all of the above and then put him in a household with two mamas, and he will still manage. But put him in a movie with Ann Sheridan, when a better-looking and more honest man is opposite him, and he will lose, hands down. Even so, Bogart will surface a better man, though the person he impersonates has two identities and he will spend the rest of his life in prison.

Such, in brief, is Bogart in *It All Came True*, a gangster movie, a comedy, a musical, and, at least technically, a romance. It's hard to imagine that the movie will be all those things when it starts, showing a quaint old-maidish lady walking down the street and believing that a fine gentleman with a hat on and cigar in his mouth is following her. The gentleman turns out to be a cigar salesman with "Toro Cigars" emblazoned on his vest. The lady is Miss Flint, who lives at a boardinghouse inhabited by eccentric renters. They are led in oddity though not in status by a washed-up magician named Mr. Boldini (Felix Bressart), who finds it easy to cheat at cards and play worn-out hat tricks and who possesses a clever black pooch that stands while greeting the guests coming in, a bow tie fixed above his eyes. The dog ends up being the best comedian in the story. There is also a poet, Mr. Salmon (Grant Mitchell), later to display his verbal mastery in iambics, and a dreamy gentleman, Mr. Van Diver (Brandon Tynan), who composes encomiums to nature and to life and who lives in the past, as all of them seem to.

The spacious boardinghouse belongs to an aforementioned mama, Nora Taylor (Jessie Busley), the motherly and cheerful type who might have welcomed the devil himself (he comes in later) with a red rug spread before her door. Her friend, Mrs. Maggie Ryan (Una O'Connor), a waspish and sour-looking woman of years, lives with her. She constantly complains about everything, and especially when the two ladies face a lawyer who tells them the apartment will be foreclosed unless owed back taxes are paid to the bank. "The bank wants money," the lawyer tells Mrs. Ryan, who responds, with a contemptuous, "As if they didn't have enough!"

The peaceful atmosphere of the boardinghouse is interrupted by a raucous verbal exchange outside the door, and when Mama Taylor opens it, Sarah Jane (Ann Sheridan), Maggie Ryan's daughter, is shown man-handling a small man, pulling his hat down to his shoulders and unceremoniously kicking him down the stairs. He is seen running for his life, overturning a trash can as he scampers away. Sarah storms in and starts telling the stunned group that the fellow had been a crooked talent agent who had called her into his office for an interview, promising to "discover her." The rambunctious Sarah declares to her stunned audience that the man had a "gat" (gun) with him, which she tosses on the table to show that she is no easy prey to small-time crooks. She had been promised jobs, had been around for five years, and nothing had come of it. Naturally she collides with her ill-tempered mother, who accuses her of a worthless and penniless existence, but Sarah is not the type to let a mom intimidate her. She readily asks her for twenty dollars. "What a breath of spring!" exclaims the dreamy Mr. Van Diver, impressed by Sarah's stormy entrance into the boardinghouse with its hibernating inhabitants. He might have called her a gust of gale-force wind, for that is what Sarah's entrance into the establishment resembles.

At that point, the two main male characters enter—Bogart in the person of Chips Maguire, the gangster owner of the nightclub Cairo Club, and his disillusioned pianist and musician, Tommy Taylor (Jeffrey Lynn). This is the Bogart that we all know (at least up to that point), a tough guy who kills or is killed in quick gunfire. That's not very far from the truth here, though he stays alive for the duration of the movie, and he goes to jail at the end, instead of being gunned down by a Robinson or a Cagney. He is first shown inside his club, talking to his disgruntled musician, when loud knocks on the door announce the appearance of cops, who are breaking down the door with axes. Before he exits, Maguire manages to burn important documents; then he and Taylor exit from a back door. Maguire sees Monks outside, the gangster who informed the cops, and shoots him. He has used the gun, which he had registered in Taylor's name, "for security," and forces the latter to take him to his mama's place to hide.

Having no other option, Taylor complies, and he knocks on his mother's door, where he receives an ecstatic hug from her, as she had not seen him for five years. He explains that the gentleman next to him, introduced as "Mr. Grasselli," needs a place to stay, and she, full of smiles at seeing her son, takes them to a back room. Grasselli explains that he is recovering from a "nervous breakdown" and needs peace and quiet. She assures him he will have both, delighted to have such a distinguished guest in her quarters. She is motherly and takes a cigarette out of his mouth the next morning, telling him that a man in his condition shouldn't be smoking, and then empties a tray full of cigarette butts in her trash can. A bit later, though, as she unpacks one of Grasselli's suitcases, she discovers an arsenal of guns there. Coolly, Grasselli explains that he is a hunter (!) and that he intends to go hunting when his health improves. Naively and good-heartedly, Mrs. Taylor accepts the explanation and promises to keep mum.

But before we forget, this is also a love story, and the principals, as one would expect, are Sarah and the young Tommy Taylor, lovers in their youth, who are reunited after all those years. Both are failures, as both had been pursuing careers, she as a singer, he as a songwriter, to no avail. This is not an easy reunion, for Sarah knows who Grasselli is and knows her lover boy has been in bad company. But both Taylor and Sarah are on the verge of an unexpected break, which will give them a chance to exhibit their talents: to break the monotony of the torpid daily existence of the houseguests, their mamas propose an evening of recreation, a performance starring their

gifted guests. Grasselli scoffs at the idea, but he attends out of sheer bore-
dom. First comes Mr. Salmon, who waxes grandiloquent, reciting flowery
verses, going on and on; he is asked for an encore from Boldini, who has to
go "inside" to put on his costume. When he comes in wearing it, one cannot
decide whether he looks like a Roman guard from *Julius Caesar*, a Spartan
in half-uniform, or an escapee from a lunatic asylum. He produces a rabbit out of a hat, one among his various antics, while his dog hops around
purposelessly—until the dog pulls Boldini's toga away, revealing his rear,
where a cooking pan is attached. He runs away, his rear rattling, and that
provokes a laugh even from Grasselli, who finds himself amused at last.

But wait. The main event is yet to come—the musicians, and when their
turn comes, wham! The tone of the whole ridiculous show changes. Ann
Sheridan as Sarah appears in a black low-cut gown that reveals a sexy, vo-
luptuous woman with dancing talent and a singing voice! She croons away,
pulsating and shaking, reminding of Rita Hayworth's dance in *Gilda*, but
without Rita's morose mood. In short, Sheridan as Sarah rocks! And Grasselli is struck by an idea: why not transform the parlor into a nightclub and
invite real guests to enjoy the show! The idea takes root, and pretty soon an
Italian master chef is brought in, the parlor is transformed as if by magic
into a spacious showroom, and the show begins with lots of pizazz and glitter. The show is to be called "The Roaring Nineties," a name that fits the
antiquated surroundings.

The informal nightly shows continue for a few weeks without incident—
until one day Miss Flint, an avid reader of detective magazines, sees photos
in one and finds out that their guest Mr. Grasselli is the notorious Chips
Maguire. Ready to reveal the exciting news, she is stopped by Sarah, who
tells her about the horrors awaiting those who squeal on gangsters—extraction of gold teeth, death by strangling, feet placed in cement and being sunk
into the river, and so on. Terrified, Miss Flint stays silent, until the night
of the "The Roaring Nineties" performance. Then she shakes with terror
at the thought of her imagined torment, gets drunk, and flees to the police
station, where she bubbles about Grasselli, but accidentally spills the name
Chips Maguire, and the police instantly send two of the detectives to the
party to seize him. Maguire, knowing this is the end, tells them to stay on
and enjoy the show, since he went into so much trouble to put it together.
They do.

Meanwhile, "The Roaring Nineties" goes on. Boldini performs magic
tricks, and his dog is in top form, pulling his toga. Then things get professional: several real well-known ensembles come in to perform, playing
themselves. Crowds roar in applause, as this turns out to be first-class enter-

tainment, and one wonders how those ensembles were persuaded to come into such an outlandish environment. One pair is missing though: Sarah Jane and Tommy Taylor. By now lovers, they plan to make their big debut and go on to better and bigger things. But Tommy gets terrified when he sees the police arriving and hides on the roof. It takes a lot of convincing on the part of Sarah—including a passionate kiss—to get him down to the ballroom. She sings and is a sensation. He plays the piano, and he proves a master of the keyboard, not to mention the music he wrote. Now Maguire, suddenly feeling generous, tells Tommy he will admit he killed Monks so the musical pair of lovers can go on to a glorious future. "I have one hundred twenty years coming to me," he says. "Adding thirty more won't make any difference." Once more, Bogart gives up the girl to a better man—that's going to be a habit from now on, at least on the screen. Maybe living in a household of honest folk humanized him, and that's the end of it.

For the record, this is a movie where Bogart gets top billing with Ann Sheridan, a gal his character Maguire/Grasselli lusted after, and though he does not get the girl, he proves that he can do anything, including playing a buffoonish gangster who, just to amuse himself, turns people's lives around. By the way, the room he was forced to hide in had been rented by a "naturalist," Mama Taylor explains, as he jumps back in fright every time he turns around and a stuffed animal flashes before him. "He died on this very bed," Mama Taylor remarks, as Grasselli sits on the dead man's bed. On occasion audiences need a kick, and they get it, watching a gangster cringe in fright at the sight of a stuffed monkey. And Bogart is at his comic best in a movie of floundering wannabe artists until he, a mobster, walks in to pave the road to love repair and domestic amity. God bless them bad boys, as Mama Taylor might have said. As for Miss Flint, she will probably sleep calmly, knowing that she will not lose her gold tooth or sink in the river, her feet in cement.

⑩

THEY DRIVE BY NIGHT

(Warner Bros./First National, 1940)

★ ★ ★

Director: Raoul Walsh
Screenplay: Jerry Wald, Richard McCauley, adapted from the novel *Long Haul* by A. I. Bezzerides
Executive Producer: Hal B. Wallis. *Associate Producer:* Mark Hellinger.
    Cinematographer: Arthur Edeson. *Music Score:* Adolph Deutsch. *Editor:* Thomas Richard
Cast: George Raft (Joe Fabrini), Ann Sheridan (Casey Hartley), Ida Lupino (Lana Carlsen), Humphrey Bogart (Paul Fabrini), Gale Page (Pearl Fabrini), Alan Hale (Ed Carlsen), Roscoe Karns (Irish McGurn), Charles Halton (Farnsworth), John Ridgley (Hank Dawson)
Released: August 3, 1940
Specs: 95 minutes; black and white
Availability: DVD (Warner Home Video)

The main reason for including *They Drive by Night* in this volume is its unintended ironies. Although their careers mixed only twice on the screen, Raft and Bogart had a rivalry that extended beyond the screen. At this point, 1940, Bogart was still considered second rate compared to the stars at Warners—Robinson, Cagney, Muni, *and* Raft. Things changed rapidly a year or so later, as Raft rejected two meaty roles that went to Bogart— *High Sierra* (1941) and *The Maltese Falcon* (1941)—and put Bogart on the map, as from that point on Bogart received top billing, the surest sign of star status (in *High Sierra*, both Lupino's and Bogart's names were in the opening credits, but Bogart's name appeared below Lupino's, which meant that his costar was still ahead of him in top billing status). In *They Drive by*

Night, however, Bogart was still in the shadows, and Raft got the girl at the end, while Bogart becomes incapacitated halfway through the movie and is hardly seen after that.

Directed by Raoul Walsh, *They Drive by Night* is an absorbing tale and, in its own way, fun to watch. It is a quickly paced, well-acted movie that offers entertainment on several fronts: it is a road movie that shows the perils of truck drivers at night and the trucker culture in general; it offers romantic interest with two love triangles centered on two of the most likable (for different reasons) actresses of the time, Ann Sheridan and Ida Lupino; it has moments of humor, albeit of the crude kind; and it is a murder story, climaxing in a trial that showcases the brilliant talents of Lupino. For Bogart, the movie leaves little room for action, although his part in it is still worth mentioning. He plays second banana to George Raft, with whom he had been paired before in *Invisible Stripes* (1939), the man Bogart was to leave in the dust one or two movies later.

The two, Raft and Bogart, as Joe and Paul Fabrini, respectively, are loving brothers, truck drivers who drive mostly at night, but, evidently, Paul is the weaker member. He has a wife, Pearl (Gale Page), who pleads with him to find an ordinary job, come home in the evening for dinner, and raise a family. But Paul is loyal to his brother, an enterprising fellow who wants to pay off his rig, expand if he can, and stay in the business. But the two struggle to make ends meet, and their rig is about to be repossessed if they don't make payments on time. Paul, who is pushed to drive one night to give a break to his equally tired brother, falls asleep at the wheel. The rig crashes into a canyon, and Paul loses an arm after barely surviving the accident. Joe comes out of the accident with only a scratch on the head, while Paul is left an amputee and out of action for half of the movie.

During a stop at a truckers' roadside café, Joe meets a smarty-pants waitress, Cassie Hartley (Sheridan), who, unable to survive the rough environment of truckers' stops, quits and walks away in the rain, only to be picked up moments later by Joe and then share a motel room with him, surprisingly uneventfully. Here Raft's character proves a gentleman, though evidently falling for the attractive Cassie. But he also has to deal with Ida Lupino's Lana, an egotistical woman who is not satisfied with her marriage to the older Ed Carlsen, played with gusto by Alan Hale,[1] who is boisterous, crude, and drunk most of the time. He likes one-liner wisecracks of his own making; when his wife, Lana, tells him to stop drinking or he will end up with a bloated liver, he responds, "Live and let liver!" (A more ghastly one is "Early to rise, early to bed makes a man healthy but socially dead.") But he is the wealthy owner of a truck company, and Lana has married him for his money. She has an eye for the unattached Joe, and she uses her wiles to get him an executive job in the company. As the boisterous Carlsen takes his guests around to show them his new house, which he has built as a gift to his glamorous wife, he demonstrates how his garage doors can be opened and closed if he breaks an invisible beam by walking across the driveway.

Here the tale takes a turn, almost becoming a different movie.[2] When a few nights later Lana takes her drunken husband home from a party, she is struck by an idea. Instead of turning off the engine, she leaves it on and exits. She pauses a moment, vacillating, then crosses the beam to close the door. A day later, at the district attorney's office, wearing a black veil and looking shattered with grief, she explains how she couldn't carry the heavy man upstairs and left him in the car. He must have turned the engine on, but his drunkenness kept him pinned to his seat resulting in his death by carbon monoxide fumes. The DA buys the story and begs her pardon for bothering her at such a moment, and Lana goes off, scot-free.

She sees this as a chance to accost Joe, asking him to take over the management of the company, on a fifty–fifty basis. He accepts, under the condition that there will be no "interference." That, of course, is not what she intends. Lana makes it clear in several meetings that the only reason she made Joe a manager was to get a slice of him. As he keeps saying no, she displays all the fire and fury of a rejected woman. When Joe announces that he is marrying Cassie "next Friday," Lana takes an extreme step. Going back to the DA's office, she confesses that she murdered her husband and implicates Joe as well, stating that he was behind the plan so he could take over the company. In the ensuing trial, Lana displays the phobia she developed during her imprisonment when she sees doors opening and closing when a beam is crossed. Called to the stand, she looks haggard and aged, and when asked questions, she looks straight ahead and starts sputtering incoherent phrases of guilt and fear, screaming out, "The doors made me do it!" "Remove the witness," says the judge, and she is taken out in a straitjacket.

Joe, of course, is free to marry Cassie, but he feels he has no right to be the head of the company, so he turns over his share to his friends and employees. With one voice they coax him to stay, and he does. Bogart's Paul is standing with the others, one-armed but with a steady job at the office that allows him to go back to his wife in the evening. He announces they are expecting a baby. Paul, now under the sheltering wing of his prosperous and happy brother, will have a quiet and happy life, what he always wanted. Maybe the loss of one arm—in a movie—showed the real Bogart that he still had work to do. But it was Raft's witlessness that gave Bogart a leading role in the next two movies and made him a top star.

Lupino's performance, by the way, was so stunning that she was offered a seven-year contract by Warner Bros. and was readily paired with Bogart in *High Sierra*, and this time Bogart got top billing, appearing in the opening credits, though his name appeared below Lupino's because he had yet to supersede her in star status. She couldn't get Raft, but she did get Bogart next time around.

And for trivia seekers, Joe and Paul wore their hats with the rims turned up, like truck drivers who want to have full vision of what lies ahead. But when Joe became a traffic manager, he wore his hat with the rim down, on the left side, an attraction for Lana. When Bogart became Sam Spade, he turned the rim of his fedora down, on the right—and that was his trademark from then on. One could say that the rim makes the man.

⓫

HIGH SIERRA

(Warner Bros./First National, 1941)

★ ★ ★ ★

Director: Raoul Walsh

Screenplay: John Huston, W. R Burnett, adapted from the novel by W. R. Burnett

Producer: Hal B. Wallis, Mark Hellinger. *Cinematographer:* Tony Gaudio. *Music Score:* Adolph Deutsch. *Editor:* Jack Killifer

Cast: Humphrey Bogart (Roy Earle), Ida Lupino (Marie Garson), Joan Leslie (Velma), Alan Curtis (Babe Kozak), Arthur Kennedy (Red Hattery), Henry Hall (Doc Banton), Barton MacLane (Jake Kranmer), Henry Travers (Pa Goodhue), Cornel Wilde (Louis Mendoza), John Eldredge (Lon Preiser), Donald MacBride (Big Mac), Willie Best (Algernon), Pard (Zero, the Dog)

Released: January 21, 1941

Specs: 100 minutes; black and white

Availability: DVD (Warner Home Video); streaming (Amazon)

Just as *The Petrified Forest* had placed Bogart on the Warners payroll six years earlier, thus jump-starting his film career, so did *High Sierra* become the vehicle that turned him from a second-rate hood to a major movie star and a screen icon. Despite a second billing to Ida Lupino, Bogart is the real lead in this one, and *High Sierra* became a movie that turned his fortunes around; from that point on Bogart received top billing, which in those days determined the status of an actor as well as the size of his salary. The role had been offered first to George Raft, who rejected it, thus unintentionally helping to promote Bogart's career to bigger things. The script was based on a novel by W. R. Burnett and was coauthored by Burnett and John Huston, who was to direct several of Bogart's top movies in the next decade. It was one of those rare instances where the actor and director/author saw eye to eye, knew each other's mind, and produced masterpieces together, becoming close friends in the process.

Bogart gives a convincing performance as Roy Earle, fresh from prison, graying at the temples and looking like an ex-con with a mission. In the Burnett novel, the hero was Roy "Mad Dog" Earldon, changed to Earle in the movie, a character based on the notorious John Dillinger, "the Last Desperado," dominating headlines in the midthirties.[1] Earle is an infamous bank robber, suddenly pardoned from a life sentence through the intervention of Big Mac (Donald McBryde), the mobster and financier of a new operation out west. Before he leaves, Earle sees a connection, Jake Kranmer (Barton MacLane), who gives him the keys to a car, money, and the general idea of what the new setup is and where he is to go. Kranmer is an ex-cop and knows Earle's past, and when he makes a crack at Earle's expense, Earle slaps him in the face twice before he leaves. That brings to mind Bogart's tough persona already established in his thirties movies, but with some new twists here. Having spent eight years in prison, Earle is still living in the era of John Dillinger, becoming an anachronism, as the era of notorious killers on the loose has come to an end. Slowly, the new Bogartian persona emerges. Freed, Roy Earle is set up for another fall, as he drives west for a new adventure. Tough and bitter, he can also be nostalgic, as when he stops at an Indiana farm that used to belong to his family, meets an old man who recognizes him, and talks to a young boy who is going fishing, giving him a word about the right spot, a small lagoon where fish used to abound.

When he reaches the California-Nevada border, Earle stops a moment at a gas station, where a garrulous old attendant talks about Mt. Whitney of the High Sierras, the tallest peak in the country at nearly fifteen thousand feet high. As Earle talks, a car he had passed on the road soon arrives, driven by an old man and full of family inside. A few moments earlier, Earle had swung around it to avoid it, as the old man himself had swung to his right to avoid hitting a rabbit. Inside the car is a young girl, Velma (Joan Leslie), who is traveling west with her grandpa, Pa Goodhue (Henry Travers), and some other members of his family. Earle is struck by her beauty, but he soon learns that she is a clubfoot, born that way, and Pa informs him she could be cured if Pa had the money. Earle dreams of a future with the young lady, after he is done with his job, when he could marry and settle down and have a family of his own.

Earle reaches his destination, near the High Sierras, where he meets two young men, Babe Kozak (Alan Curtis) and Red Hattery (Arthur Kennedy), who live in a hut with Marie, a girlfriend of one of them. A black youth, Algernon, does domestic chores for them, spending most of his time fishing and training an amiable dog, Pard, to perform clever tricks. Earle soon visits Big Mac, seemingly a genial man who is bedridden because of hepatitis, but who keeps drinking against the advice of his doctor, Doc Banton (Henry Hall), who is in the plan and cooperative. The gang of Earle, Babe Kozak, and Red Hattery is joined by Louis Mendoza (a young Cornel Wilde), who is the receptionist of a posh hotel in Los Angeles, where the heist is to take place. Babe and Red are two undisciplined young toughs, fighting over Marie (Lupino), and Earle has trouble putting this amateurish group together. To complicate matters, Marie insists on coming along, with Pard (Bogart's own dog, Zero), a lovable animal that adds both color and trouble. The heist takes longer than expected and things go wrong during the escape, as Earle is forced to kill a hotel guard. There is a chase, during which Babe and Red are killed as they fail to negotiate a turn on the road. Mendoza is injured and captured, while Earle and Marie get away carrying a shoe box where the stolen jewels are kept.

Roy Earle (Bogart) negotiates the heist with Louis Mendoza (Cornel Wilde), as his co-conspirators Babe Kozak (Alan Curtis) and Red Hattery (Arthur Kennedy) look on, with Marie Carson (Ida Lupino) watching from the side. *Warner Bros. Pictures/Photofest © Warner Bros. Pictures*

Before delivering his treasure to Big Mac, Earle wants to stop by Pa Goodhue's family to see how Velma is doing; she is still bedridden but the operation, which Earle had funded with the money he had initially received from Kranmer, was a success and she expects to be walking normally in a few days. But when Earle asks her whether she will marry him, she turns him down. She will be his friend, but she is not in love with him. Velma will marry Lon, a man she knew back in Indiana.

Things turn for the worse from now on. When Earle returns to Big Mac's to deliver the treasure, he finds Big Mac dead. Earle gets into a scuffle with Big Mac's partner—the same man, Jake Kranmer (Barton MacLane, who became Bogart nemesis is several movies to follow), who had initially given Earle money and a car to reach California; Earle kills Kranmer and he himself suffers a light wound on the side.

Earle and Marie are now fugitives. Earle, who is now a notorious outlaw called "Mad Dog Earle," puts her on a bus with Pard to Las Vegas, and he takes off to find some cash. But when he attempts to rob a convenience store, he is recognized by the owner and that sets up a chase by police on cars and motorcycles. Earle drives to the Sierras, and when he reaches a "Road Closed" sign, he takes off with his guns and hides behind rocks. Marie hears the news and hurries back to the place with Pard, who, hearing Earle's voice, runs up to him. Earle knows that Marie is there and gets into the open and shouts at her, but he is killed by a sniper, and his body rolls down the rocks at the foot of a hill. "He has crashed out," a reporter named Healy (Jerome Cowan) whispers, looking at the dead body. "What does that mean?" Marie asks. "Means he is free," says the reporter. "Free, free . . ." Marie smiles in her tears, and she walks away, holding Pard.

By the end of the movie audiences were rooting for Earle. Here is Bogart, still a gangster, but with a refashioned image, one tough guy with vulnerabilities, holding on to his code that there is "honor among thieves," but unable to control his environment and his own feelings. When he meets Pa's family and gets to know them, he is sentimental and even delusional. A Bogart character is rarely afflicted with illusions, setting them aside for pragmatic choices. Here, however, it is illusion that sidetracks him and brings about his tragic end. He thinks the planned heist would enrich him, that he would be able to settle down to a quiet life and marry Velma, the crippled girl who is cured because he had financed her operation; however, he falsely assumed that her friendship and gratitude are love. Velma will not marry Earle; she chooses Lon (John Eldredge), despite the fact that he is evidently ordinary. But so is she, Earle now concludes, despite the image she projected earlier when they first met and he talked to her about the stars.

Earle is not wrong, however, about the gang of Babe, Red, and Mendoza. He sees through them as quarrelsome amateurs, not big enough for a big job. But he likes Marie, a victim like him of itinerant life. The dog's devotion to her is also affecting both the actions and feelings of Earle. All three seem rootless and victims of fate. All three are misfits. Marie could have made Earle happy, if circumstances were different, something it takes him too long to realize. Ida Lupino's performance is carefully modulated to set her character and Earle apart from both the criminal milieu they are mixed with and the law-abiding social class they can't fit in with or adapt to. Roy Earle belongs to the world of crime, which he entered when young, and into which he is trapped for life. His illusion that one more crime would set him up for life is shattered. He does not lack abilities, and with more competent partners, he could have achieved his goal of gaining riches. But a safe, happy life after that, perhaps an idyllic agrarian existence, would not have been guaranteed. The movie illustrates that the road to crime has no exit.

⑫

THE MALTESE FALCON

(Warner Bros./First National, 1941)

★ ★ ★ ★ ★

Director: John Huston
Screenplay: John Huston, based on the novel by Dashiell Hammett
Executive Producer: Hal B. Wallis. *Associate Producer:* Henry Blanke.
  Cinematographer: Arthur Edeson. *Music Score:* Adolph Deutsch. *Editor:*
  Thomas Richard
Cast: Humphrey Bogart (Sam Spade), Mary Astor (Brigid O'Shaughnessy),
  Gladys George (Iva Archer), Lee Patrick (Effie Perrine), Gerome
  Cowan (Miles Archer), Sydney Greenstreet (Casper Gutman), Peter
  Lorre (Joel Cairo), Elisha Cook Jr. (the "gunsel," Wilmer), Barton
  McLane (Lieutenant Dundy), Ward Bond (Detective Tom Polhaus),
  John Hamilton (District Attorney Bryan), Walter Huston (Captain
  Jacobi)
Released: October 18, 1941
Specs: 100 minutes; black and white
Availability: DVD (Three-Disc Special Edition; new digital transfer of the 1941
  original movie. Disc 1 contains a commentary by biographer Eric Lax.
  Discs 2 and 3 contain the two previous movie versions: *The Maltese
  Falcon* from 1931 and *Satan Met a Lady* from 1936); Blu-ray; available to
  watch streaming through Amazon.com, Ps3, Xbox, Kindle Fire, iPad, PC

We are such stuff that dreams are made on,
and our little life is rounded with a sleep.

—William Shakespeare

The Maltese Falcon is about a black bird statuette—the length of a football, weighing fifty pounds, and encrusted with fabulous jewels—that is pursued by a gang of thieves and a clever detective and that proves a fake when it is finally found. The movie's subject is supposed to illustrate human avarice, a motive practically existing in most of us, the movie suggests. The movie could possibly be renamed, "How to Acquire Wealth without Really Trying," for, though the principals expend a great amount of energy, none of them possesses either the wit or the will to get money by achieving something else; instead, they wait, as the leader of the gang says to them that he has waited for seventeen years for the prize to fall into his lap. They are rewarded with failure, but instead of taking it in stride and doing something worthwhile, they continue pursuing their goal—"another year on the quest," their leader says—proving the limitless horizons of human illusion.

The story was written by Dashiell Hammett, who was a detective but gave that up due to pulmonary tuberculosis; he was content to collect eighty dollars a month from disability insurance and write short stories and crime novels. Most of his stories were published in a pulp fiction magazine, *Black Mask*, and one, "The Maltese Falcon," was purchased by Warner Bros.,[1] who filmed it three times. First, in 1931, Warners produced a film that starred Ricardo Cortez and Bebe Daniels, stayed close to the Hammett original, and did well enough with public and critics, but it did not blaze any trails in movie history. Warner Bros. tried again in 1936, doing the movie, titled *Satan Met a Lady*, as a comedy, with William Warren and Bette Davis, who was so hopeless in it ("So you knew all the time I had killed him!") that it nearly wrecked her career. Finally, a clever producer at Warners, Henry Blanke, brought the subject back in 1941, and the company tried again, this time with an unproven first-time director, John Huston, only known as a screenwriter up to that time. Huston saw the potential of the story and decided to reproduce it exactly as it was, retaining the same terse dialogue and the clipped pace of the novel. Luck brought in Humphrey Bogart to play Sam Spade, as George Raft, the initial choice, turned the role down, not wanting to entrust his career to the hands of a novice director. The movie was a smashing popular hit and won a nomination for a Best Picture in a crowded field that included *Citizen Kane, Sergeant York, The Little Foxes,* and Hitchcock's *Suspicion*. Huston was nominated for Best Screenplay and Sidney Greenstreet for Best Supporting Actor. Bogart was passed over, but there was no doubt in anyone's mind that his status at Warners had been impacted dramatically and that he was now a major star.

The Maltese Falcon was also regarded as a powerful introduction to the film noir era, setting the tone for films that came after, such as *The Big*

Sleep, Double Indemnity, The Postman Rings Twice, and dozens of others with dark themes that filled the screen in the 1940s. The premise of film noir, according to Roger Ebert,[2] was that people fall due mostly to their own flaws—an idea that comes close to Greek tragedy. In elaborating on film noir, the film historian Foster Hirsch gives primacy to the sleuth, who operates in an urban environment of crime,[3] in the dark alleys speaking street language, rather than in the aristocratic salons where upper-crust guests exchange more jokes than gunshots. The sleuth is an ambiguous character, single-minded, smart, and ruthless, bouncing back from momentary setbacks and capable of operating on both sides of the law. As film noir, *The Maltese Falcon* also introduced visual techniques, such as contrasts of black and white, low camera angles, slick camera movements, and asymmetrical compositions, derivatives of the German expressionism abounding in Orson Welles's *Citizen Kane*, arguably a film noir itself.

Bogart was paired with Mary Astor, whose stellar performance as the femme fatale Ingrid O'Shaughnessy added both glamor and intrigue. Astor almost stole the show by constantly changing her tale, confusing both Spade and the audience, simultaneously being pleading, fearful, seductive, and sweet-talking, and though Bogart's Spade figures her out as a liar, he falls for her charms and seems to struggle to keep his thoughts straight.

Of the other players, Peter Lorre had already appeared in several films and established his credentials in Fritz Lang's *M* and Hitchcock's *The Man Who Knew Too Much* (1935), but was not yet a major star in Hollywood. Here he was member of a gang of three, led by Sydney Greenstreet, a stage actor who was making his movie debut at the age of sixty-one, playing the main pursuer of the falcon, Caspar Gutman. He was a man of size (over three hundred pounds) and imposing presence, and he had the manners of a gentleman and the lethal elusiveness of a cobra. His other partner was Elisha Cook Jr. as the "gunsel"[4] Wilmer, slight in size but vindictive and lethal, the "lightest heavy," as Hollywood gossip had it. The action comes mostly in stagelike dialogue in small episodes, with occasional bursts of violence; yet the pace is quick, the dialogue crisp, both complicating and revealing, spun like a yarn of a maze, with Bogart's character hunting an elusive goal. These five characters, appearing in sequence—Spade, O'Shaughnessy, Cairo, Wilmer, Gutman—remain in place from start to finish, forming the nucleus of the plot and giving it coherence and symmetry.

There are several peripheral characters: Miles Archer (Gerome Cowan), Spade's partner; Effie Perrine (Lee Patrick), Spade's secretary; Iva Archer (Gladys George), his partner's wife with whom Spade was carrying on an affair; Sergeant Tom Polhaus (Ward Bond); Lieutenant Dundy (Barton

MacLane); District Attorney Bryan (John Hamilton); and Captain Jacoby (Walter Huston). Aside from Effie, these peripheral characters appear sporadically, though importantly, at crucial points of the plot, which is based on a story that Spade learns piecemeal, very little from O'Shaughnessy and the rest from Gutman, who is behind this plot and who outlines its essentials when it is convenient to him. Several absent characters are only known by name—Floyd Thursby, General Komidov, Charilaos Costantinidis—and references are made to historical personages such as the Templars of Malta and the King of Spain. This arrangement gives the plot clarity and economy. In contrast to *Casablanca*, which is populated by an amoral cosmos of (mostly uncredited) actors thrust together in Rick's café, and *The Big Sleep*, where characters appear and are committed to oblivion moments later, *The Maltese Falcon* is a detective story and a puzzle, where all the main pieces fit together from beginning to end.

Of the main characters to appear at Spade's office, the first is Brigid O'Shaughnessy, who presents herself as Wonderly, beautiful and distressed, telling Spade a tall tale—that she has lost her younger sister, who left New York and is now in San Francisco. The sister has been enticed by a Floyd Thursby, a dangerous man, whom Wonderly hires Spade to shadow. Spade's partner, Miles Archer, undertakes to do so but is killed mysteriously the same night. Spade knows he is a suspect, as he is carrying on an affair with Archer's wife, and has to shake off two policemen, Lieutenant Dundy and Detective Tom Polhaus, who visit him the night of Archer's murder, telling him that Thursby, too, has been killed. In the morning, Spade visits Wonderly at her apartment, where she tells him that the story she told him was "just a story," and that her real name is Brigid O'Shaughnessy. She desperately pleads for his support, but gives him little to go by, and he soon guesses that he is dealing with a compulsive liar. Spade seems fascinated by her, nonetheless.

In comes Cairo to further complicate things, startling Spade with his bizarre appearance. His card precedes him, brought in by Effie, who utters the word *gardenia*, as she hands the card to Spade, who smells it knowingly. Cairo is small—almost a toy man—impeccably attired, his hair curled in ringlets; he is holding a cane and gloves. He is ostentatiously polite, his large eyes rolling innocently as if he is pleading his case, and speaks in a whisper, with the manner of an aristocrat who has fallen on hard times. Cairo offers Spade a $5,000 reward to find a lost statuette, if the latter can obtain it "with no questions asked." Then, as Spade is momentarily busy with the phone, Cairo pulls a gun, demanding that he be able to search the place. It takes only a moment for Spade to knock him out with a few punches, and he then goes through Cairo's pockets. He finds several passports, a wallet with about $200 in it, various other objects, and a perfumed handkerchief. Spade pays no particular attention to this detail, but knows—as the audience does—that Cairo is a homosexual. Hammett calls him "a fairy," but in those times of movie censorship that word was taboo. Coming around, Cairo protests, "Look what you did to my shirt!" he exclaims, and he renews his offer. Before Cairo departs, he asks for his gun; Spade gives it to him, and Cairo turns it on him and says he intends to search his room. Spade puts his hands behind his neck, laughs, and lets him do so.

The third character, Wilmer, whom Spade calls a "gunsel" (a "boy" in the Hammett book), is seen shadowing Spade, but the latter spots him instantly, catches him in a hotel lobby, and has him expelled, but not before he gives Wilmer a message for his boss, the "fat man," who is behind all the manipulations. Spade soon receives a phone call, a sign that Gutman wants to see

Sam Spade (Bogart), Joel Cairo (Peter Lorre), and Bridget O'Shaughnessy (Mary Astor) look greedily on as Gaspar Gutman (Sidney Greenstreet) holds the falcon. *Warner Bros./Photofest* © *Warner Bros.*

him. Gutman, massive and attired in black, sits immobile in his chair; photographed from a low-angle camera, he fills the screen with his solid bulk. His face is round, his eyebrows are curved, and his eyes look down at his opponent with disdain, as if at a rat. But he welcomes Spade with affected geniality, offering him a drink and saying, "I like a man who likes to talk." Yet he is reluctant to give Spade any information, and Spade storms out of the room faking a violent temper outburst. His right hand shakes as he approaches the elevator, a sign that he is himself affected by the turn of events.

Soon afterward, Spade is approached by Wilmer, who, holding a gun, leads him up to the hotel room, but Spade disarms him easily before they get there. Gutman is now ready to talk, offering Spade a drink. In a lengthy tale (shortened from the novel), Gutman tells Spade that he is in pursuit of the Maltese Falcon, a statuette of a black bird filled with precious jewels that supposedly had been sent by the Templars of Malta to Charles, King of Spain, in the sixteenth century as a token of their obedience to him. The statuette was stolen by pirates along the way, was passed from hand to hand for nearly three centuries, and found its way to Istanbul in 1923, when it came into the possession of a Greek named Charilaos Costantinidis, who understood its real value (as Hammett's novel had been published in 1929, the original date of the events in the novel happen seventeen years earlier). But when Gutman and his gang, Cairo and Wilmer, were headed to Istanbul to get it from Costantinidis, the latter had already been murdered and the Falcon stolen. A Russian, General Komidov, was now the new owner. Gutman attempted to buy it from Komidov, but the latter, possibly understanding its value, did not sell. Gutman asks Spade to procure it, in exchange for $25,000, but as they are talking, Spade's vision blurs and he blanks out, the result of knockout drops in his drink. As he is lying on the floor, Wilmer delivers a vicious kick to his head.

When Spade comes to hours later, he calls Effie, his secretary, and tells her, "Let's do something right for a change." Quickly, he finds a marked-out news item in a newspaper, concluding that the three were headed for *La Paloma*, a liner that had arrived that afternoon from Hong Kong. When he gets to the harbor, the ship is on fire, and after making sure that everyone in it was evacuated, Spade returns to his apartment. Moments later, a man stumbles in, drops a newspaper-wrapped bundle to the floor, mutters "Falcon," and falls on a chair, dying seconds later. Spade registers the bundle in a storage depot and drops the deposit ticket into a mailbox, addressed to a PO Box number. When he returns to his place, O'Shaughnessy is waiting for him outside, and together they enter his apartment. Gutman is there and so are Cairo and Wilmer, both aiming guns at him.

What follows is a long, highly theatrical scene, about one-third of the film (thirty-five pages of the script), where Spade knows he is playing his final card. The group are there because they had failed to get the bird, as Captain Jacobi (played by Walter Huston, John Huston's father, in a cameo role) had brought it to Spade's place, even while near death. Gutman explains that this failure is to be attributed to Miss O'Shaughnessy, who had been difficult in negotiating with him where the bird had been delivered. Spade knows he is under threat of death, so he agrees to deliver the bird in exchange for the money he had been promised, though this seems a ruse to gain time. Gutman hands him an envelope with $10,000 in it, as a first payment for the bird. But then Spade outmaneuvers Gutman by saying that he has to have "a fall guy," to safeguard against the police, and he points to Wilmer. After Wilmer is disarmed and held captive, Spade demands more details about what happened and who is responsible for what murder. Gutman sees no reason to hide anything at this point and tells him the full story of the theft of the bird; as daylight approaches, Spade calls Effie, tells her where the bird is, and asks her to bring it to his place.

One of the most visually compelling cinematic scenes follows. Five people look on as Gutman frantically cuts the strings and removes several layers of covers, until he sees the bird. "At last, after seventeen years," he says, as greed shines on all faces, including that of Spade. But in a moment the illusion vanishes. As Gutman scratches the enamel surface of the falcon, he realizes that the bird is a fake! He touches his collar with his fingers, showing signs of having an apoplexy. At the same time, Cairo bawls at him—an unusually energetic moment for the passive Cairo—calling him "fathead," "a bloated idiot," and other such decorative adjectives, blaming him for his blunder of attempting to buy the bird from Komidov, arousing suspicions in him that this object must have been of great value. But Gutman momentarily recovers and tells Cairo, who is sitting on a chair, dejected, that he is going to Istanbul to spend one more year on the quest, and asks Cairo if he is going with him. Cairo weakly murmurs, "Are you going?" quickly adding, yes in answer to Gutman's question. Gutman also asks Spade, but the latter won't buy the offer. Pistol in hand, Gutman demands the envelope with the $10,000 and Spade complies, but asks to keep one of the ten bills, for his "time and expenses." That was not his purpose for keeping the bill though.

Now, the final confrontation is at hand—Spade versus O'Shaughnessy. She has been left behind, helpless and in her lover's hands. She is certain that her wily charms will keep them friends. To her surprise, she hears Spade saying that he "will send her over." In disbelief she pleads, but he repeats to her that she is "taking the fall." Dramatic intensity rises, but now on a different emotional level. Spade has called the police and told them how to track down the fugitives. That is the right move, since now he can prove he has the killers. But not all the killers. He is by now convinced that his partner, Miles, was not killed by Thursby or any of the others. Archer was too experienced to be killed by a man he was following. But he was "dumb enough" to fall for the woman, who had reasons to have him killed, and thus Thursby could be blamed. So, when the bird arrived with Captain Jacobi of *La Paloma*, O'Shaughnessy would have it all to herself. Soberly, Spade explains to her the reasons for sending her over: a man whose partner had been killed has to do something about it. If he doesn't, then he hurts all detectives in the business. And, second, he cannot trust her. As he explains, if she has something on him, he is not sure she is not going to use it against him; and if he has something on her, he is not sure she is not going to put a bullet through him at some point. As she pleads, the police arrive, announcing that the three fugitives have been captured. "Here's another one for you," says Spade, handing O'Shaughnessy to them, pointing to the guns on the table as physical evidence. The curtain falls, so to speak, as the police take her to the elevator and she looks at Spade (and the audience), her eyes full of tears of shock and despair—but not of repentance. When asked by Tom Polhaus, who is holding the fake falcon, what this was all about, he takes the bird and walks off, misquoting Shakespeare by responding, "The stuff that dreams are made of."[5]

Bogart's Sam Spade has become the archetypal detective who left his traces on all screen detectives to follow. The detective's struggle is not the result of an assignment (as in *The Big Sleep*), but of self-preservation. He outsmarts opponents on the three sides: the police, who are first to suspect him of the murders of Archer and Thursby; Gutman and his gang, who see him as a means of getting the falcon but who remain a menace throughout; and a lethal enchantress, who has honed the art of deception to a tee but who fails to trap her man at the end. The result has left Spade a winner, but not necessarily a happy one. He has gained nothing that can be of use to him, outside of a moral victory. In the Hammett novel, the following morning he goes back to his office, greets Effie, and then he resumes his relationship with Iva Archer.

But that would have been not only amoral but distasteful to the audience. Wisely, John Huston shows Spade disappear from the screen holding the fake falcon in his hands. He is a man who lost in winning. No girl, no money, no fee (he pocketed some money from O'Shaughnessy, so don't feel too sorry for him). Bogart's performance as a detective is as brilliant as any, before or after. He is the man who dares step into the danger zone, who gets the shakes, whose face twitches often, but who shows toughness combined with the savvy of a fox. He is a force on the screen, a force that cannot even be stopped by a kick in the head strong enough to incapacitate another man. He is left only with knowing what he has stood against: a momentary brush with illusion.

⓭

ALL THROUGH THE NIGHT

(Warner Bros./First National, 1942)

★ ★ ★

Director: Vincent Sherman
Screenplay: Leonard Spigelgass, Edward Gilbert, adapted from a story by Leo
    Rosten
Producer: Jerry Wald. *Executive Producer:* Hal B. Wallis. *Cinematographer:* Sid
    Hickox. *Music Score:* Adolph Deutsch. *Editor:* Rudy Fehr. *Art Direction:*
    Max Parker. *Special Effects:* Edwin Du Par
Cast: Humphrey Bogart (Gloves Donahue), Conrad Veidt (Hal Ebbing),
    Kaaren Verne (Leda Hamilton), Frank McHugh (Barney), Peter Lorre
    (Pepi), Judith Anderson (Madame), William Demarest (Sunshine),
    Jackie Gleason (Starchy), Phil Silvers (Waiter), Wallace Ford (Spats
    Hunter), Barton MacLane (Marty Callahan), Edward Brophy (Joe
    Denning), Jean Ames (Anabelle), Ludwig Stossel (Mr. Miller)
Released: December 2, 1942
Specs: 107 minutes; black and white
Availability: DVD (Warner Home Video: *TCM Greatest Gangster Film
    Collection*); streaming (Amazon)

All Through the Night was a timely vehicle for Bogart, when his screen image was transforming from the gangster/hood of his thirties movies to a romantic hero, lover, and defender of the Star-Spangled Banner. The movie was shot at Warner Studios, with exteriors and some of the action filmed by a second unit in New York City. Vincent Sherman[1] specialized in group scenes that gave the impression of organized chaos, adding to the movie's zaniness and slick action. *All Through the Night*, which came after the smashing success of *The Maltese Falcon* and just before *Casablanca*, features Bogart as Gloves Donahue, a prospering sports gambler surrounded by a friendly gang of nitwits, including neophytes Jackie Gleeson (doing next to nothing); a bespectacled Phil Silvers, who plays a waiter; and several others who go along for the ride. The movie is meant to be a comedy, abounding in verbal gags, wacky mix-ups, close escapes, hateful villains, and a pretty woman in distress whom Bogart feels obligated to rescue. Being made as World War II started, the movie appealed to audiences looking for a laugh at the expense of the Nazis and a spy thriller featuring one of their favorite actors. However, spoofing the Nazis in any form gave a movie a patriotic tint, something audiences wanted to cheer about.

Right from the start, comedy takes a serious turn when an elderly baker, Mr. Miller (Ludwig Stossel), who provides Donahue with his cheesecake, is murdered for refusing to cooperate with his Nazi connections. Donahue's mother, Ma Donahue, has a "feeling" that a girl who used to be a customer at Mr. Miller's knows something about the murderers. Donahue and two of his buddies, Sunshine (William Demarest) and Barney (Frank McHugh), trace her to Marty Callahan's (Barton MacLane's) high-class nightclub, where the girl, Leda Hamilton (Kaaren Verne), sings. The nightclub is a nest for a group of Nazis, with whom the manager of the place, Joe Denning (Edward Brody), has connections. But when Donahue finds Denning staggering out of a closed door, he smells foul play as the dying Denning shows him his opened five fingers. Though at first Donahue fails to recognize the sign, following events make him guess that the gesture symbolizes a fifth-column Nazi ring.

As events unfold in the midst of disorderly action, Donahue discovers that his adversaries are an underground group of fifth columnists intent on recruiting and using Nazis from Germany and American sympathizers to assemble enough explosives to blow up American warships in New York Harbor. They are headed by Hal Ebbing (Conrad Veidt was to reemerge in *Casablanca* as Major Strasser), who affects an auctioneer of antiques, accepting bids for various art items by an audience swarming with spies; his underling is Pepi (Peter Lorre), the executioner of Mr. Miller, the baker who had refused to stay in the Nazi ring. Judith Anderson, already established as arch-villainess in *Rebecca*, is the hostess of the fake auction proceedings and adds little to the action, but her expressions lend a mask of menace to the scene. Pepi is also the piano accompanist to Leda Hamilton, the young woman forced to work for the Nazis to keep her father alive at Dachau. Among the sympathetic characters one notices Jane Darwell as Ma Donahue, dominant in the few scenes she is in; this is a rare occasion when Bogart's character, usually a loner, has a family connection on the screen.

Sunshine (William Demarest) and Charles Donahue (Bogart) in the Nazi stronghold, with Pepi (Peter Lore) lurking in the background. *Warner Bros./Photofest © Warner Bros.*

After several twists and turns, Donahue, who is suspected by the police of murdering Denning, manages to penetrate the Nazi conclave as an American Nazi from Detroit, along with Sunshine. When he is called to the podium to deliver the plan of attack, Donahue solves his bewilderment by asking Sunshine, who readily uses nonsense words like *scadavan* and *paratoot*, to which Donahue adds, "We get the rillera." While the police and Donahue's friends raid the place, Strasser, after killing Pepi, forces Donahue at gunpoint to drive a boat with explosives to hit an American warship at the New York Harbor. Donahue manages to turn the wheel of the boat at a crucial point, Ebbing falls overboard, and the boat hits a barge, blowing it to pieces. Donahue jumps out just before the explosion.

By the time the movie was released, Pearl Harbor had already occurred, so the comedy succeeded in spoofing the Nazis at a time when many Americans had not yet fully grasped how dangerous the world was becoming. Here the Nazis, murderous as they are, become the butt of jokes; this ridicule is one way for the moviemakers to make their point. (It was the year after Charlie Chaplin had made his famous spoof of Hitler in *The Great Dictator*.)

While Veidt remains the same character as in *Casablanca*—a despicable Nazi—Bogart is markedly different from Rick Blaine. Blaine is a truly heartbroken man and suffers the pangs of jealousy, albeit with a touch of class. Donahue is an amoral profiteer, comfortable with his socially lowly status, hardly paying attention to the buffoons that surround him, and seems more interested in his cheesecake than the girl he will eventually save from peril. Depending on the occasion, he will exchange fists and shots with bad men or parley nonsense at the auctioneer's, bidding "two Gs" to a puzzled Ebbing, who asks for clarification if this means "two thousand." No risk seems to faze him, no Nazi stands a chance, and Donahue is a patriot on his own soil and not in some godforsaken geographic outpost. In the midst of chaos, Bogart's character rises above the madding crowd when he is forced at gunpoint to drive a boat with a bomb in New York Harbor to sink an American warship. Veidt made the mistake of giving him the wheel.

14

ACROSS THE PACIFIC

(Warner Bros./First National, 1942)

★ ★ ★

Director: John Huston
Screenplay: Richard Macaulay
Producer: Jerry Wald, Jack Saper. *Cinematographer:* Arthur Edeson. *Music
Score:* Adolph Deutsch. *Editor:* Frank Magee. *Special Effects:* Byron
Haskin, Willard Van Enger
Cast: Humphrey Bogart (Captain Richard Leland), Mary Astor (Alberta
Marlow), Sydney Greenstreet (Dr. Lorenz), Charles Halton (A. V.
Smith), Victor Sen Yung (Joe Totsukio), Roland Got (Sugi "Should-
a-Be"), Lee Tung Foo (Sam Wing On), Frank Wilcox (Captain
Morrison), Paul Stanton (Colonel Hart), Lester Matthews (Canadian
Major), John Hamilton (President of Court-Martial), Roland Drew
(Captain Harkness), Monte Blue (Dan Morton)
Released: September 5, 1942
Specs: 97 minutes; black and white
Availability: DVD (*TCM Greatest Classic Legends Film Collection: Humphrey Bogart*)

The motto "Hollywood Helps the Cause," part of the "Extras" in the DVD
edition of the film, was typical of many Hollywood releases of films with
emphatic war themes designed to lift the spirits of embattled Americans
in their fight against a double enemy—Hitler in Europe and the Japanese
in the Pacific. The film, directed by John Huston, his last before he enlisted in the war effort,[1] reunites three of the principals of *The Maltese
Falcon*—Bogart, Sidney Greenstreet, and Mary Astor—and though the
circumstances are entirely different, there are some parallels, as Green-

street is as elusive and colorful a villain as ever, perhaps more malignant than Gaspar Gutman of the *Falcon*. Astor is also a charmer whose loyalties seem to fluctuate, though in the end she turns out a victim rather than a duplicitous villainess.

This movie was made just before *Casablanca*, but Bogart's persona seems to have evolved since *The Maltese Falcon*. As Richard Leland (he is called Ricky in the movie), he is no longer indifferent to any cause but his own, and the first part of the plot does not allow the viewer to guess what his motives really are. When the movie opens, he is shown as a disgraced naval officer being stripped of his rank as Captain Leland; he subsequently tries to enlist in the Canadian Navy but fails, as his record has followed him in Canada. It is a few weeks before Pearl Harbor, as the calendar in the trial room shows November 21, 1941, so when Leland decides to take a ship to Panama Canal, the viewer suspects that something is brewing in the Pacific front. Leland embarks on a Japanese vessel named *Genoa Maru*, which is scheduled to make a stop at New York before it proceeds to its final destination. Among his fellow travelers there is a rotund gentleman dressed in white, Dr. Lorenz, and an attractive lady who answers to the name of Alberta Marlow, both traveling to Panama, with a stop in New York. Leland soon learns from Dr. Lorenz himself that he has been a professor of social sciences at the University in Manila for the last thirty years, that he has studied the Oriental cultures, and that his sympathies (professionally speaking) lie with Japan. Dr. Lorenz has a young Japanese escort, T. Oki, who occupies a cabin next to him. Leland accepts the services of an obliging young Japanese, Sugi, who points out to him the facilities in his cabin, constantly repeating the phrase "Should-a-be," so Leland decides to call him that. As for Ms. Marlow, it doesn't take him long to insinuate his romantic feelings for her, though she gently but steadily repulses his advances.

But they become friendly enough, and when they stop at New York, he asks her to wait for him momentarily, saying he is going to visit a friend and get some money. As he leaves her, Leland notices a tall man with a hat is shadowing him, something that he reports to Colonel Hart in the latter's office moments later. There we learn that Leland is on a secret mission and that his dismissal is a cover, to throw enemies (the Japanese) off the track. Leland tells Hart that Ms. Marlow is harmless, but that Lorenz may be the lead in a big operation in Panama.

When they are back on the ship, a man who took a cab to Pier 16, where the *Genoa Maru* was anchored, intends on assassinating Lorenz, but Leland runs after the man and prevents the attempt. The police are not brought in (it would delay the sailing, Leland is told), and Lorenz, in gratitude, invites Leland to his cabin for a drink. Marlow alerts Leland to the fact that T. Oki is not the same man who was on the first part of the trip, but a look-alike. Also a new passenger comes aboard, Joe Totsukio, who wears thick glasses and boasts that he is second generation Japanese.

In due time, Leland, who pretends to be disgraced and unemployed, receives money from Lorenz, who expects some services in return. While they sail to Panama, the Japanese crew entertain themselves reading haikus in Japanese, which, as Lorenz explains, is a distilled form of poetry expressing the Japanese ability to do much with the least effort. A judo exhibit stresses the point as well; when Leland brags that a right swing would do more damage to an opponent, Joe Totsukio challenges him to prove it. Leland asks Joe to remove his glasses before he hits him, but is quickly upended by a swift jujitsu move by Joe. Joe calmly resets his glasses, as Leland gets a premonition of what is to come.

When they arrive at Cristobal at the Panama Canal, they are informed that the *Genoa Maru* cannot go through. It is December 6, 1941, and the Japanese attack on Pearl Harbor is imminent. The Japanese have made preparations to destroy the American air bases from where planes would take off on patrol missions that day. Preparations by the Japanese in Panama have been laborious and are being revealed to the viewer gradually. Leland knows much of this, but not all. He sees packages being loaded from the Canadian port of Halifax, addressed to Dan Morton, owner of Bountiful Plantation—something that looks harmless enough. But the Bountiful Plantation has been taken over during the last few years, and it has been turned into a camp from which an airplane will carry a bomb that will damage the air base at the Panama Canal severely. As they settle at the Pan-American Hotel that morning, Lorenz asks Leland for information about the American schedules of the patrol planes. He offers Leland $1,500 if he can get this information by five o'clock.

Leland, who is known to the friendly owner of the hotel, Sam (Lee Tung Foo), fails to get any information from him, but proceeds to his connection A. V. Smith (Charles Halton), who provides him with the schedule for Lorenz, assuring that Leland's cover will be protected. But, as the latter negotiates with Lorenz about the price due to him, he is hit from behind by Joe Totsukio and is dragged behind a partition, where Lorenz delivers two violent blows with his cane—not shown to the viewer—something that would have left a lesser man dead or incapacitated.

But not Bogart as Leland, who comes to a bit later and takes matters in his own hands. It is now past five o'clock, and he calls A. V Smith to ask him to change the flight schedule, but before Smith has time to do so, he is shot dead by an unseen executioner. The action, leisurely up to this point, quickens amazingly. Leland goes downstairs in the hotel, where his friend Sam takes care of his wound and gives him a gun as well as a tip to go to a certain Japanese cinema, where a comedy is shown. There, Leland is approached by a man who tells him to go to the Bountiful Plantation immediately. But before that can happen, Leland is attacked by several Japanese, and he evades them by shooting back, opening doors to block deadly knives thrust against him, and climbing scaffolds and leaping over roofs with the agility of Gene Kelly in *The Pirate*.

But when Leland arrives at the plantation, some surprises await him: Lorenz is there, who congratulates Leland on his powers of recuperation, as is Joe, who is holding a gun on him; Alberta Marlow is also there and reveals that the drunk and demoralized man next to her is her father, alias Marlow. His farm had been converted to a war camp, where, piece by piece, the materials needed to build a large bomb had been assembled. T. Oki makes his appearance, but Lorenz bows to him, calls him "his highness," and exits with his group. T. Oki (whose switch of identity Alberta had noticed and told Leland) is to fly the place with the large bomb that will destroy or damage the American bases. Leland is left alone with Joe, Mr. Marlow, and Alberta. But it takes him no time to land a right on Joe, get his gun, run out, knock out a Japanese guard who has a machine gun, and start firing rounds against the plane taking off, killing T. Oki, whose plane explodes, and then razing each and every Japanese in sight. Only Lorenz escapes, going toward the building. The camera shows him unsheathing a blade, muttering some words and ready to commit hara-kiri. But as Leland, escorted by Alberta, arrives at the scene, Lorenz begs him to plant a bullet in his head, "as one soldier to another." Leland answers in the negative, taking Lorenz to face the authorities.

Needless to say, Bogart again plays a hero of many sides, and there are no real weaknesses in this one. The leisurely gentleman on board the *Genoa Maru* who poses as an unscrupulous war profiteer is transformed into a formidable war hero, fast, hard to catch or keep down, coming back from a severe beating to conquer a pack of hostiles to his country, single-handedly ensuring that the US planes will fly for their patrol missions—as they do indeed at the very end of the movie. In agility and bodily might, the small-sized and potentially vulnerable Leland becomes alternately Tarzan and Gene Kelly, leaping over chasms, and finally a Rambo type, defying a whole army and killing at will and without the slightest scruple. But this was wartime; America had been attacked, the outcome at that point very much in doubt, and the country needed an uplift, which, if nothing else, Hollywood could provide. Hollywood knew the power of the moving picture—that movies could help in times of need. And Bogart did his part in the war effort, though he never wore a uniform. Bogart's persona could be adapted to anything, and when it came to playing a tough guy, he had been there before. By not killing Lorenz, Leland also shows that he is an astute action hero who knows that delivering a high-value prisoner alive is preferable to just delivering his corpse. Besides, Lorenz deserved the onus of defeat.

15

CASABLANCA

(Warner Bros./First National, 1942)

★ ★ ★ ★ ★

Director: Michael Curtiz
Screenplay: Julius J. Epstein, Philip G. Epstein, Howard Koch, based on the
    play *Everybody Comes to Rick's* by Murray Burnett and Joan Alison
Producer: Hal B. Wallis. *Cinematographer:* Arthur Edeson. *Music Score:* Max
    Seiner. *Art Direction:* Carl Jules Weyl
Cast: Humphrey Bogart (Rick Blaine), Ingrid Bergman (Ilsa Lund), Paul Henreid
    (Victor Laszlo), Claude Rains (Captain Louis Renault), Conrad Veidt
    (Major Heinrich Strasser), Peter Lorre (Ugarte), Sidney Greenstreet
    (Señor Farrari), S. Z. "Cuddles" Sakall (Carl), Madeleine LeBeau
    (Yvonne), Dooley Wilson (Sam), Joy Page (Annina Brandel), Marcel Dalio
    (Emil, the Croupier), Leonid Kinsky (Sascha), John Qualen (Berger)
Released: November 26, 1942
Specs: 102 minutes; black and white
Availability: DVD (Two-Disc Special Edition, 2003, on the occasion of
    Casablanca's sixtieth anniversary, with audio commentaries by critic
    Roger Ebert and historian Rudy Behlmer. The second disc contains a
    featurette with Lauren Bacall, reminiscing about her husband's life and
    career); Blu-ray (A 2012 one-disc Blu-ray edition was issued on the
    occasion of the seventieth anniversary of *Casablanca*, in DTS Master
    Audio sound containing all the materials of the 2003 DVD edition.
    Also in 2012, the *Casablanca* Ultimate Collection was issued, and it
    comes as a package containing three discs—a Blu-ray version in an
    all-new 4K transfer, a regular DVD, and a third Blu-ray disc with
    a lengthy history of Warner Bros. written by Richard Schickel and
    narrated by Clint Eastwood; it also includes other materials, among
    them a deluxe sixty-page production book with never-before-seen
    photos, archival documents, and personal memos)

Casablanca *was and remains a phenomenon, and it shot Bogart into an orbit in which he still floats, serene, above the lesser drudges who toil before the cameras.*

—Nathaniel Benchley[1]

The above tribute by Nathaniel Benchley, Bogart's friend and biographer, though written forty years ago, defines the durability of *Casablanca*, which today (2015) still ranks third in the American Film Institute's list of the one hundred best films of all time, after *Citizen Kane* and *The Godfather*. In the various editions of his *Movie Video Guide*, Leonard Maltin defines *Casablanca* as "our candidate for the best Hollywood movie of all time," and also, "A kiss is only a kiss, but there is only one *Casablanca*."[2] Similar statements have been made by critics, viewers, reviewers, and commentators for seventy-plus years now. Such fame has been bolstered by virtual worship on college campuses, where students swarm classes in which it is shown, or ask professors why they do not include *Casablanca* in the syllabus if it happens to not be there. *Casablanca* has so far survived the slings and arrows of outrageous oblivion, the cloud that ultimately obscures all glory. One can turn back the clock and look at the movie with the paraphernalia of modernity: Blu-ray/DVD commentaries, online streaming, and a glut of reads by biographers, critics, foes (it has some[3]), and other strangers.

A great many factors contributed to the making of *Casablanca*, but luck might be considered one of the most important. By 1942, Bogart had at last reached the status of a top movie star at Warners after six years of slave labor as a thug who was shot dead in the seventh or eighth reel. The tough guys who had precedence over him at Warners in the previous decade, mainly in gangster roles, were James Cagney, Edward G. Robinson, Paul Muni, and George Raft.[4] Raft turned down the leading role in *High Sierra* (1941), and subsequently the role of Sam Spade in *The Maltese Falcon* (1941), which catapulted Bogart to stardom, so elusive until then; as one film historian observed, "Raft, single-handedly, handed stardom to Bogart."[5] Even for *Casablanca*, Raft, who was not in the run but had the backing of Jack Warner,[6] was left behind, as the clever producer at Warners, Hal Wallis, now an independent producer of selected films of his own and saw to it that Bogart was the right choice for Rick Blaine. After *Casablanca*, Bogart was propelled into the sphere of superstardom, becoming not only a romantic lead but an unforgettable screen presence. He was forty-three years old when that happened. Of course, his embodiment of Rick Blaine, the most memorable of his characters, worked to his benefit, but also to the benefit of *Casablanca*. The two are not mutually exclusive; on the contrary, when one thinks of *Casablanca*, one also thinks of Bogart, and vice versa. In 2006, Richard Schickel, in his encomium to Bogart, wrote, "If he had not played Rick Blaine it is doubtful that we would be gathered here to mark the 50th anniversary of his passing."[7] This is as true as is its opposite: Where would *Casablanca* be today if Bogart hadn't been in it?

Of course, his presence alone would not have been enough without a worthy female lead, and the choice of Ingrid Bergman to play Ilsa Lund was no less fortuitous. Several actresses were considered, among them Hedy Lamarr, the French actress Michele Morgan, and Ann Sheridan. But Lamarr, who had made an impression as an exotic beauty in *Algiers* (1938), was tied up at MGM, which was in no mood to loan her out to anyone. The others gradually fell out of favor for one reason or another,[8] and Wallis turned his eye upon the Swedish import Ingrid Bergman, who had made a few good movies so far—*Intermezzo* (1939) and *Dr. Jekyll and Mr. Hyde* (1941), among others—but had not yet gained the status of a big star. Bergman was under contract to David O. Selznick, who kept a zealous eye on his imported beauties (think of Vivien Leigh in *Gone with the Wind*). Aside from that, as A. M. Sperber and Eric Lax point out, Bergman at the time (1942) was considered "damaged goods," because there were reports that Sweden was going to join the Axis[9] (it never did). So Selznick grudgingly said yes, though not entirely for those reasons only,[10] and Ingrid became Ilsa and, as they say, the rest is history.

Luck was also a factor in the selection of character actors in the making of *Casablanca*. Because of Hitler and Nazism and the defeat of France in 1940 (a crucial event in the story of *Casablanca*), scores of good men and women, and more than a few actors, had fled Europe, and many of them sought refuge in Hollywood, which took advantage of good, but largely unemployed, players. Of those included in *Casablanca*, the ones in key secondary roles will be mentioned here as well as a few of the others who worked uncredited. First and foremost is Conrad Veidt, whose etched features and vain swagger suggested the archetypal Nazi villain, but who had actually fled Hitler's Germany because his wife was Jewish,[11] and had already appeared with Bogart in *All Through the Night* (1942). As Major Strasser, Veidt is the perfect foil for Claude Rains's Captain Renault, who maintains a precarious balance between him and Rick, in whose Café Américain Renault wins large sums of money and sells visas; for attractive women, visas are provided in exchange for sexual favors. For those reasons, he offers cover for independent-minded Rick, who affects indifference to any cause but his own: "I stick my neck out for nobody," he says frequently. Strasser already has a dossier on Rick ("Don't worry, we are not going to broadcast it," he says to him), but he allows his café to remain open, for he is looking for a bigger fish to catch—Victor Laszlo, an escapee from the concentration camps—and he knows the latter will sooner or later make his appearance at Rick's, looking for an exit visa. Strasser's presence at Rick's, and that of his Nazi cohorts, adds to the menacing undercurrents that pervade the jovial atmosphere at Rick's café. In reality, Veidt was an affable man and excellent actor who relished displaying the mind-set of a despicable Gestapo leader.[12]

Other expatriates include Marcel Dalio, a noted French actor who played Emil, the croupier, a bit role considering that he had distinguished himself in Jean Renoir's *The Grand Illusion* (1937) and *The Rules of the Game* (1939) and had fled France after its occupation by the Germans. Madeleine LeBeau, playing Yvonne, Rick's casual girlfriend, adrift in the amoral cosmos of Café Américain, was a Frenchwoman in exile and had real tears in her eyes while Victor Laszlo led the independent-minded crowd at Rick's in singing *"La Marseillaise,"* the French national anthem. Other European imports fleeing Hitler were the Hungarian S. Z. "Cuddles" Sakall, playing the jowly and sentimental Carl, the waiter, and Leonid Kinsky, a Russian actor who is known as Sascha, the love-struck bartender ("I love you, but he pays me," he tells Yvonne when she asks for another drink). These and other bit players lend color and authenticity to the crowd at Rick's Café Américain, a gathering place of hopefuls who traveled to Casablanca, where they sought exit visas for Lisbon, and then to America.

Luck had something (but not everything) to do, too, with the assemblage of other important characters. Peter Lorre and Sydney Greenstreet had already gained status at Warners after their outstanding performances in *The Maltese Falcon* (1941), in which they were two of the five major characters. They were well fitted here, Greenstreet as Señor Ferrari, owner of the Blue Parrot, the rival spot across the street from Rick's café, and Lorre as Ugarte, the black marketer who sold visas at "cut-rate" prices, as Rick cynically tells him. In *Casablanca* Lorre has only two short appearances: one when Ugarte delivers the letters of transit to Rick, with the request to hide them for a short time, and another when he is captured while trying to escape. Ugarte's brief appearances set off a chain of events that last from that point to the very end, as the letters, which Rick hides under the piano cover, become the objects of interest to all parties concerned: the police; Victor Laszlo, to whom Ugarte planned to sell them; and Rick, who has reasons to keep them for himself.[13] And, of course, Strasser, who is intent on discovering who killed the German couriers from whom the letters were stolen.

As Victor Laszlo, Paul Henreid was an Austrian aristocrat who also had fled Hitler's Germany, as some of his ancestors might have been Jewish.[14] He had previously made *Night Train to Munich* (1940), in England, playing a handsome Nazi, winning the attention of female audiences worldwide. Subsequently, he came to Hollywood, where he established a notable career. When *Casablanca* started filming in May 1942, he was still making *Now, Voyager*, with Betty Davis, and arrived on the set late. In his first scene, he enters Rick's, side by side with Bergman—she in a plain white dress, he in off-white suit—just after Ugarte had been arrested and order restored. Arthur Edeson's camera captures the couple in a long panning shot that makes him look a hero with a princess at his side. They have the stamp of Europeans, elegant upper-class people who dominate their environment just by entering it. His elegance and her beauty immediately draw the attention of patrons, Strasser, and the vigilant Captain Renault. Visually, they are splendidly matched, and everything changes in the café after their entrance. Laszlo has come there to look for a connection, evidently with Ugarte, to obtain the letters of transit and exit visas. As Laszlo and Ilsa sit at their reserved table, a man, Berger, approaches them and asks Laszlo if he wants to buy a ring, which Ilsa recognizes as a sign of the French underground resistance, and Laszlo goes to the bar to talk to him. Berger is played by John Qualen, born Johan Kvalen, in Illinois, from Norwegian immigrant parents (Berger tells Laszlo he is a Norwegian). Qualen looks foreign, and he fits the character ambiance in the film. As they sit at the bar, Berger tells Laszlo that Ugarte has just been arrested. But neither of them suspects at this point that the letters had already been delivered to Rick.

Other bit players, almost all uncredited, look or act like foreigners: the wonderful Corinna Mura, the guitarist, singing an entrancing Latin song, as the camera captures Ilsa's worried face in profile; the pickpocket warning two naive customers, crying "Vultures, vultures," while lifting the man's wallet; the Hungarian couple learning to speak English, as their compatriot, Carl, has a drink with them—"What watch?" "Ten watch?" "Such much?" Add the suspicious-looking, whispering traffickers who offer bottom prices for diamonds to anxious ladies; the omnipresent uniformed policemen who overcrowd Rick's café; the heavy-accented Colonel Heinz (uncredited) screeching, "Can you imagine us in London?"; and others, such as the portly Arab (Dan Seymour) wearing the fez and opening Rick's door, and Sam (Dooley Wilson), like a chorus leader, intoning "As Time Goes By" and pounding on the piano, which the real Dooley Wilson could not play.[15]

Aside from Ugarte's arrest and a couple of shots fired at the beginning and end of the movie, there is no violent action in *Casablanca*. It's an anomaly in the age of gangster and subsequently war and film noir movies dominating the screens at the time. Witty dialogue provides relief to the underground tension, in a place of merriment where danger simmers and intrigue dominates.

Of the principals in the story, only Rick is an American (aside from Sam, of course), an expatriate for unknown reasons[16] in a foreign land, running his joint with a steady hand, and yet he is alone, alienated, wearing a cynical mask ("I am a drunkard," he says to Strasser when asked by the latter to state his nationality), though the viewer cannot quite accept this facade. With the entrance of Laszlo and Ilsa, the configuration changes, as the glittering, high class Europeans come face-to-face with the tough owner of the Café Améri-cain. Bogart had been born into privilege, the son of a wealthy doctor and an artist mother, and he had reached maturity as a stage actor and New Yorker of good social standing. But that image had just about been eradicated by his playing hoods and tough guys at Warners in the previous decade. Now, weathered and practically resurrected from that image, Bogart, who had been spruced up for his role here wearing a white tuxedo and black trousers, could be looked upon as his own double: "Don't believe what I wear; I'm still tough when I need to," as evidenced in Rick throwing out a German banker, an undesirable in the gambling room, and later stopping a German officer fighting with a French policeman for the graces of Yvonne. And of course he sheds this mask altogether when he shoots Strasser at the end.

Luck had also a hand in the screenwriting of *Casablanca*. At the time filming started, May 1942, Pearl Harbor had already been bombed by the Japanese in December 1941, and America had entered the war, the out-come of which was very much in doubt at that point. Patriotism was needed and expected by everybody, and Hollywood was contributing its share. Warners had in fact already produced *Across the Pacific* and *All Through the Night*, both Bogart vehicles earlier in 1942 and both with anti-Japanese and anti-Nazi themes, and was getting ready to film *Watch on the Rhine*, by Lillian Hellman, whose play had been a hit on Broadway. Hal Wallis had picked up a play, *Everybody Comes to Rick's*, written by Murray Burnett, a schoolteacher with writing aspirations who had visited Europe, Vienna in particular, in 1938, when the Hitler had annexed Austria. Horrified by the anti-Semitism there, he had fled to the south of France, where he saw a black man playing the piano at a nightclub. The idea of a play with an American facing crucial decisions, set in a nightclub seething with prewar turmoil, came to him, and upon his return to America, he teamed with Joan Alison, who added important details to it, for instance, the famous letters of transit. The play lay dormant in New York for a while, though Warners had purchased it for $20,000. No one else had any use for it, until the idea for Lillian Hellman's play for a movie fell through momentarily, and Wallis saw the opportunity to use *Everyone Comes to Rick's* instead. Though written before the war, it had a perfect war theme—a man with an independent spirit who owns a café, a black pianist who is his friend, and a woman, a lost love who keeps the man cheerless and cynical, although his patriotism is aroused when the war comes. Wallis would model it on *Algiers* (1938), the prewar movie, set in an exotic land rather than in Europe, and he renamed it *Casablanca*. Though no one really believed that it would become the classic it did, *Casablanca* retained most of the trademarks of the Burnett play: resistance to evil, a potentially destructive love story, a subjected crowd looking for a leader making a big, selfless decision—timely themes that ultimately found their way to glorious fruition.

The first version of *Casablanca* was coauthored by Wally Kline and Aeneas McKenzie, based on the Burnett and Alison play, and soon after the attack on Pearl Harbor in early December 1941, the project gained momentum. Wallis handed the script over to the Epstein brothers, Philip G. and Julius J., known for their witty and cynical repartee ("My heart?" says Renault seeing Rick aiming a pistol at him. "That is my least vulnerable spot."), having worked on previous Warners' projects, such as *Yankee Doodle Dandy* (1942), also directed by Michael Curtiz. Two other authors were added: Howard Koch, whose writing credits included *The Sea Hawk* (1940) and *Sergeant York* (1941), was brought in to strengthen the political aspects of the script, bolstering Rick's character as a patriot finally moved by the plight of fugitives in his saloon, and Casey Robinson, a regular at Warners, helped build up the romantic ties between Rick and Ilsa, especially the scene when Ilsa finally breaks down and tells Rick that she still loves him. Only three names appear in the final credits—the Epstein brothers and Koch—while Kline and McKenzie were altogether omitted. Robinson, used to solo credits, refused to be credited, thus missing out on the Oscar *Casablanca* won for Best Screenplay. The names of Burnett and Alison appear at the bottom of the screen, as authors of the play on which the script is based. Hal Wallis deserves credit for assembling the team that contributed to one coherent whole, but it was Michael Curtiz, the Hungarian-born director, who is most responsible for delivering what in lesser hands might have been a chaotic exercise in filmmaking instead of a classic, and his efforts won him the Oscar for Best Director.[17] Two Hollywood stalwarts, Max Steiner and Arthur Edeson, were responsible for the music score and photography, rounding up the number of contributors responsible for *Casablanca*'s longevity.

Rick (Bogart) and Ilsa (Bergman) meet again at Rick's café, as Renault (Claude Rains) and Laszlo (Paul Henreid), puzzled, look on. *Warner Bros. Pictures/Photofest © Warner Bros. Pictures*

Casablanca was released in November 1942, shortly after the Allies landed in Algiers and Morocco, in the real Casablanca. Soon after that, the three Western leaders of the war—Winston Churchill, Charles de Gaulle, and Franklin D. Roosevelt—met in Casablanca, Morocco, for a conference. *Casablanca* means white house (*casa blanca*) in Spanish, and FDR invited the cast to the White House, in Washington, DC, where he viewed the film with them. When Bogart and his then wife Mayo Methot visited Casablanca, Morocco, in 1943 on a North Africa tour in support of the troops, one of the men, recognizing Bogart, asked him, "Where's Rick's?" The legend had begun.

Aside from favorable circumstances in its making, *Casablanca* would not have been the classic movie it became without its two celebrated leads. Ingrid Bergman's Ilsa Lund, with all her luminous beauty, is a troubled woman with hard choices to make. When she and Rick Blaine first met in Paris, neither of them knew much about one another's past. In a joking manner, Ilsa tells Rick that ten years ago she had her braces fixed and that he was trying to get a job. Prodding her, he asks if there was another man before him. "That's simple," she says. "There was." "He's dead," she adds. On their last day together, when the Germans are coming into Paris, she cries when Rick suggests that they marry on the train on their way to Marseilles, almost giving herself away. Rick, waiting for her at the station, drenched in the rain, gets a letter saying that she is not going with him, offering no explanation. When, entirely by chance, she sees him again at his café, in Casablanca, she rekindles the flame in Rick's heart, breaking it for the second time. Her dilemma is obvious and immediate, and she chooses the worst possible way to mitigate it. As Rick is trying to drown his sorrow in drink, upstairs in his apartment at night, she enters, a white scarf on her head, looking like an apparition. When she tries to explain to him that she had left him for a much superior man, she was twisting a knife into his still raw wound. With pointed sarcasm, he asks her if "there were others in-between." Next morning, when Rick tries to make up for his rudeness the previous night, she is hardened and tells him plainly that Laszlo "was, and is" her husband. Spurned by Rick, she now concentrates on supporting Laszlo to obtain visas, having decided that Rick was not the man she thought he was. When she and Laszlo try to seek help from Ferrari, the letter tells them that he can only arrange for one of them to leave—her. Laszlo and Ilsa confer and decide they will seek visas for both. Ferrari, a cynic who softens when he sees their devotion to each other, tells them that Rick may be the owner of the letters. "He is a difficult customer, that Rick. One never knows what he will do next," he adds.

When Laszlo attempts to entice Rick into selling the letters to him with a generous offer, Rick refuses, and when Laszlo asks the reason for the refusal, Rick tells him, "Ask your wife." When she learns of this, Ilsa decides that it is now up to her to get the letters from Rick; she goes to his apartment, first pleading, and then pointing a gun at him. She also tells him that he is cruel and a coward. He still refuses, provoking her to shoot him: "You would be doing me a favor," he says. At that moment, she lowers the gun, breaks into tears, and tells him she still loves him. When he observes, "This is still a story without an end," she tells him that from now on, he has to think for both of them.

With this, Rick has regained his status as the power man, back in charge and in his element, the one who moves the chess pieces on the board. It is interesting to recall a little scene between him and Laszlo, as the latter returns from a secret meeting slightly wounded and tying a bandage around his wrist. Rick asks Laszlo whether he thinks what he is doing is "worth all of this." Laszlo responds that fighting for liberty is like breathing. Then he scolds Rick for trying to hide who he really is, saying that every man has a destiny and that Rick is ignoring his. "You seem to know all about my destiny," Rick answers sarcastically. Rick never really liked Laszlo, thinking him pompous and full of himself. Laszlo had actually done nothing heroic during his stay in Casablanca, aside from leading the café band in singing the French national anthem. Rick's disdain of him looks justified. But at this point Laszlo does something that seems admirable, even to Rick. He says he knows that Rick loves the same woman as he, but as no one was to blame, he demands no explanations. But since Rick has what he wants, the letters of transit, he proposes that Rick uses them to escape, taking his wife along, so that Ilsa would be saved. To Rick's question of whether he loves her that much, Laszlo replies that he is not only a fighter for a cause, but also "a human being," adding, "yes, I love her that much."

This is the critical point that turns things around in Rick's mind. Had he decided to do what Laszlo suggested, he would be responsible for a man's death, the very man Ilsa loved just as much, though in a different way. Laszlo could not have escaped Strasser and the Gestapo. Perhaps Rick's decision was also based on the prospect of himself going away and living with a woman who was someone else's wife, as her guilt would weigh against any future normal relationship. Perhaps he also did not want to go back to America, from where he had fled, for reasons unknown. Still, his decision to send her off with her husband has its perils, for he has to navigate through Renault and Strasser, something he manages with admirable skill—and some luck. Renault complies with his demands under threat; it seems not without some relish, saying he didn't like Strasser's face either. But he warns Strasser by phone, and the latter rushes to the airport to circumvent Laszlo's departure, he thinks, unable to guess, as nobody else did, the final twist of the story. But after Laszlo and Ilsa are on the plane and Rick shoots Strasser, Renault does not give orders to the arriving policemen for Rick's arrest, and he famously says to them, "Major Strasser has been shot. Round up the usual suspects."

The convergence of all five major characters in the last scene at the airport gives *Casablanca* its great power as a drama. So far, the viewer has had a great deal to unpack: a delightful ensemble of minor characters, each with his or her own concern; witty dialogue; a rousing rendering of the French national anthem; comedy and intrigue; tension mounting about the outcome; and unforgettable love scenes. But the resolution demands that all main players—the cogs that have turned the machine, so to speak—be brought together before the plane takes off in the foggy night. Outside one couple, the others are in conflict with each other, forming polar opposites, and such conflicts come to a head in the final scene. Strasser, for instance, is there with one purpose: to arrest Victor Laszlo or possibly kill him. Laszlo is there to escape, but to do so he needs the letters of transit, which Rick possesses. That creates another polar opposite, for Rick is in no mood to hand them to Laszlo, resenting the fact that Ilsa prefers him. Isla is caught at a crossroads, forced to make a choice between husband and lover. And Renault knows his self-interest lies in helping Strasser to seize Laszlo. In and of themselves, the letters are of no interest to Renault, just a means of handing Laszlo to Strasser. And Rick, now free from his grudge knowing Ilsa loves him, is burdened with the task of moving the chess pieces to obtain a checkmate.

Who wins, and who loses? Strasser loses, and the audiences cheers, for he is the hated enemy. Renault has a crucial change of heart, turning from an amoral temporizer to a French resistance fighter. The corrupt official, whose heart is his "least vulnerable spot," shows he has a heart. And Laszlo? Well, one can say things are handed to him on a platter: he gets the letters and his passage to freedom with them, and whether he deserves the big prize or not, he also gets his wife, the woman he loves. As for Rick, he says he is "not good at being noble" at the very moment he is. Half mockingly, Renault tells him what he thought about him from the first: that Rick is a "sentimentalist"; now he knows Rick is also a patriot. A tearful Ilsa mutters a "God bless you," to Rick, understanding that she must do as he says, go away with her husband. Claude Rains, brilliant by any measure as Renault, throws the Vichy bottle into the waste basket and the kicks it, thus sealing his change from temporizer to patriot. And Rick sends a good but wavering woman away with her husband, showing that he has achieved what he lacked throughout the movie: a healing of his wounds and a restoration of his self-respect. He *has* been noble, while steering his way through the perils of love and war. To the audiences of his time, Bogart as Rick gave them what they wanted—a man with a heart, but one who had also saluted the colors. Audiences of today still continue to applaud him, though their reasons may not be as clear.

⑯

ACTION IN THE NORTH ATLANTIC

(Warner Bros./First National, 1943)

★ ★ ★

Director: Lloyd Bacon
Screenplay: John Howard Lawson, adapted from the novel by Guy Gilpatrick.
   Additional Dialogue: A. I. Bazzerides, W. R. Burnett
Producer: Jerry Wald. *Cinematographer:* Ted McCord. *Music Score:* Adolph
   Deutsch. *Editor:* Thomas Pratt. Art Direction: Ted Smith. *Special
   Effects:* Jack Cosgrove, Edwin B. DuPar
Cast: Humphrey Bogart (First Mate Joe Rossi), Raymond Massey (Captain
   Jarvis), Alan Hale (Boats O'Hara), Julie Bishop (Pearl), Ruth Gordon
   (Mrs. Jarvis), Sam Leven (Chip Abrams), Dane Clark (Johnny Pulaski),
   Dick Hogan (Cadet Robert Parker), Minor Watson (Rear Admiral
   Hartridge), Kane Richmond (Ensign Wright), William von Brinken
   (German Submarine Captain)
Released: June 12, 1943
Specs: 126 minutes; black and white
Availability: DVD (Warner Home Video: *TCM Greatest Classics Films Collection*);
   streaming (Amazon)

At 126 minutes, *Action in the North Atlantic* is a war epic showing an Allies convoy with war supplies, led by the United States, trying to reach the Russian port Murmansk after crossing the north Atlantic and the Norwegian Sea. The movie begins with a caption, quoting the words of Franklin D. Roosevelt, which includes his famous war cry: "Damn the torpedoes, full steam ahead!" The convoy consists of converted merchant ships or tankers from many nationalities—Australian, British, Mexican, Cuban, and many others. In this way the movie manages to convey the enormity of the Allied effort to defeat the Nazis, which included the necessity of supplying Russia (no Soviet Union was mentioned), a staunch ally of America and the other allied forces at the time. (In the same year, Warners also made a well-meant war movie, *Mission to Moscow*,[1] which caused the company much grief when the House Un-American Activities Committee investigations began several years later.) It is assumed that the audience knew enough about the common war effort to defeat Nazi Germany, and the movie does not go into specifics as to who is doing what for whom—just the urgency of the mission and its dangers are emphasized. This is a war adventure, with tension mounting as the cat-and-mouse game between a submarine and one of the tankers is played out. And, of course, count Bogart in as a war hero, as he was from now on as long as the war lasted.

The plot of the movie comes in two parts: the first part is getting acquainted with the main characters; the second concerns the effort of the Allied convoy to reach the Russian port of Murmansk, which also comprises the main action of the story. All civilians, plus one Cadet Robert Parker (Dick Hogan), who works in *The Northern Star*, a tanker torpedoed by a German submarine and sunk. All but one were saved, escaping from an exploding ship and burning oil in the seawater, as the tanker carried high-octane gasoline used to supply tanks and airplanes. The boat they are in was shot to pieces too, so they spend eleven days in a raft, until they are spotted by an American plane and subsequently rescued and returned home. Captain Jarvis (Raymond Massey) returns to his wife of twenty years, Mrs. Jarvis (Ruth Gordon), while Joe Rossi (Bogart), who had the reputation of being a womanizer at every port, meets Pearl (Julie Bishop), a young singer at a nightclub who is singing Cole Porter's "Night and Day." Despite a brief flare-up after they meet, they make up quickly enough to be shown married when Captain Jarvis visits Rossi in his apartment. Several others of the same old crew receive new commissions and join the convoy to help the national cause. There is character interplay, joking and horsing around, as the old shipmates reunite, some with mixed feelings for the new life-and-death adventure. They are a colorful bunch—Boats O'Hara (Alan Hale), Johnny Pulaski (Dane Clark), Chip Abrams (Sam Levene), and several others who are uncredited—and lax in discipline, but they eventually become a tight group, conscious of the importance of their call to reach the Russian port and deliver the much-needed supplies to the Russians. The most effective German weapons in those days were submarines—hard to spot and seemingly ever-present in the waters of the north Atlantic.

The mission starts promisingly, as the captains receive their ships' numbers with sealed orders as to their destination, not to be opened until they are at sea. There are seventy-three vessels in the convoy, most of them Liberty ships built during the war by the hundreds and known for their large tonnage and capacity to carry anything and everything, their main assets being their maneuverability, plain quarters, and small crews, thus ensuring maximum efficiency. Captain Jarvis, whose ship is called the USS *Seawitch*, has most of his old crew back, First Mate Joe Rossi being one of them, in addition to a naval gun crew who know to handle antiaircraft guns and the one five-inch cannon in the ship. There is some initial friction between the two groups—the ones from the old crew and the newcomers who came aboard for the mission to Murmansk—but when danger comes they learn to cooperate. The ships in the convoy, accompanied by a small number of destroyers and fast-moving torpedo boats, can communicate only visually, by flares and loudspeakers if close enough, but war conditions demand absolute radio silence. If forced to disperse, they will not try to rejoin the convoy, but each ship will proceed to its destination alone.

Things go smoothly for a while, but soon the viewer is shown a "wolf pack" of German submarines underwater near the convoy formation, and soon enough German crews are shown counting and pressing buttons, letting torpedoes fly out, and hitting several ships, which are blown up. Quickly, Rear Admiral Hartridge (Minor Watson) gives orders for the convoy ships to disperse, while several swift-maneuvering torpedo boats drop large numbers of depth charges, destroying most of the submarines. But one of the submarines, commanded by its German captain (William Von Brinken) survives and continues tracking the *Seawitch*, setting off a cat-and-mouse game, the most exciting and suspenseful part of the movie. The Germans are heard and seen as they operate, and though subtitles are not given, the viewer surmises what they are saying. There are some intimate shots of the Germans, for instance, when the submarine captain is offered a scarf and heavy coat and a warm cup of coffee from a Thermos when the submarine surfaces.

At this point, it becomes obvious that First Mate Rossi begins to show leadership. He makes an astute suggestion that instead of attempting to outdistance the German submarine they apply complete silence by turning off the engines and keeping quiet for an entire night. But this is easier said than done. One of the crew members has brought a kitten with him, and he makes a noise while chasing it around; meanwhile, the boisterous Boats O'Hara runs over a chain while trying to punch the cat owner. Both noises alert the German captain, who understands the Allies' ruse and counters with one of his own. O'Hara is also responsible for the one literary line in the film: "Next time we are on port, I will take an oar and walk until somebody asks me 'What is this?' Then I will plant it on the spot and stay there until the end of my life."[2]

When the German submarine surfaces next morning, its captain knows he cannot catch up with the faster Liberty, and he radios to the Luftwaffe headquarters, requesting an air attack on the American vessel. And soon enough two hydroplanes appear and start strafing and bombing the ship. The planes are eventually shot down, but not before inflicting severe damage on the ship and killing eight of its men. Captain Jarvis is wounded on the leg and assigns command of the ship to Rossi, who virtually becomes the ship's captain from now on. He proves perfectly capable of his new assignment, ramming the German submarine and getting rid of it for good, and even operating on the wounded captain, removing the bullet from his leg with the skill of a surgeon. At half speed and escorted by Russian planes, the *Seawitch* is captained by Rossi until it reaches the Russian port Murmansk, and the mission is brought to its triumphant conclusion.

Thus, Bogart's character once more accomplishes a goal to which, as he stated earlier more than once, he is indifferent: to captain a ship. Jarvis had reminded him more than once that he has the qualifications to do so, but Bogie as Rossi says it's too much paperwork and responsibility for him. But during the trip, and even before he is forced to take the helm as captain, Rossi shows leadership qualities during the dangerous mission: he is hard-working, knows the ways to quell trouble among a disorganized crew, and is vigilant and inventive at the most perilous moments—more so than Jarvis himself. He even performs the burial rites of the eight men killed during the battle with the submarine; he reads the appropriate passages from the Bible, recites the Lord's Prayer, and then delivers the obligatory patriotic funeral oration as part of his duty. The usual clichés of wartime speeches sound genuine coming from his mouth, even more so than the opening caption of FDR's words at the start of the movie. Rossi "earned his stripes," so to speak, but manages to stay modest and unassuming. Most importantly, the casual womanizer at every port turns out to be a man with a purpose. Of course, now that he has joined the ranks of matrimony, he has someone to go back to. He has scored a victory in every sense—and along with him the United States Navy.

Perhaps it is also worth reminding the reader that Bogart had been in the US Navy during the First World War, and even appears with the white naval cap while still in the first ship, *The Northern Star*, which curiously reminds of Bogart's earlier appearance when he was in the navy decades earlier, at the Pelham Park Reserve Training Station, with the rank of coxswain.[3] Also worth noticing is the fact that Bogart himself was an able sailor, and at the start World War II he offered his services, signing up with the Coast Guard Patrol and using his boat *Sluggy* for patrolling, as did many boat owners after Pearl Harbor.[4] In later years, he perfected his skills as a sailor and captained his luxury yawl *Santana*, so he was man of the sea in every sense of the word. This may have been a factor in his flawless performance as a significant part of a perilous naval war expedition. Bogart was in his element.

SAHARA

(Columbia Pictures, 1943)

★ ★ ★ ★

Director: Zoltan Korda
Screenplay: John Howard Lawson, Zoltan Korda
Producer: Harry Joe Brown. *Cinematographer:* Rudolph Maté. *Music Score:*
    Miklos Rozsa. *Editor:* Charles Nelson
Cast: Humphrey Bogart (Sergeant Joe Gunn), Bruce Bennett (Waco Hoyt), J.
    Carroll Naish (Giuseppe), Lloyd Bridges (Fred Clarkson), Dan Duryea
    (Jimmy Doyle), Rex Ingram (Tambul), Richard Nugent (Captain Jason
    Halliday), Carl Harbord (Marty Williams), Patrick O'Moore (Ozzie
    Bates), Louis Mercier (Jean Leroux), Guy Kingsford (Peter Stegman),
    Kurt Krueger (Captain Von Schletow), John Wengraf (Major Von
    Falken), Hans Schumm (Sergeant Krause), Frank Lackteen (Arab Guide)
Released: November 11, 1943
Specs: 97 minutes; black and white
Availability: DVD (Sony Pictures Home Entertainment); streaming (Amazon)

Sahara takes place in Africa, where the German units of Marshall Erwin
Rommel's Afrika Korps had taken key towns and had dampened the spirit
of the fighting in the Allied African front in the early 1940s. The movie, ably
directed by Zoltan Korda and brilliantly photographed by Rudolph Maté,
was shot in the Mojave of Southern California near the Mexican border, in
a stretch of the Borrego Desert that perfectly simulated the African Sahara.
The movie, which was shot under harsh physical conditions, was aided by
units from the US Armored Force of Southern California that traveled a
hundred miles south to simulate German troops. Bogart, then on loan to
Columbia Pictures, delivers one of his most intense performances in a series

of patriotic-themed movies he made during the war years, including *Across the Pacific, All Through the Night, Casablanca, Action in the North Atlantic,* and *Passage to Marseille.* Dozens of war movies filled the screen after the war was over, but those made during the war have an air of authenticity and urgency difficult to capture later. The movie was well received by both public and critics, made good money for Columbia, and received three Oscar nominations: Best Sound, Best Cinematography in B&W, and Best Supporting Actor (J. Carroll Naish). It was dedicated to the IV Armored Corps of the United States Ground Forces, in recognition of their support. As a Bogart vehicle, it shows Bogart at his best, as a leader in firm command of a group of fighters for the Allied cause, enduring life-and-death situations, and standing up for patriotic principle.

The story begins at a time when Tobruk, a key town in North Africa, has just fallen, and all units have been ordered to go south and join the Allied Forces for a new defensive initiative at El Alamein. This is still the beginning of the war for America, and a few American armored units had joined the British forces in order to render help and to gain experience in desert warfare, which became essential in order to drive the Germans out of Africa. The crew of a lone American tank, nicknamed "LULUBELLE," is given orders to retreat under a barrage of shells exploding around them. It is commanded by Sergeant Major Joe Gunn (Bogart), who prepares to obey the order with his crew of two men, Jimmy Doyle (Dan Duryea), the radio man, and Waco Hoyt (Bruce Bennett), the machine gunner, driving south and out of harm's way. Soon they are joined by a small group of English soldiers, survivors of a German attack that had decimated their unit. The ranking officer of this group is Captain Jason Halliday (Richard Nugent), who, for the sake of unity, yields leadership to Gunn, the tank commander when Halliday's group joined Gunn's. Halliday is also a doctor, of the Army Medical Corps, something that comes in handy later. Several other characters from different ethnicities and geographical latitudes are added to the unit, among them the French corporal Jean Leroux (Louis Mercier), called "Frenchie," a member of the Free French Resistance group in Africa.

Gunn decides to take them along in the tank, though there is an inadequate supply of water. The group becomes enlarged when a black soldier, Sergeant Major Tambul (Rex Ingram) from the Sudanese Battalion, joins the group, along with a captured Italian soldier, Giuseppe (J. Carroll Naish), who carries Tambul's baggage. Gunn takes the Sudanese, who speaks fluent English and is useful with tracking water wells, and leaves the Italian behind, using some harsh words—"I don't want a bundle of spaghetti"—to describe the hapless captive. But as Gunn sees him trudging on the sand behind, certain to die, with vultures circling above him, he changes his mind and allows Giuseppe to join them. Bogart is good at showing change of heart, and this is one of the most touching instances. Naish is good playing the sentimental Giuseppe pleading while showing a photo of his wife and little daughter.

The group has by now jelled and is driving along in the desert when this momentary calm is broken by a German plane attack that strafes the crew in the tank repeatedly, wounding Clarkson (Lloyd Bridges, playing a British soldier), one of those in the group. The plane is downed by the tank gunner Waco, and the German pilot, the much decorated Captain Von Schletow (Kurt Krueger), is captured. He is a fanatic Nazi, who pretends not to understand English but who looks suspicious to Gunn and to Frenchie. But Gunn decides to take him along as a "high-value" prisoner of war. Clarkson, seriously wounded during the air attack, soon dies, and they stop to bury him, planting his rifle and helmet on the sand. They proceed with their trek, having almost lost all hope of finding water, as Hassan Berani, the well they

Sergeant Joe Gunn (Boggart) confers with English captain Jason Halliday (Richard Nugent) after the capture of German pilot Captain Von Schletow (Kurt Krueger), who is standing to the right. *Columbia Pictures/Photofest* © *Columbia Pictures*

were driving to, is found dry. Tambul recommends that they try to reach
Bill Acroma, which requires another fifty miles of hard travel, and they
arrive there in a sandstorm. Tambul finds a well and climbs down to the
bottom in search of water. There is none but some rocks are dripping, and
they gather enough in canteens to have a few swallows each and of necessity
wait until enough water is gathered for them to resume traveling.

Forced to camp there for days, they are attacked by a five-hundred-
strong German battalion, but knowing the Germans are also thirsty, they
negotiate with them, asking them to surrender their guns in exchange for
water, but to no avail. Waco Hoyt undertakes to drive a captured German
scout vehicle to find and notify Allied forces of the plight of his besieged
companions, and after a trek in the desert, where he nearly dies of thirst,
he manages to do so. Meanwhile, his companions at the well fight desperately for their lives, until all but two survive. Gunn and two others of his
companions are still alive and think themselves doomed, when, as if by a
miracle, one of the exploding shells uncovers the well and water springs
out. The remaining Germans rush to the water, having thrown their guns
away and capitulated. Easily, Gunn and his two men capture them, take
them prisoners, and make them march to join the group, with the tank right
behind them. Waco, now with an army unit, sees them in the distance. He
announces that the battle of El Alamein has been fought and won by the
Allies, and Gunn and Waco are soon saved by the advancing Allied forces.

The movie is sprinkled with patriotic dialogue, and even the usually
taciturn Gunn delivers a speech, extolling the bravery of the Allies and
the necessity of fighting even against enormous odds. He sees most of his
companions killed one by one. Frenchie is shot when he turns his back after
negotiating with the treacherous Major Von Falken (John Wengraf), Jimmy
Doyle is hurt and then blown to pieces along with Doctor Halliday, who is
trying to help him, as the fort is demolished by a shell. Giuseppe is killed by
Von Schletow for refusing to go along with him, but not before he delivers
an angry outburst against Hitler and the Nazis. In turn Schletow is killed
by Tambul, in a graphic scene in which Tambul leaps over the German
and buries his head in the sand. Krueger, an actor who specialized playing
Nazis, complained later that Ingram, who played Tambul, was so eager to
be realistic that he almost choked the actor to death.[1] This set of colorful
characters gives the movie its sense of ethnic diversity and shows the urgency of fighting the Nazis. One of them, Marty Williams (Carl Harbord),
is a typesetter who has educated himself by reading the books he set, and
he learned to like poetry. While in the trench with Gunn, Williams starts
reciting a line from "The Rubáiyát of Omar Kayyám"—"A book of verses

underneath the bough/A jug of wine"—but he hasn't time to finish the second line, "a loaf of bread—and thou," as a bullet silences him. He falls forward before Gunn even realizes what has happened.

All characters have geographical roots—one from Dublin, another from Brooklyn, one from Texas, another from a French village, one from South Africa, one from Torino, Italy. Only Gunn says from "nowhere," when asked to identify his place—"From the army," he mutters tersely. Bogart's fans are used to his screen characters' rootlessness. Much too often, they don't know where he has come from—except in the vaguest of terms—or where he is going to go, unless he dies, as in many of his early movies. Gunn is a child of the army, and he goes where he is ordered to go. He has no wife waiting for him, as Waco has, waiting for him back in Texas. Bogart does his job, and very well, with no regrets or complaints. Often one thinks he is an abstraction: he exists only while his screen persona lasts. In this one Bogart is a trooper when patriotism is concerned and he does all the right moves—he is brave, cunning enough to outmaneuver the dumb and vain Germans, as a film of that time describes them, and above all, tough in tough circumstances. He cannot save his entire unit but all of those killed die bravely and thus provide an example for those who must and should fight against enormous odds.

⓲

PASSAGE TO MARSEILLE

(Warner Bros./First National, 1944)

★ ★ ★

Director: Michael Curtiz
Screenplay: Casey Robinson, Jack Moffitt, based on the novel Sans Patrie by
    Charles Nordhoff, James Norman Hall
Producer: Hal B. Wallis. Cinematographer: James Wong Howe. Music Score:
    Max Steiner. Editor: Owen Marks
Cast: Humphrey Bogart (Jean Matrac), Michelle Morgan (Paula Matrac),
    Claude Rains (Captain Freycinet), Sydney Greenstreet (Major Duval),
    Philip Dorn (Renault), George Tobias (Petit), Peter Lorre (Marius),
    Helmut Dantine (Garou), John Loder (Manning), Eduardo Cianelli
    (Chief Engineer), Charles La Torre (Lieutenant Lenoir), Hans Conreid
    (Jourdain), Billy Roy (Mess Boy), Corinna Mura (Singer)
Released: March 11, 1944
Specs: 109 minutes; black and white
Availability: DVD (Turner Classic Movies: Humphrey Bogart: The Signature
    Collection, Volume 2)

By the time Bogart started filming *Passage to Marseille* in 1943, Bogart had already been in a movie dealing with French resistance against the Vichy government, the famous *Casablanca*, and was to do so again, joining the cause of French independence in *To Have and Have Not*, which followed a year after *Passage*. But the primary theme of *Casablanca* and *To Have and Have Not* is romance, which in both cases dominated the action on the screen. In *Casablanca*, patriotism comes in full force, but eventually it is the love story that keeps center stage. In *Passage to Marseille* (spelled without the "s" by the studio), Bogart plays not only a supporter of the cause but a

Frenchman—American accent and all—who was falsely convicted of murder, was incarcerated in Devil's Island, led an escape through the jungle, and fought the Germans as a gunman, both on a ship and on air raids over Berlin. He was joined by three stalwarts of *Casablanca*, Claude Rains, Sydney Greenstreet, and Peter Lorre, all of them playing divergent roles, rounding up an excellent cast of mostly men.

Passage to Marseille was produced by Hal B. Wallis and directed by Michael Curtiz, both of whom had won Oscars for *Casablanca*. The movie screenplay was written by Casey Robinson, who adapted it from the novel *Sans Patrie* ("Without a Country") by Charles Nordhoff and James Norman Hall, whose novels had inspired the Oscar-winning movie *Mutiny on the Bounty* (1935), starring Charles Laughton and Clark Gable. Hal Wallis had ambitions of turning *Passage to Marseille* into a blockbuster of epic sweep, but the movie fell just short of that goal due to its convoluted plotline and several flashbacks that impaired continuity of action. Still, each one of its episodes is powerful drama, and in the end the strands connect.

The movie opens with an action sequence, showing a squadron of bombers returning to their base in England after a successful air raid over the Rhineland. One of the planes flies low over the French town of Romilly, and a crew member, Jean Matrac (Bogart), drops a white flag attached to a steel tube containing a letter, picked up by a woman. It turns out that she is Matrac's wife, Paula (Michelle Morgan), who still lives in France with the couple's five-year-old son. It appears that the war has separated them, and this is their only means of communication.

The action shifts to the English countryside dotted with haystacks, fences, and cows grazing in the fields. A civilian, a war correspondent called Manning, is being driven by a young officer, who takes him to one of the buildings hidden inside the haystacks. There he meets Captain Freycinet (Claude Rains), eye-patched, elegant in his white uniform, and courteous to his visitor, offering him aperitifs and lunch. Freycinet explains to his guest that the agrarian appearance of the landscape is a camouflaged airdrome, where a squadron of the Free French, named the Victoire, flies missions against the common enemy, Germany. Manning is curious about Matrac; talking briefly to Freycinet prior to his flight that night, Manning asks his host about him. Freycinet, whose physical limitation, being blind in one eye, has confined him to a noncombatant role, is quite willing to talk, and he begins his long tale of Jean Matrac, who has incredibly survived persecution, imprisonment, escape through the jungle, a trip through the ocean on a canoe, and air attacks while on a naval cargo ship, helping it and its crew to reach its destination in England. He is now a gunner in the squadron of "flying fortresses," flying missions over Germany. That is a packed story and it comes in flashbacks by several narrators, with Freycinet's voice-over picking up the thread at crucial points.

Freycinet starts his narrative going back in time, just before the war, when he was a passenger in a cargo ship carrying a load of nickel ore to Marseilles. It was captained by Captain Malo (Victor Franken), whose small circle of passengers included Major Duval (Sydney Greenstreet), a martinet who believes that discipline is the essence of fighting, not free-thinking men. As soon as *Ville de Nancy* goes through the Panama Canal, news arrives that the Maginot Line, then thought impregnable, was outflanked by the Germans, who were rapidly advancing toward Paris. Captain Malo continues his course toward his destination, the port of Marseilles, but as soon as it is announced that France lost the war and an armistice was signed by Marshall Petain, now the head of the collaborative government of Vichy, Malo changes his course and heads for England. Meanwhile, the crew has spotted a small vessel in the distance, which turns out to be a canoe with five men near death from starvation and lack of water. Captain Malo welcomes them, believing their tale that they are workers trying to return home from Venezuela. But Duval, who says he "smells" convicts, believes they are escapees from Cayenne, where he had served earlier, and recommends that they be detained. Captain Malo asserts his authority, stating that as the ship's captain he will allow the rescued men to mix and work with the crew.

But Freycinet, who too has guessed that the five men are prison escapees, is eager to learn their true story, so he befriends them, and as they share a drink from his cabin, he hears their tales. The five men consist of Renault (Philip Dorn), Petit (George Tobias), Garou (Helmut Dantine), Marius (Peter Lorre), and Matrac (Bogart). Renault starts by describing the horrid conditions in the penal colony, where men are forced to labor in the mosquito-infested jungle, building a road they call "Route Zero," which is going nowhere and is meant only to punish the prisoners, who die or go mad trying to escape. Renault had noticed an elderly man who always saluted when the French flag was hoisted every morning. Gradually, he and his companions, minus Matrac, became acquainted with the old man, called Grandpère (Vladimir Sokoloff), who tells his story. He had been in Devil's Island for thirty-five years, had served his sentence, but was not allowed to leave the place. He used his spare time to catch butterflies, which he sold to tourists and then saved the money, always planning to find a way to escape. He bribed the guards with money or cigarettes, and one evening he managed to join the small group, as he overheard them say that they wanted to go back to France. He had a canoe in the swamp, but wanted someone to navigate it through the swamp and reach the ocean. Renault mentioned Matrac, who at that time was serving a two-month sentence in solitary confinement for having knifed a guard who defiled a letter he had received from his wife. He was in St. Joseph Island, called the "Rock," where each cell is made of four bare walls with iron bars overhead, where men go mad. Grandpère wanted to leave right away, but Marius observed that Matrac was the man to lead the group and that he would wait not just two months but two years, if necessary.

Renault also tells Matrac's story before he was a convict, and he tells it to the old man, and we are now on the fifth level of flashback storytelling, if that does not sound confusing. Grandpère learns Matrac's story from Renault, who has already told Freycinet who the others are and the conditions of the prison. Freycinet is continuing to tell the story to Manning (occasionally we hear his voice-over), who has been listening to all this, although we don't see him again until the story is over. But the crucial story of Matrac as a nonprisoner comes right at this point, more than halfway through the movie. It is a rather lengthy interlude, not unlike that of *Casablanca*, going back several years, when Matrac and Paula were still unmarried. As Renault starts his tale, there is a cut to a scene at the airport in Paris, where the French premier, Edward Deladier, is received by applauding crowds after his return from Munich, where he and Neville Chamberlain, the English prime minister, had signed a peace treaty with Germany after it had invaded parts of Czechoslovakia. Considering this an act of treason, Matrac is seen dictating his news to Paula, who is working for him, from a telephone booth. Right after that, Matrac's newspaper is seen rolling out of the press, accusing Deladier of treason. Moments later a mob is seen breaking into the newspaper office and smashing everything to pieces. Paula pulls Matrac out of a back door, fearing for his life. Two policemen outside the office just look on, doing nothing. Soon they are seen driving through the countryside, looking as happy and as much in love as Rick and Ilsa did when they drove through the streets of Paris. Matrac and Paula are headed for Romilly, Paula's town, and stop at a café and dance, while Corinna Mura, the exotic singer in *Casablanca*, sings them love songs. They marry, but happiness is brief. Paula sees in a newspaper that there is an order to arrest Matrac and they rush away on a train, but soon her husband is picked up by the police.

The rest of the story is easier to follow, but a few points are worth mentioning here. Bogart's Matrac is a bitter man who does not want to go back and help liberate France, as his four other companions do when they get into the boat. He hates France for having imprisoned him, an innocent man. He only agrees to lead the others in their escape in order to go back and be reunited with his wife. So when Grandpère gives his place to Matrac in his boat, he asks all five fugitives to raise their hand to take an oath to help liberate France; Matrac says nothing. When they are rescued, and asked by Captain Freycinet to tell their tales, Matrac does not tell his, and Freycinet hears it from Renault, who had told it to Grandpère in the scene mentioned earlier. Thus, the entire story of Matrac before he is rescued is revealed to the viewer indirectly before they are on the ship.

Matrac remains this way, that is, determined to return to France to meet his wife and son, whom he has never seen. But once he is on the *Ville de Nancy*, a turn of events brings on a change in him. When the wireless radio picks up the news that on June 23 Marshall Petain had negotiated an armistice with Germany and established himself at Vichy, Captain Malo decides to change course; instead of going to Marseille, he will go to London to deliver his valuable cargo there. But Major Duval notices the change, and he and a few other men loyal to him attempt to take over command of the ship.

Marius (Peter Lorre), Garou (Helmut Dantine), and Petit (George Tobias) stand behind Jean Matrac (Bogart), as they watch a German plane approach. *Warner Bros./Photofest* © *Warner Bros.*

But as soon as they announce their decision, the mess boy cries, "Vive la France!" and Matrac springs to action. Bullets fly, but the four companions and the loyal members of the crew fight and soon subdue the rebels. Duval and his associates are detained, but not before Jourdain, the radio operator, transmits a massage giving the ship's position.

This is the turning point for Matrac, who changes from a bitter man to a fighter for the resistance. Even as this happens, he shows some ambivalence, which, if anything, makes Bogart's projected image even more intriguing. Here, for instance, when a German bomber, responding to the message received by the operator, attacks the ship, killing some of its men, among them Marius and the mess boy, it is Matrac who fires back with the ship's machine gun and downs the German plane. But then, despite the protests of Captain Malo, he shoots the three Germans who survived and stand on the floating plane. This goes against war conventions to spare men who are surrendering and are to be taken war prisoners.

The conclusion comes with a return to Freycinet as the narrator of his tale to Manning at the French airdrome. The large air squadrons of flying fortresses that flew to over Berlin earlier are expected to return from their mission that night. One by one the planes land, but the one flown by Renault, with Matrac as the gunner, is delayed. Radio signals are sent to it, but there is no response. A short sequence shows Paula Matrac and her young son waiting to hear the familiar sound from a plane approaching. The young boy, who has never seen his father, is now five, and he is preparing to blow out the candles of his birthday cake. After they hear a sound and the mother goes outside as usual at such times, she comes back. The father is not to fly overhead.

Back at the airdrome, signals arrive from the missing plane that it has suffered damage and casualties. Renault brings it in, but when Matrac is carried out on a stretcher, he is already dead. But the steel cylinder found on him contains a letter to his young son, urging him to be proud to be French and to stand up for the defense of liberty everywhere. The letter is read a day later by Freycinet, as the casket of Matrac is lowered into the grave.

Passage to Marseille lacks the humor and love interest of *Casablanca* and *To Have and Have Not*, though all three movies promote the cause of the Free French and resistance to Vichy and to the scourge of Europe, Hitler. But *Passage* comes closer to the reality of war than the other two. It also shows the horrors of a penal colony and the bitter divisions among the French, some of whom chose to side with the Nazis and the compromisers at Vichy. As the narrator Claude Rain's Freycinet is a totally different from Captain Renault of *Casablanca*, who at times sounds frivolous, amoral, and as he says himself, a man who "blows with the wind." Here, as Freycinet, Rains is deeply patriotic, humane, an astute judge of character, and above all, a man who wants to tell the truth, valuing the valor and sacrifices of the men who joined the fight for French freedom. As for Bogart, the hero of the story, his persona seems divided. As a newspaper owner and lover, he is the man most viewers know, wearing his fedora with the lowered front rim, a figure he adopted since *The Maltese Falcon*. Though unconvincing as a Frenchman, we have no problem accepting him as the lover and then husband of Michelle Morgan, a French beauty who had been considered for the role of Ilsa Lund in *Casablanca*. Bogart as a convict is a different man, bitter, antagonistic, with a fiery temper that lands him in the solitary. The Devil's Island is no playground for Matrac and his four loyal companions. The movie shows not only the patriotism but also the crimes of France— man's inhumanity to man, in the most vivid colors. No wonder that Matrac is bitter, forced to live through this inferno for just speaking his mind freely. Even when placed in the straitjacket of three different personalities, and despite the flashbacks and convoluted story line, Bogart in the end emerges as a hero, the man we know.

TO HAVE AND HAVE NOT

(Warner Bros./First National, 1944)

★ ★ ★ ★

Director: Howard Hawks
Screenplay: Jules Furthman, William Faulkner, based on the novel by Ernest
    Hemingway
Producer: Howard Hawks
Photography: Sid Hickox. *Music Score:* Franz Waxman. *Editor:* Christian Nyby.
    Art Direction: Casey Roberts. *Costumes:* Milo Anderson
Cast: Humphrey Bogart (Harry "Steve" Morgan), Lauren Bacall (Marie "Slim"
    Browning), Walter Brennan (Eddie), Dolores Moran (Helene de
    Brusac), Walter Molnar (Paul de Brusac), Hoagy Carmichael (Cricket),
    Marcel Dalio (Gerard "Frenchie"), Dan Seymour (Captain Renald),
    Sheldon Leonard (Lieutenant Coyo), Walter Sandy (Johnson)
Release: October 11, 1944
Specs: 100 minutes; black and white
Availability: DVD (Warner Home Video)

To Have and Have Not launched Lauren Bacall's career, led to her romance
and marriage to Humphrey Bogart, and made Hollywood history for those
reasons alone. But it took the combined efforts of a great director, Howard
Hawks, and two of the ablest Hollywood writers, William Faulkner and
Jules Furthman, to convert a lesser Hemingway novel into a brilliant movie,
regarded as one of Bogart's best both now and then, not to mention Bacall's
memorable debut that made her an instant star. The movie is fun to watch,
as sparks fly between Bogart and the newcomer Bacall, with plenty of witty
dialogue, erotic innuendo, and mounting suspense.

Hemingway's novel *To Have and Have Not*, published in 1937, shows an American drifter in Cuba who is entangled with drug traffickers and killed at the end. For political reasons,[1] Hawks and Warners directed Faulkner and Furthman to change the locale to Martinique, which, along with many French colonies, was ruled by the Vichy regime after the defeat of France in 1940. Vichy's functionaries and goons were running the city, which was also teeming with insurgents, supporters of De Gaulle, who were organizing an underground resistance. As in *Casablanca*, much of the action takes place in a café run by a Frenchman, Gerard, or Frenchie (Marcel Dalio, the croupier in *Casablanca*), here heavily involved with revolutionaries, so his café is watched by Captain Renald, played by the plump and sinister-looking Dan Seymour, who enters the café at will.

Port-de-France, the capital of Martinique, was also a hot spot for fortune hunters, tourists, pickpockets, and all kinds of riffraff seen at Frenchie's café, where suspicious types mixed with customers. The café had a band and a singer/pianist, Hoagy Carmichael[2]—known as Cricket—to provide entertainment and add a lighter note to what could otherwise have been a rather gloomy tale. Cricket is the equivalent of Sam in *Casablanca*, and it might not be unreasonable to suggest that Hawks was cashing in on the success of that movie, in which Bogart had made his big switch to a great lover. Frenchie's café was part hotel, with rooms to rent upstairs and a basement, a hideout for fugitives where illegal activities were conducted. If not in Harry Morgan's (Bogart's) boat, most of the action happens at Frenchie's. It was shot at Warner Bros. Studios, of course, with some establishing shots of a map of Martinique.

Though Bogart had reached the status of superstar at the time, he was well matched with the newcomer, Betty Bacall,[3] as she was called when she arrived in Hollywood. Betty had appeared as a model in *Harpers' Bazaar*, but had no other experience on stage or screen. She lived alone with her mother, and she had come from the east on the recommendation of Hawks's wife, whose name was Slim, a name that was later adopted as a nickname for Bacall's character in *To Have and Have Not*. It took many months for Hawks to groom her for an important role, signing her up with Warners on a multiyear contract when she was only eighteen. Hawks also looked for a new first name that fit her persona better; he dug into her family background, and he chose Lauren, which was Bacall's great-grandmother's name.[4] Hawks asked her to take numerous tests so she could know how to behave before a camera, and he and his wife took her to Hollywood parties where she met celebrities and acquired Hollywood gloss. Even at that young age, she understood that Hawks was making special efforts to advance her career, so she knew she had to try to meet his standards and worked hard to play to her strengths—lowering her voice by reciting prose pieces in some desert spot

Harry Morgan (Bogart) lights a cigarette for Marie Browning (Bacall). *Warner Bros./Photofest* © *Warner Bros.*

and behaving with masculine aggression when expected to be paired with a star who was reputedly the screen's toughest guy. Despite stiff competition for the role of Marie Browning in *To Have and Have Not*—Ann Sheridan was Warners' first choice[5]—Bacall was given a role that dreams are made on. She also developed "The Look," which became her trademark—head lowered, an intense glance shooting arrows at any challenger. Here is how she explains, in her own words, how The Look came to be during her first real test for a famous opening scene for *To Have and Have Not*:

> "Action," said Howard. This was for posterity, I thought, for the real theaters, for real people to see. I came around the corner, said my first line, and Howard said, "Cut." He had broken the scene up—the first shot ended the first line. The second set-up was the rest of it—then he'd move in for close-ups. By the end of the third or fourth take, I realized the one way to hold my trembling head still was to keep it down, chin low, almost to my chest, the eyes up at Bogart. It worked, and it turned out to be the beginning of "The Look."[6]

The scene created not just The Look, but the image of a young female who refuses to be patted or cornered and keeps a physical distance between her and any male, as in her first scene alone with such a man as Bogart.

At their first meeting, she asks, "Got a match?" standing by the door. He tosses her a matchbox; she catches it adeptly, lights her cigarette, and tosses it back: "Thanks," and exits.

The movie placed her opposite Bogart, who had at the time reached the status of a megastar and a great screen lover. Initially, Bogart was polite to the newcomer, acting on his established principle not to flirt with his female costars. At the time, he was on his third marriage, to Mayo Methot, whose career had taken a plunge as his had risen spectacularly. Methot was extremely jealous of his costars, and she was known for her drunkenness and domestic violence, often throwing crockery at him and stabbing him in the back once.[7] He said he had the scar to prove it. That marriage was collapsing rapidly, but Bogart had no intention of divorcing her, being as loyal a husband to her as he had been to his two previous wives. He treated Bacall with consideration, knowing that she was a newcomer, somewhat overwhelmed by her first big role and needing encouragement on the set, despite the audacity she showed on the screen, which Hawks had managed to draw out of her. Her feelings for Bogart had been spontaneous, as were his for her, but it was not a romance that sparked instantly. It took three weeks or so before Bogart became familiar enough and asked for her phone number.[8] She gave it to him, written on the inside cover of a matchbox, and soon they were lovers, to the amazement of Hawks, who was touchy on costars' affairs and a bit jealous, for he was a notorious woman chaser, in addition to being the best known Svengali[9] in Hollywood—a Pygmalion[10] who did not foresee that his Galatea would fly in a different direction.

On the surface, the movie is a story of survival in a hostile environment, at time of war, when France had fallen to Hitler and the Vichy government had spread its tentacles to the French colonies, no matter how remote. Like *Casablanca*, it projects patriotic traits, showing such a man as Harry Morgan, a boat owner who makes money renting his fishing boat to tourists and who cares for no one but himself. Here the attraction between man and woman is sexual, not weepy and sentimental, as in *Casablanca*, without any pretense of nobility in it. The characters feel the oppression of a brutal regime and use their wits to stay alive. Hawks plays down sentiment, uses humor to deflect it, and has his characters scramble for pennies, rather than the mythical sums needed in *Casablanca* to buy exit visas. Instead of isolated gunshots that seem a momentary annoyance to the customers of Rick's café, here the nightclub is riddled with bullets and bullies kill or are killed. Harry runs a fishing business, owning a boat and employing a drunk and limping Walter Brennan as

Eddie, loyal and amiable during the moments he managed to stay sober. An American, Johnson, fails to catch a big fish, but intends to skip town without paying Harry. Harry notices that a young girl in the café has picked Johnson's pocket. Harry makes the girl, whom he calls Slim, give the money back to Johnson, but before he can collect, Johnson is killed during a raid led by Captain Ranald (Dan Seymour) against the resistance group at Frenchie's café, which the captain suspects is a nest of revolutionaries. Harry and Slim, whose actual name is Marie Browning, are taken to the police station, where his passport and money ($825-plus owed him) are confiscated.

Forced to seek money to flee town, Harry accepts a job picking up and transporting a man from Haiti to Martinique, but the man, Paul de Brusac (Walter Molnar), who is escorted by his beautiful wife, Helene (Dolores Moran), is wounded when the boat runs into a patrol boat. De Brusac's mission is to connect with an important resistant fighter, Pierre Villemans (the equivalent of Victor Lazlo in *Casablanca*), who is kept prisoner at Devil's Island, and bring him to Porte-au-France, in Haiti, and to freedom. The wounded man is brought to Frenchie's café, hidden in his basement, the center of operations, with a bullet in his right shoulder. Medical attention is urgently needed, and Frenchie asks Harry to operate and pull the bullet out. Cool and methodical, lit only by the dim light of a kerosene lamp, he does the job, paying little attention to the man's wife, who swoons when she is told to hold a chloroform bottle near the sick man's face. De Brusac recovers soon and is well enough to travel to his destination the next day. Helene, who had up to that time considered Harry a fraud, asks for his forgiveness, but in a manner just shy of flirtation. Not wanting the audience to be confused as to who is the lady of Bogart as Harry's heart, Hawks cut some of Dolores Moran's lines out. But Moran adds a touch of enchantment to the dreary basement where all this happens and also suggests that Harry could take an insult from a lady without flinching. After all, he has two beautiful women offering their hearts on a platter to him—and the luxury of choosing the one he likes best. Still grateful for Harry's action, Helene gives him a handful of jewelry belonging to her family, enough to pay his way back.

The sexual dominance of Bacall in the movie had to be balanced with Bogart's image as a tough guy, which comes to prominence in the second part of the movie, when Harry decides, albeit out of necessity, to help Frenchie and his undercover friends. To be in his element, Bogie has to look a bit worn out, weary of the world, with more than a touch of cynicism in him, cracking lines of derision, but generously souled. And Bacall is really more like him—run down and broke—than the beautiful and elegant Helene de Brusac, who, like Ilsa Lund, is there for her husband's noble cause. As Slim, Bacall is far from innocent, challenging Harry with jokes like "To whistle, just put your lips together, and blow." Mimicking her, Harry whistles! Slim also sings at the bar, liking the man at the piano, Cricket, who writes a song for her—Bacall actually sings. But when a new crisis crops up, Harry shows clearly who moves the chess pieces, and as Bogart frequently did in real life (he was a first-rate chess player), he scores a checkmate. After Harry brings the wounded man and his wife back and they are making preparations to leave the hotel and Martinique, Renald and two of his goons enter his room, telling him that they hold Eddie, knowing that Harry would not leave without him. Eddie, a practically useless old "rummy," had been Harry's friend for a long time and he could not survive without his regular dose of booze. He would get the "shakes," and, worse, would tell all. Harry gets out of the tight spot quickly and decisively. Pretending he is looking for a match in his open drawer, he grabs a hidden gun and shoots one of Renald's men and, with Frenchie's help, disarms and handcuffs the others. Harry's action is so quick it catches Renald and all present by surprise. He forces the two villains to step over the corpse of the dead man and makes them sit on a couch, threatening to beat or kill the one who refuses to make the phone call to free Eddie. In a moment, Renald is shown, a gash on the side of his head, making the call. Harry has vowed not just to flee to freedom but escort de Brusac and his wife to the Devil's Island to help free Pierre Villemans and bring the group to Porte-au-France. He has joined the French resistance, and the war effort. As they say, déjà vu all over again.

Hawks does not care so much for a moral tale as for presenting a symmetrical composition. All elements work. Bacall as Slim entices Bogart's character and the audience with suggestive sex; Bogart as Harry, though always a bit differently, displays his ability to come out of a tight spot, side with the right course of action, showing again that, when the chips are down he can stand and deliver; and Faulkner and Jules Furthman deconstruct Hemingway's novel, bringing it to the level of a movie with a contemporary and relevant theme. There is no moral to the story. Perhaps, one can say this is a tough world, and most guys don't care for the right course, so if you are to survive, keep your eyes open. Harry Morgan is a good man, though. His buddy, Eddie, needs his sheltering wing. Harry cares for him. And Slim captures his imagination—she is much like him, despite her young age. She proves that age has nothing to do with being young. A runaway, she is the female Huck in the chaos of the Caribbean, at times of turmoil. Whether they will settle down and raise a family is not even hinted in the movie. It is enough that they joined forces to flee a little hell boiling with atrocities, where life has little value. They survive.

20

THE BIG SLEEP

(Warner Bros./First National, 1946)

★ ★ ★ ★ ★

Director: Howard Hawks
Screenplay: William Faulkner, Jules Furthman, Leigh Brackett, based on the
    novel by Raymond Chandler
Producer: Howard Hawks
Cinematographer: Sid Hickox. *Music Score:* Max Steiner. *Editor:* Christian
    Nyby. *Art Direction:* Carl Jules Weyl. *Set Decoration:* Fred M. McLean.
    Costumes: Leah Rhodes
Cast: Humphrey Bogart (Philip Marlowe), Lauren Bacall (Vivian Rutledge),
    Martha Vickers (Carmen Sternwood), Charles Waldron (General
    Sternwood), John Ridgely (Eddie Mars), Theodore Von Eltz (Arthur
    G. Geiger), Dorothy Malone (Acme Book Owner), Peggy Knudsen
    (Mona Mars), Regis Toomey (Bernie Ohls), Charles D. Brown (Norris,
    the Butler), Bob Steele (Canino), Elisha Cook Jr. (Harry Jones),
    Louis Heydt (Joe Brody), Sonia Darrin (Agnes), James Flavin (Captain
    Cronjager), Dan Wallace (Owen Taylor), Tom Rafferty (Carol
    Lundgren), Theodore Von Eltz (Arthur Gwynn Geiger), Joy Barlowe
    (Taxi Driver), Trevor Bardette (Art Hunk), Carole Douglas (Librarian),
    Joseph Grehan (Medical Examiner)
Released: August 31, 1946
Specs: 116 minutes; black and white
Availability: DVD (Warner Home Video, with "Special Features,"
    "Documentary: *The Big Sleep*, 1945/1946 Comparisons," by Robert
    Gitt, 1997); Blu-ray (*Humphrey Bogart: The Essential Collection*; contains
    twenty-four Bogart movies, 2010); streaming (Amazon)

The Big Sleep has retained its status as a classic movie of the highest order for generations, and it is still widely viewed, written about, and shown in college classes and other film venues. A testament of its longevity is the fact that as recently as December 2014, Richard Brody wrote a laudatory piece in the *New Yorker*, as this Howard Hawks movie, featuring Humphrey Bogart, was shown at the New York Film Forum series of film noir movies. The title of Brody's essay was "The Bigger Sleep," implying that the film's reputation is perhaps greater today than at the time it was made. For this and other reasons, *The Big Sleep* is a must for Bogart devotees and other film buffs.

Drawn from Raymond Chandler's 1939 novel, the screenplay of *The Big Sleep* was fashioned by William Faulkner, Leigh Brackett, and Jules Furthman, and directed by Howard Hawks, who was known to mix genres and to build scenes for their own inherent interest. As a result, *The Big Sleep* is notorious for its labyrinthine plot, leaving viewers wondering about who's done what to whom, and what strands have been left hanging loose. A few comparisons between the original Chandler novel and the film may help to explain some of these discrepancies and fill in gaps. In both film and novel, many minor characters, especially in the first part of the story, come in, are shot dead or left behind, and are never heard of again. This is a far cry, however, from saying that the plot is incomprehensible or that an occasional muddle slows the pace or affects the story's importance. In fact, tension increases and, as a puzzled viewer tries to make connections, things begin to shape up, and a resolution comes that explains most, if not all, questions. Meanwhile, it is great fun for those who like to watch Bogart as an intractable detective, lover, and tougher than the tough guys who happen to cross his path.

Perhaps few people realize that there were two versions of this film: the first was supposed to be released in 1945 but never was, and the second version, with some of its scenes reshot to make the film more sexually appealing, was released in 1946, and that is the one that is generally known to the public—then and now. Jack Warner was hesitant to release the 1945 version because Lauren Bacall, after her impressive debut on the screen in *To Have and Have Not* (1945) with Humphrey Bogart, had subsequently received terrible reviews for *Confidential Agent* (1945), a movie she made with Charles Boyer that bombed at the box office. (Ironically, *The Confidential Agent* was shot after *The Big Sleep*.) So Warners kept *The Big Sleep* unreleased, afraid it too would bomb. But after a letter from his agent, Charles K. Feldman, who had introduced Bacall to Warners, Jack Warner reconsidered, and he had some of the crew reassemble and reshoot scenes, mostly between the two principals almost a year later, when the two had already been married. The new version enhances the presence of Bacall, giving her additional scenes with Bogart, some famous for their racy exchanges. The story, considered a prime example of film noir, features seven murders/deaths, several off camera, one solved only in the final minutes, while another is reputedly never explained.

The plot may seem—but is not—episodic. This may be due to both Chandler's novelistic style and to the storytelling of Hawks, both emphasizing tone over plot design and both treating individual scenes as wholes in themselves. Although the plot appears to evolve with total disregard for sequential logic, nevertheless, it has a beginning, a middle (or several middles), and an end. Here are some important highlights:

1. Marlowe probes the Geiger establishment; Geiger dies; Marlowe gathers clues as to the Sternwoods.
2. Marlowe investigates the mystery of Owen Taylor's death.
3. Marlowe follows a trail to Eddie Mars; Shawn Regan's disappearance is explained.
4. Marlowe is shown in relation to the women in the story, especially in the added scenes with Vivian.
5. Marlowe acts in a way that enhances Bogart's persona as a "tough guy."

After Marlowe gets his assignment from General Sternwood, who is sitting in a wheelchair, bundled up in his hothouse though the temperature/ humidity is melting the flowers, he moves quickly to his assignment. The general reveals to him that his younger daughter, Carmen (Martha Vickers), had written large promissory notes to one Arthur G. Geiger, who then sent those notes to the general along with a handwritten card complaining that these, being gambling debts, ought to be honored. The general also mentions that he had paid a check of $5,000 some months earlier to a man called Joe Brody, made out to Brody by Shawn Regan, the general's handy man (in the novel Regan is Vivian's current husband), who used to work for the general and had left him abruptly a month earlier without any explanation. Regan had commanded a brigade during the Irish Rebellion, the general says, and Marlowe recognized the name as he and Regan, who used to import rum from Mexico, had exchanged gunshots sometime in the past but had stayed on friendly terms. Marlowe's assignment is to get rid of Geiger, leaving it to Marlowe to choose the way of doing it. The general is cynical about his daughters, whom he cannot save from their own corruption, as they have inherited his own corrupt blood, he says. He describes his older daughter, Vivian, as "exacting, smart, and ruthless," while Carmen is "a child who likes to pull wings off flies." Self-reproachfully, he adds, "A man who engages in parenthood at my age deserves all he gets." As if to confirm the general's bitter remarks about his daughters, Marlowe tells him that Carmen had tried to sit on his lap while he was standing, just after he had entered the building. Before he leaves the general, Marlowe recommends that he pay Geiger the promissory notes and undertakes to find out what this is all about. As Marlowe leaves, Norris, the butler, asks him to see Mrs. Rutledge (Lauren Bacall), Mrs. Regan in the Chandler novel, who worries about her father, and she begs that Marlowe treat him with consideration. But her motives, not to mention her insolent manner, don't ingratiate her with Marlowe, who leaves her abruptly.

Marlowe's first step is to go to the Hollywood Public Library to take some notes on rare editions to use as a ruse to visit Geiger's bookstore. When he asks Agnes (Sonya Darrin), the salesgirl at Geiger's, for a copy of an 1880 third edition of *Ben-Hur* and a *Chevalier Audubon* from 1840, the woman becomes uneasy and dismisses him rudely.

Marlowe then enters a real bookstore across the street, named Acme, run by a bespectacled young Dorothy Malone (otherwise nameless), and she informs him that the book he asked for does not exist. "But the woman in Geiger's place did not know that," explains Marlowe. Then she does give him a good description of Geiger—middle-aged, medium height, fattish, a glass left eye, chauffeured by a man called Carol Lundgren. By that time the rain is coming down, and as she doesn't seem too eager to let him go, he mentions a bottle of rye he carries with him, and she accepts his offer. When he asks her, "Do you have to wear these?" pointing her spectacles, she takes them off, looks at the mirror, loosens her hair, rolls down the blinds, brings two paper cups . . . and we are left to imagine the rest.[1] In the Chandler novel, this woman, still nameless, is "an intelligent Jewess," who gives Marlowe the information on Geiger mentioned in the film, but nothing else happens between them.

Geiger is seen leaving his place, the rain pouring, accompanied by a young man who holds an umbrella over him. Marlowe follows him in his car and settles outside his house, waiting. He watches a woman go in, and a bit later he hears a scream and three shots, and sees someone driving away, another car following the first. Marlowe breaks into the house by kicking a window in and finds Geiger dead on the floor and Carmen drunk and doped on a chair. A photograph has been stolen from the head of a statue concealing a camera, the film gone, so he surmises someone took a picture of Carmen. Marlowe searches Geiger's desk and finds a book with codes and with the Sternwood name on it. He is certain it contains the names of those he blackmails, for by now it appears to him that Geiger runs an extortionist racket. In the Chandler novel, the bookstore is a front for pornographic literature and extortion, with a list of customers to be black-mailed later. Also in the novel, Carmen is not just doped and incoherent, but stark naked—something that, of course, would make a juicy visual detail in current cinema, but at that time unthinkable due to the Breen Code. Marlowe takes Carmen, barely conscious of what's going on, back to her father's but tells Norris the butler and her sister, Vivian, to let her lie in her bed and keep mum about the whole thing. He tells Vivian that he will not report this—he is hired to protect them. Her sister would be implicated if someone found out that she was at the crime scene. But when he goes back to Geiger's place, the body has disappeared. The appearance of Vivian in this scene exists only in the 1946 film version; in the novel only the female servant, Mathilda, comes out to help him with Carmen.

Back in his office, while Marlowe is trying to decipher the contents of the booklet, certain it contains names of those Geiger blackmailed, Chief Inspector Bernie Ohls (Regis Toomey) drops in. Ohls informs Marlowe that a car is being dredged out of Lido Pier, with a body in it. Ohls is a friendly cop, and he already knew that Marlowe had an assignment from General Sternwood; Ohls himself had recommended him. They drive to the scene of the crime, as the Packard, a car that belongs to Vivian, is being dredged out. The dead man inside the car is Owen Taylor, the Sternwoods' chauffer, who, an officer tells Ohls, had suffered head wounds when the car plunged into the pier. Later in the story, Marlowe learns that Taylor "was sweet" on Carmen—she used to seduce every man who came near her, but mostly reserved her sweetness for the revolving set of chauffeurs her dad hired. Taylor had followed her to Geiger's, either because he wanted to protect her from extortion or because he was jealous; we never learn for sure.

Much has been said about Owen Taylor's killer, and a story that some consider apocryphal[2] has it that Hawks and William Faulkner, not knowing the answer, called Chandler to ask who killed the chauffer. Bogart also, his wife tells us, asked Hawks one day, "Who pushed Taylor off the pier?"[3] Chandler reputedly said that he did not know. Well, if he didn't know, he certainly gives enough clues for the reader of his book, and possibly the viewer of the film, to reach some conclusions. For one, the novel describes a man standing at the pier and wiping his face with a towel, the very man who had gone underwater to place the chains on the hauled car. As the others speculate whether it was murder or suicide, the man is called to offer an opinion. Without much hesitation he says it was suicide. The tread marks of the tires show a straight furrowed line; the car was speeding when it hit the broken rail, and it landed squarely in the water, right side up. His words have irrefutable logic, for it is hard to imagine that someone had pushed the car in, in which case it would have been moving slowly and plunged into the river headlong, going down vertically.[4]

This is consistent with what Brody tells Marlowe later, as both Marlowe and the police have suspicions that he, Brody, had been the killer. When Brody tells his story to Marlowe, he admits that he was the last man to see Taylor alive. In the film he says that he had followed Taylor after the latter had shot Geiger, played "copper," and as Taylor seemed nervous, Brody "sapped him down," took the negatives, and then left him alone near Beverly Hills. In the film Brody does not have time to finish his point to Marlowe, because he answers the door and is shot by Lundgren, Geiger's handyman. In the Chandler book Brody tells just about the same story, with one important detail that was left out in the film: Brody says that he had lifted the plate holder while Taylor was still unconscious, but then Taylor came to, knocked Brody off the car, and sped away, leaving him there. That was the last Brody saw of him. That explanation in the 1945 movie version is also consistent with what Marlowe told the district attorney, Taggart Wilde, as he was being questioned about Geiger's and Brody's murders in the first version (1945) of the film, as well as in the novel. Captain Cronjager, a suspicious policeman, and Ohls were there, too, as Marlow made his statement to the DA.

The above scene from the 1945 version and the novel was totally omitted in the 1946 released film, and was replaced with the sexually charged scene between Bogart and Bacall at the café.[5] Marlowe is asked why he believes that Brody did not murder Taylor. Though Marlowe's answer is basically the same in the book and movie, in the novel it is more amplified. He explains that he thinks that it is physically possible but "morally impossible." Brody was not the killer type. Brody was interested in having something on Geiger, whose activities he knew through his girlfriend, Agnes, so he was watching his house that night. Marlowe points out that if Brody had killed Taylor, aside from taking the negatives that Geiger was taking of the nude Carmen Sternwood (which he did), he would have had to plant the gun on Taylor, and push Taylor off the Lido Pier, thirty-five miles away—a physical impossibility. One could also argue that, if the car had sped off the pier, as the man who had placed the chains on the car said, Brody should have been inside the car with Taylor.

On the other hand, a Taylor suicide is plausible. He had just killed a man out of jealousy, and he had lost the photos of Carmen, whom he presumably might have been trying to protect. Besides, he had a record of arrest in

Indiana and had spent six months in jail. With Brody presenting himself as a copper, Taylor might have thought the police were after him. The word *suicide* was mentioned briefly in the film, and a clear, though still speculative, case is made in the novel. The facts, as presented in the novel, suggest that nobody could have killed him. And that suicide remains the most likely explanation.

With the Geiger matter behind him, Marlowe is now pursuing a new path, not altogether unrelated to the events of the first part of the story. For one thing, the hasty, albeit generous, payment he received from Vivian Rutledge alerted him to the idea that she was trying to stop his prodding into her affairs. In their sexually charged banter at the restaurant, after she pays him, she acts as if she believed that that was the end of it, but she suddenly changes her expression as soon as the name of Eddie Mars is mentioned. Marlowe is now convinced that Mars has something on her. Soon enough after that, he gets a warning from Bernie Ohls that the DA had ordered Marlowe to stop inquiring into the Sternwood affairs. The request had come from the elder daughter, Marlowe is told. Then, there is the matter of Shawn Regan's disappearance. At first, Marlowe had not bothered to pay attention to this part of the story, but now he suspects that all of these matters are connected.

And sure enough, Marlowe's suspicions are realized. He pays a visit to Eddie Mars's establishment and finds Vivian there playing the roulette and winning a large sum, as Eddie Mars looks on. She asks Marlowe to drive her home but when she comes out of the casino into the parking lot, a man holds her up and grabs her bag. Marlowe easily overcomes this man and gives her back her handbag. But he has guessed that this whole scene was a setup. As they drive home, he challenges her to open her bag and show him the $28,000 she was supposed to have won. Mars let her win, he implies, and then she handed the money back to him. As Marlowe sees it, Vivian had gone to lengths to prove that Mars had nothing on her. In the same car drive, Marlowe kisses her, to assure her that both his feelings and his motives are genuine.

Despite all that, Marlowe soon receives a phone call from her that she has found Shawn Regan. He is in Mexico, and she is going there to meet him. Things don't stop there. As he crosses a dark alley, Marlowe gets a sound beating by two men, no doubt Mars's goons. Marlowe had also spotted a car shadowing him and had learned that the driver was one Harry Jones. The latter soon shows up and renders help. The little man is played by Elisha Cook Jr., who had also appeared with Bogart in *The Maltese Falcon*, a vicious punk there, but a rather harmless shadowy figure here who is out to make a quick buck for his girlfriend, Agnes, the same one who had lost Brody and who had then complained that she could never in her life find a man smart enough "to go around the course once." Back at his office, still sore from the beating he took, Marlowe negotiates to meet Jones at his place in an hour, give him the two Cs ($200), in exchange for whatever news she could give him on Mars's wife, who is supposed to have eloped with Regan.

But when Marlowe gets there, Jones has company, the most vicious killer in the entire movie: Canino (Bob Steele), Mars's top gun, who is questioning Jones on the whereabouts of Agnes. Jones gives him a false address; Canino forces a poisoned drink on him, and Jones dies laughing, in one of the most bizarre scenes in movie. Marlowe is hiding behind a partition, watching the entire scene without interfering. But as soon as Canino is gone, he goes into the room and finds Jones dead. He calls the address where Agnes is supposed to be, but the man there tells him that no such person exists. But when his phone rings, Marlowe answers it. It is Agnes as he has anticipated; he tells her Jones is dead and agrees to meet her. In exchange for the $200, Agnes provides him with the information that Mars's wife is being kept secretly in a house behind a garage, in a remote area. Marlowe drives there, pretends he has a flat tire, and knocks on the garage door. He is held at gunpoint by a man, Art Hunk, and knocked unconscious by Canino, who swings at him with a fist full of coins.

When Marlowe comes to, he finds himself in a room attended by Mona, Mars's wife (Peggy Knudsen), and soon Vivian also comes in. Marlowe tells Mona that her husband is a crook, not just a gambler, and that he kills "by remote control." Angrily, she throws water in his face and leaves the room. Vivian cuts his ropes, but he is still in handcuffs. As a car arrives outside, he tells her to count to twenty and then scream. He slips outside and gets his gun from his car, which has been brought there by the two men in the garage, and when she screams, he fires a shot. Art panics and runs away. When Canino comes out, holding Vivian in front of him for protection, she cries out, "There he is!" Canino shoots in the wrong direction, and Marlowe shoots Canino three times. Quickly, Marlowe searches Canino's pockets and finds the keys to the handcuffs; then both he and Vivian go inside, from where he calls Mars. Marlowe tells him that he is at Geiger's former place. He drives to Geiger's ahead of Mars and waits for him; when the latter comes in, Marlowe holds him at gunpoint and fires a couple of shots to warn Mars that he means business. Mars exits the door crying "Do not shoot!" But his men outside fire, he is riddled with a streak of bullets, and Mars falls back through the door. Marlowe calls the cops, but before they arrive he tells Vivian that she needs to put her sister, who is a sick woman, in a place where she can be cured. "They have places like that," he assures her. "What about me?" she says. "What's wrong with you?" he replies. "Nothing you can't fix," is her answer.

Explanation: Carmen had killed Regan as revenge when he started showing interest in Mona Mars. That is the secret Mars had on Vivian, holding her hostage—in more ways than one—and she had acted to protect the reputation of her family. The cover-up still remains. Marlowe told the police on the phone that Mars had killed Regan.

Two points will be added to this rather extensive plot synopsis. First, as said earlier, any viewer will notice how many young and pretty women have eyes for Marlowe, Hawks having crowded the screen with as many young fresh faces as one would want to count. He has added many more than in the book—for example, the girl taxi driver (Joy Barlowe), who is a young man in the book. Many others have been mentioned already. Why is that? In the

Philip Marlowe (Bogart) telephones the police, after Eddie Mars has been killed by his own men, while Vivian Rutledge (Bacall) looks on apprehensively. *Warner Bros./Photofest © Warner Bros.*

Chandler novel, Marlowe is rather ascetic, so these young ladies, with the exception of the leads, were intentionally placed in the script. The answer can only be a guess. The young, pretty females add a comedic/sexual touch to the rather gloomy plot, and Hawks was known for mixing genres. One can add that Bogart as Marlowe has undeniable sex appeal. The string of ladies early in the movie testifies to that, and Carmen had a lustful thought when she sneaked into his apartment (nude in the Chandler novel), expecting to sleep with him. Marlowe treats her with revulsion, both in book and film, but his reasons here are both professional and personal. In all other occasions he seems to enjoy the attention he gets from the opposite sex—and in one case, the girl at the Acme bookstore, he seems to have capitalized on it.

Second, how does Bogart come off as Philip Marlowe, a role played by several other actors?[26] In some ways, his image here is a continuation to that established in *The Maltese Falcon*, where Bogart also plays a tough-guy detective. But while Sam Spade can be, and has been, called amoral, it is hard to make the case that Marlowe is so too. Sam Spade had adhered to his code in the end, but in between he had sided with Gutman and his clan, possibly for monetary reasons. We will never know, of course, what he would have done in the end, had the falcon not proven to be a fake. Spade also was sleeping with his partner's wife, having no scruples about that, only wanting to get rid of her. Marlowe, on the other hand, is intent on protecting his clients, and he tells the police what he has found, though he keeps his distance from them. He is a man of his word to General Sternwood, in the end protecting both him and his family's name. If romancing Vivian means going off the moral path, he is as guilty in that as countless other private eyes and screen heroes.

Marlowe also has certain personal idiosyncrasies worth mentioning here. He is tough, inventive, and undeterred by the obstinate refusals of Vivian to tell him what bothers her. He has the instincts of a hound, staying on the trail until his efforts yield something. Here he drinks and smokes less than in *The Falcon*, grabbing and holding his right ear when momentarily perplexed. In fact, occasionally, he will snap his fingers when he rushes into action. He can take a beating and recover quickly, but he is no James Bond, who always seems unruffled by what would seem incredibly painful setbacks. Marlowe seems done for before his final confrontation with Mars, and his hands shake as he reloads his gun. He's tough but vulnerable, but also foxy and undaunted when going after a top-notch mobster like Mars, who lacks neither cunning nor the means to put down lesser rivals. Marlowe, like the ancient voyager, passes through the straits of temptation and menace, barely staying alive, wounded but getting the girl—a rich one in this case. To her, he is the man who can "fix" anything.

21

DEAD RECKONING

(Columbia Pictures, 1947)

★ ★ ★

Director: John Cromwell
Screenplay: Oliver P. Garrett, Steve Fisher
Producer: Sidney Biddell. *Cinematographer:* Leo Tover. *Music Score:* Marlin
    Skiles. *Art Direction:* Morris W. Stoloff
Cast: Humphrey Bogart (Rip Murdock), Lizabeth Scott (Coral "Dusty"
    Chandler), Morris Carnovsky (Martinelli), Charles Cane (Lieutenant
    Kincaid), William Prince (Johnny Drake), Marvin Miller (Krause),
    Wallace Ford (McGee), James Bell (Father Logan), Charles Jordan
    (Mike, the Bartender), George Chandler (Louis Ord)
Released: January 16, 1947
Specs: 100 minutes; black and white
Availability: DVD (Sony Pictures)

While on a loan to Columbia Pictures, Bogart made *Dead Reckoning*,
a movie with recognizable film noir traits; in many ways, its hero, Rip
Murdock, was a replication of Sam Spade, a persona that kept resurfacing throughout Bogart's career. The movie has an archetypal villain, a
duplicitous femme fatale, and a plot with enough twists and turns to keep
a viewer's attention throughout. The film was shot mostly at night, in dark,
slippery lanes with action occurring during downpours, complete with car
chases and plenty of violence. Bogart's presence in nearly every shot trans-
forms this dark melodrama into a thriller, equal to any on the screen of that
time. There is no treasure hunt here, as in *The Maltese Falcon*. Bogart's
character aims to restore the reputation of a wronged friend, while he himself is dodging dangers, including the wiles of a woman used to derailing

men. Like Sam Spade, Murdock does not get the girl in the end, but as he said before, that will pass.

The story begins near the end, when Murdock is first seen hunted and injured, seeking refuge at a church, where he confesses his tale to a military priest, Father Logan, in voice-over flashbacks. Captain Rip Murdock had been in the war as a paratrooper, serving in the air force alongside Johnny Drake, an ex-college English professor who had developed a liaison with a woman before the war, with whom he had planned to reconnect. He and Murdock ride on a train that will transport them to Washington DC, where Johnny is to receive the Congressional Medal of Honor for his bravery in the war. Murdock is to be decorated too, for outstanding services. But when, during a stop in Philadelphia, he is told that he is to receive the medal, Johnny becomes uneasy, and soon Murdock sees him running to catch at train going in the opposite direction.

Murdock learns that Johnny is not his real name from an object that he dropped while on the train, a senior class pin from Yale, which bears an inscription: *John Joseph Preston.* He finds out from a newspaper that Johnny had been tried and convicted for the murder of Stuart Chandler, a real estate magnate whose wife was Coral Chandler, Johnny's former girlfriend. Another item in the newspaper shows that a man called Louis Ord (George Chandler) had been a key witness at the trial. Preston had falsified his birth certificate and had enlisted under the name of Johnny Drake in 1943. Running away from the train had saved him from jail, as receiving the medal would have exposed his true identity.

Murdock travels to Gulf City, a fictitious Southern town,[1] where a room has been reserved for him in an upper-class hotel. He finds Coral Chandler at a casino, the Sanctuary, run by a mobster, Martinelli, and as Murdock reveals to Coral who he is, she asks him eagerly if he knows Johnny's whereabouts. As they dance, Murdock tells her that he had found Johnny that morning in the city morgue burned to a crisp after a car accident he was involved in, and then watches her reaction as she wilts in his arms. Murdock also makes a connection with Louis Ord, the bartender, who has a letter from Johnny to deliver to him, but is unable to do so because he is watched by Martinelli's henchman, Krause (Martin Miller). Martinelli (Morris Carnovsky) is an impeccably attired middle-aged man, a gallant with graying temples and an authoritative voice that demands immediate compliance. Murdock senses that there is a connection between him and Coral and looks for clues to find out what it is. When Coral loses a large sum at the roulette, Murdock suggests a game of dice, and after he wins back all the money she lost, Martinelli invites the two to his office for a drink and to deliver the money to Coral. Louis Ord brings in the drinks, but pulls back his tray momentarily, to warn Murdock that his drink has knockout drops in it. To save Louis, Murdock pretends he did not see anything, and he swallows the drink. He falls to the floor unconscious.

When he comes to, he finds himself in his hotel room, with Louis in the bed next to him, his neck broken. Quickly, Murdock hides the body in an adjoining laundry room, so when two policemen knock on his door a few moments later, they find nothing. Murdock now knows that he is hunted by both the mobsters and the police. When Coral calls him, Murdock asks her to meet him at the hotel lobby at one o'clock, where she waits for a long time, conscious that she is being watched by Lieutenant Kincaid (Charles Cane), who is tracing Murdock's footsteps. The latter has in the meantime called Joe Baretta, a mobster from St. Louis who knew Martinelli, and where he himself had owned a taxicab business. Murdock learns from Baretta that a safecracker from St. Louis, McGee (Wallace Ford), now lives in Gulf City and practices a "legitimate" business: collecting and selling arms. Murdock, accompanied by Coral, visits McGee at the address given to him, but McGee balks when he hears that Martinelli is in the picture. But he gives Murdock some useful advice on how to crack the safe himself. Murdock also notices that McGee has in his collection some incendiary hand grenades his son had brought from Japan after the war.

As he and Coral are driving to Martinelli's, Murdock tells her that the body of Ord is in her car trunk. That startles her enough to speed, crossing a stop sign and soon a cop on a motor bike catches up with them. When he asks for Coral's driver's license, the latter fumbles in her purse but fails to produce it. The cop lets her go when Murdock comes up with a timely remark that they are on their way to the mayor's office to get married, and he hates to keep "His Honor" waiting. She sped as he was proposing to her. The cop buys the lie and lets them go.

Murdock unloads Ord's body at Martinelli's beach house, and then drives with her to his regular residence. He leaves Coral in her car and goes upstairs, where he finds the safe open; he locates Johnny's letter and starts reading it. It is in code, and he will need some moments to decode it. He smells jasmine behind him, and he is hit from behind. When he comes to, both Martinelli and Krause are there. Krause beats him severely but Murdock does not give in. He asks for the time—it is 10:45—and he tells Martinelli that if he is not let go by that time, the hotel manager will hand the police a letter he had given to him. This is a ploy, for such a letter does not exist. The phone rings, and Martinelli instructs Krause to drive the severely beaten Murdock to the hotel and get the letter, then bring him back.

But as they arrive in front of the hotel, Lieutenant Kincaid is there looking for him. Murdock tells him that Krause has a gun, and as the police chase him, Murdock escapes.

This is the moment Murdock ends his narrative to Father Logan; as the latter offers to go and get him some brandy—"for medicinal purposes only"—Murdock slips out and staggers to Coral's, where she takes care of him. But before he has time to tell her what happened, he falls asleep exhausted. Two days later, he wakes after a thirty-six-hour sleep, fully recovered thanks to the attention of Coral's obliging black servant, Mable. Coral proposes that they go away together, but he still wants to get Johnny's letter. After McGee brings him a bag with a gun and two of his grenades, Murdock locks Lieutenant Kincaid in a closet, with instructions to Maple to let him go at 12:45. Coral insists that they leave everything behind them and go away together—something we learn she had proposed to Johnny too—but Murdock says he needs to get the letter first. Both drive to Martinelli's, at night and in the rain, he tells her to wait in the car, and goes in, surprising both Martinelli and Krause this time. He demands not only the letter, but the gun used to kill Johnny, for by now he has had a muddled story from Coral, who said that she was present at the scene of her husband's killing but had passed out at the moment he was shot.

The gun is essential in Murdock's odyssey to find the truth. Martinelli then tells him something startling: Coral is his wife, yes, and was before she married Chandler, and they had not divorced. Martinelli adds that he had found her in the slums of Detroit and brought her with him, allowing her to marry Chandler, who had told Coral he would not live to be fifty, so she would inherit his wealth soon. Martinelli found out from Chandler's doctor that the man was in good health and would live to be eighty. So Chandler would have to be gotten out of the way. Chandler was actually accidentally killed by the bumbling and accident-prone Krause, and Johnny, who was on the scene, was accused of the murder. That was what—in large part—the letter was to reveal to Murdock. When Murdock ignites the two grenades, Krause jumps out of the window, and Martinelli tells him where the gun is, but prefers to go the police headquarters than be burned alive. Four bullets hit him as he exits the door, shot by Coral, who thought it was Murdock who was going out. Murdock joins her in the car, and as he drives she pulls a gun on him. At that point he tells her he knows she was trying to shoot him instead of Martinelli. When he presses the gas pedal, she shoots him and they crash. In the next shot after a fade-out, several heads are seen leaning over her in a hallucinatory vision. She says she wants to see Murdock before she dies.

Temptress Coral Chandler (Lizabeth Scott) pleads with Rip Murdock (Bogart) to go away with her. *Columbia Pictures/Photofest © Columbia Pictures*

In dying, Coral leaves behind her the corpses of three men—Chandler, Johnny, and Martinelli—not to mention shooting Murdock while he is driving the car. The movie is about the pursuit of justice—the vindication of Murdock's friend—but in reality it turns out to be centered on Coral and her doings. She is behind all the main action, and the story unfolds as Murdock learns about her and relates to her up close and personal. There is no doubt that he is smitten, one moment even saying, "I should never have let you sing that song." Consider a luscious beauty, displaying her open sexuality with provocative dress, exposed leg, bared arms, blond hair cascading to her shoulders, and a husky voice (an octave lower than a baritone's) singing her siren song. Murdock is at odds with himself, hesitant to let his passion show, remembering his mission to redeem his friend's name. When she tells him her tale of how she fainted when Johnny and her husband were struggling for a gun, and Murdock gives a typical Bogart stare of disbelief, she says, "You don't believe me, do you?" he says. "Yeah, but I still want that letter." He still hopes she can come clean, but she never does to his satisfaction. She fails to bend him to her will to go away with her. In the end, Murdock unmasks her, and he is also saved from her four shots and her attempt to kill him when he was driving her to the police—coincidence playing a bit role here.

Just as Bogart's character had done with Brigid O'Shaughnessy in *The Maltese Falcon*, Murdock explains to Coral the reasons why he is not going with her. When a man's friend is killed, he is supposed to do something about it, and if he went with her, he is not sure she would not plant a bullet in him, or get rid of him, as he had done with the others. He loved her, yes, but, as he tells her, "I loved Johnny more." But there is pity for her also, humanizing his feelings. He felt the waste of a beautiful woman, whom his friend had taught to speak correct English. In film noir, love is deadly, for it entraps those who fall for it. Just before she dies, Coral asks for Murdock, who is seen recuperating from a shot in his arm. He gets up to go but stops for a moment to get a phone call from Washington. It is from General Steele, in appreciation for his services. Murdock makes a request that Johnny Drake be honored too, posthumously. Lieutenant Kincaid shakes his head when he sees him go into Coral's room. After all, this was the man he had been after, whom he suspected for murder. How things do turn around! For a cop to find out that the man he suspected of murder is actually the hero is a shock, a reversal, as Aristotle said in his *Poetics* (335 BC). Aristotle liked a good, tight plot, above everything else. Film noir would have pleased him. After all, what was Greek tragedy all about? Things turn out to be opposite of what one expects, and people fall, mostly because their own actions.

At Coral's deathbed, Murdock speaks some soothing words to her, as he holds her hand, telling her to "let go," and whispering "Geronimo," the word a parachutist says when he drops from a plane into the abyss. A falling parachute is the last shot, symbolic of the death drop. Murdock has restored his friend's reputation, but he also shows some compassion for the wasted life of a fallen beauty.

22

DARK PASSAGE

(Warner Bros./First National, 1947)

★ ★ ★

Director: Delmer Daves
Screenplay: Delmer Daves, adapted from the novel by David Goodis
Producer: Jerry Wald. *Cinematographer:* Sid Hickox. *Music Score:* Franz
  Waxman. *Editor:* David Weisbart
Cast: Humphrey Bogart (Vincent Parry), Lauren Bacall (Irene Jansen), Bruce
  Bennett (Bob Rapf), Agnes Moorehead (Madge Rapf), Tom D'Andrea
  (Sam, the Taxi Driver), Clifton Young (Baker), Rory Mallinson (George
  Fellsinger), Houseley Stevenson (Dr. Walter Coley), Douglas Kennedy
  (Detective at Diner), Pat McVey (Second Taxi Driver)
Released: September 27, 1947
Specs: 106 minutes; black and white
Availability: DVD (Warner Home Video); streaming (Amazon)

Dark Passage is a quick-paced, well-plotted, suspenseful romance-adventure, with Hitchcockian overtones of an innocent man pursued for something he has not done. The movie is the third Bogart-Bacall reunion on the screen—with their final one, *Key Largo*, to follow a year later. It was shot in San Francisco, and one gets a sense of place, as the Golden Gate Bridge, the famous streetcars, and other landmarks are shown during on-location shooting. In this one, Bacall, as gorgeous and splendid-looking as ever, takes a defenseless man under her wing and nourishes him until he is able to be on his own, falling in love with him in the process. It takes awhile to see Bogart's face on the screen, as it was not shown until the movie was half over, and that was generally thought the reason why that the movie failed to attract big audiences at the box office. But it is a Bogart-Bacall vehicle, and as these were a precious few, the movie is worth revisiting for that reason alone.

Bogart plays Vincent Parry, convicted for the murder of his wife and incarcerated at San Quentin, though he has always claimed his innocence. When he escapes after three years, he is picked up near San Quentin by a small-time crook, Baker, who suspects his identity and plans to give him up and collect the large reward of $5,000. But Parry fights him off, beats him unconscious, and while exchanging his prisoner's outfit for the man's clothes, a woman shows up at the spot, picks him up, and takes him to her house, after some close calls with police at roadblocks.

She identifies herself as Irene Jansen, whose father had been wrongly convicted for the same reason—killing his wife—and had died in prison, an innocent man. But Parry does not want to get the young woman in trouble, so he takes to the streets, hires a cab, and asks the cabdriver, named Sam, to take him to a friend of his, George Fellsinger, a trumpet player, whose help he plans to seek. But the cabdriver, a talkative fellow who says he can read faces, immediately recognizes Parry in his rearview mirror and offers to take him to a "plastic surgeon" who can fix his face. They stop at Fellsinger's, and Parry asks him to let him stay in his place for a while after the operation. Fellsinger accepts immediately.

Subsequently the cabdriver takes Parry to Dr. Walter Coley, "Specialist" written on his door, who brags about his skills, which he acquired after he had been kicked out of the Medical Association for malpractice years ago; he's still practicing, just under cover. He is a cadaverous man, looking the part of a miscast Doctor Frankenstein bent on creating appalling monsters. Having no choice, Parry entrusts his life to him. Dr. Coley agrees to do a face job on him for a mere $200, and after Parry pays him, he performs the operation in the middle of the night. The doctor proves more proficient than his appearance indicates, and gives Parry clear instructions how to eat, sleep, and the date when the bandages are to be taken off. But when Parry, bandaged and hardly able to walk, goes back to Fellsinger's, he finds him murdered. He picks up his trumpet, which was the object used to kill him, leaving his fingerprints on it.

Having nowhere else to go, he staggers back to Irene's, barely making it there. She finds him at her doorstep in poor condition, hides him in her bedroom upstairs, and feeds him until the bandages can be removed. As he cannot speak, Parry writes down instructions, given to him by the doctor, and Irene follows them so well that he is able to recover in what appears to be a very short time. Before the bandages are removed, we can see Parry's head, but not yet his face. Almost all the action up to this point had been photographed from his point of view, a great deal with a handheld camera that follows closely what his eyes see. Despite the absence of Bogart's face from the screen for more than half of the movie, director Daves manages to keep the action brisk and the tension rising with every scene.

In about a week, Irene carefully scissors the bandages, and Bogart's fictitious face is revealed to the viewer for the first time. His "real" face has been displayed in posters and in print throughout the city and beyond. In those, Parry had a mustache and a square face that made him look like a fugitive of the law, seasoned by crime. When his actual face is shown, Bogart as Parry looks haggard, hunted down, barely showing his customary energy and stamina. But Irene has taken good care of him, has fed and nourished him, and now she buys him a new striped suit and he is ready to go. Incidentally, in her autobiography, Bacall recalls that during this filming, Bogart was losing his hair at an alarming pace, so she took him to a doctor (he generally disliked going to doctors), who said that Bogart was suffering from alopecia areata, meaning vitamin deficiencies, the result of many years of drinking and an "unsteady diet." As in the film, she took care of him, followed the doctor's orders for vitamin B12 injections and regular diet, and soon Bogart regained much of his hair.[1]

There is a story within a story, however, which makes Irene's job of protecting him much more difficult. Parry has an enemy, Madge Rapf, who is married to Bob Rapf (Bruce Bennett, who appeared with Bogart again in *Treasure of Sierra Madre*, a year later), but they are separated and hate each other. Bob is now making advances toward Irene, and Madge, who had a crush on Parry, had testified against him at the trial after he rejected her. But it was Madge who had killed Parry's wife in a fit of jealousy. And now, knowing he had escaped, she returns to Irene's apartment while Parry is still hiding there recuperating. Madge, played by Agnes Moorehead as almost always projecting a diabolical malice, is so persistent that Parry takes off alone, as soon as his bandages are removed. He intends to flee to South America, where he would be safe. But he is tracked down by Baker, the small-time crook who had recognized him and had been watching him ever since. After Parry had exited Irene's house, and as he was making preparations to leave town, Baker approaches him and threatens him at gunpoint, asking $60,000 for his silence. Parry says he doesn't have this sum but Baker points out that Irene is an inheritor of a large fortune, $200,000, and can easily part with the $60,000. Parry offers to go to her house and ask her, and when he is forced to drive there, Baker accidentally lets him know that his price now is $200,000. He also tells Parry to flee to Mexico, stop at a certain town, and approach a certain man, saying to him, "Baker sent me." It is at this point that Parry, already a desperate man, decides to take decisive action. He takes another route, slams on the brakes, and disarms Baker. Out of the car, they fight at a rocky spot with the Golden Gate Bridge as the background, and Baker falls to his death. Before he does, he tells Parry that a coupe with an orange color had been following them. That was Madge's car.

With that important clue, he goes to Madge's and tells her he knows that she murdered his wife and also killed Fellsinger, to further implicate Parry. During his confrontation with Madge, in a fit of hysteria she rushes to her window and falls to her death. Parry will now be accused of three murders. Rather than stay and try to clear his name, he flees to Mexico and then to Peru, after a call to Irene telling her where to find him, if she still wants him. He asks her to memorize the name of a small town, Paita, where she is to meet him. As he sits at a nightclub, having a drink, she appears at the door. End of movie.

This is not one Bogart's strongest performances. The role does not allow him to run after bad guys or expose mobsters, assorted villains, and enemies of the country. He is himself hunted, and for half of the movie we do not even see his face. He is a fugitive from justice who is not vindicated in the end. The circumstances are all stacked up against him, and the best he can do is to be an exile for life; but at least he gets the girl at the end. Still a film noir, *Dark Passage* was made at a time when the HUAC (House Un-American Activities Committee) investigations had already started, and Bogart had appeared with other actors in Washington, heading the Committee of the First Amendment, and had been harassed afterward, despite his statement later that he was a devoted American citizen and not a communist. But he remained under suspicion for a long time while the HUAC investigations that ruined so many lives of Hollywood personalities were going on. Metaphorically, the role of a fugitive and a wronged man in this movie suited him well.

But in this movie no one in particular shines bright. Agnes Moorhead's performance is perhaps the most intense—the personification of an evil mind, a face on the screen whose sharp, angular features express her inner feelings of hatred. Bacall is luminous, but here she is not the lady to exchange ripostes with a hunted and nearly wrecked man, whom she protects and falls in love with. The Look is there, though, casting darts occasionally against Madge and Bob, from whom she has to hide secrets. Occasionally, she flashes a smile at Parry, when he has a face again, provoking, pleading, or loving, in her special way. Bogart as Parry took it all in, good-heartedly, with flair and the confidence that comes with a man who knows that a woman is in love with him. Still Bacall commands the scene as the best person in the story. She is a mother/sister figure, eventually becoming his lover. Her glamor in certain scenes is a bit subdued, but she still commands the screen. Bogart, playing a weakened man under stress, has to stay back and accept her mercies, but in the end he proves he has the nerve and stamina to keep her out of harm's way, though this comes at the expense of being an expatriate for the rest of his life. But this isn't so bad—he's done that before. And it has the benefit of his getting the girl—and a rich one, too—at the exotic beach town of Paita, Peru.

23

THE TREASURE OF SIERRA MADRE

(Warner Bros./First National, 1948)

★ ★ ★ ★ ★

Director: John Huston
Screenplay: John Huston, based on a novel by B. Traven
Producer: Henry Blanke. *Cinematographer:* Ted McCord. *Music Score:* Max
    Steiner. *Editor:* Owen Marks
Cast: Humphrey Bogart (Fred C. Dobbs), Walter Huston (Howard), Tim
    Holt (Bob Curtin), Bruce Bennett (James Cody), Barton McLane (Pat
    McCormick), Alfonso Bedoya (Gold Hat), Santo Ragel (Presidente),
    Robert Blake (Mexican Boy), Jose Horvay (Pablo)
Released: January 24, 1948
Specs: 126 minutes; black and white
Availability: DVD (Warner Home Video); streaming (Amazon)

One can argue that today, *The Treasure of Sierra Madre* is more attuned to modern tastes than to those of the audiences at the time it was made. The film is about greed, selfishness, paranoia, but above all the self-destructiveness caused by the illusion of getting rich quickly. It is a return to John Huston's *The Maltese Falcon* (1941), which explored a similar theme in an entirely different context. Admittedly, today people do not try to find gold nuggets in remote mountain rocks. Movies like *Wall Street* (Oliver Stone, 1987) and *The Wolf of Wall Street* (Martin Scorsese, 2013) fit the modern mind-set of gaining easy riches more slickly, if not more expertly. *Treasure* shows average men, drifters and panhandlers without a penny (or peso) in the world, down on their luck, yet thirsty for riches, challenging the odds, working hard, making their dreams materialize, only to see them blown away by the desert storm winds. In lesser hands, Huston's allegorical tale might have seemed sheer bluster, but with a first-rate script and good actors at his command, the result was masterful. Though the film did not fill the coffers of Warners/First National as audiences stayed away because of its bleak subject matter, it was a critical success and was rewarded with three Oscars—Best Direction and Screenplay for John Huston, and Best Supporting Actor for his father, Walter—as well as a nomination for Best Picture.

This was producer Henry Blanke's and John Huston's project. Huston, whose career was disrupted by his war service for several years, had known about the B. Traven novel since 1941, but he had to wait until the war was over for his dream of filming it to be realized. The project went ahead, despite a rather reluctant J. L. Warner, who hesitated because of the potential delays and other problems arising from the conditions of filming in Mexico. But Huston won the day, and Bogart was more than eager to do the movie, as the change of pace and the complex character- ization of Fred C. Dobbs presented special challenges to him. The depth of this character bore little resemblance to the gangsters and bad guys he had played earlier in his career. He was also pleased that the film would be made for the most part in Mexico, to achieve authenticity. Making movies in the studio backlots was the practice of Hollywood for decades, but in postwar cinema this practice was changing in favor of open spaces, and Huston was a leader in this effort. Several of his films after *Treasure* were filmed in exotic locales, for example, in later years, Africa for *The African Queen* (1951), *Moby Dick* in Ireland (1956), and Mexico again in *The Night of the Iguana* (1964).

Aside from Bogart, Huston also reunited with his father, Walter Huston, who had a cameo (as Captain Jacoby) in *The Maltese Falcon*. The elder Huston plays Howard, an old fellow wizened by years of prospecting, broke and in wait for a last chance. Since he knows much more about prospecting than the two novices he joins, he assumes the leadership, rounding up the main cast. Mexican actors and what seems like a whole tribe of Indians join them. The third member of the group is Bob Curtin (Tim Holt), another American drifter willing and ready to join the others for the project. A fourth American, James Cody (Bruce Bennett), enters and exits in a short interlude, adding an important plot twist. Aside from a cameo appearance of Anne Sheridan in Tampico, the plot offers no love interest, no comic relief aside from Howard's antics—the old man dances, prances, plays the harmonica, and climbs the rugged peaks like a goat in its element. Mexican locals, including an Indian tribe, bandits, armed soldiers or *federales*, and crowds of villagers give the film its local color and aura of authenticity.

~

The film begins with Bogart, as the panhandler Fred C. Dobbs, adrift and aimless in Topico, a run-down Mexican town, asking a man in a white suit who looks like a prosperous American (John Huston in a cameo) if he can "stake a meal for a fellow American." He asks two more times. After the third time, the man in the white suit gets annoyed, tells him to get lost, but not before handing him two coins. Soon after, Dobbs is seen at a barber's, fixing himself, Mexican style;[1] then he meets Curtin, and they both work for a while for Pat McCormick (Barton McLane). McCormick is unwilling to part with his money when he pays his employers—Dobbs and Curtin learn this at a bar—and when he comes within their sight, though he is bigger than either of them, they bash him and take what he owes them, approximately $300.

Meanwhile, Dobbs had purchased a lottery ticket from a Mexican boy (played by a young Robert Blake), and when he wins an additional two hundred pesos, he and Curtin plan an expedition in the Mexican mountains to prospect for gold. They seek out the elderly drifter, Howard, who seems wise to prospecting, having done it in various parts of the world, and he is ready and willing for an expedition to the Mexican mountains. They now have enough money to buy the burros (donkeys), provisions, and some guns, to protect against bandits and hostile tribes.

The early scenes were filmed at the backlots at Warners and other studios, and then the unit traveled to Mexico for the location shooting. The three adventurers are first attacked while on the train by the bandit leader, Gold Hat (Alfonso Bedoya), and his gang and subsequently reach a village where they buy provisions and a string of burros and set out on their expedition, encountering sandstorms, jungle, and tigers (never shown). They reach a mountainside in utter exhaustion, except for the old man, who prepares beans, eats a hearty dinner, and seems to possess inexhaustible energy and zest for life, prancing about like a youth, to the amazement of his wearied fellow travelers.

Howard also can tell the difference between gold and pyrite, the shiny dust the two prospectors take for the precious metal. He leads them to a mountain top, and soon their efforts are rewarded. Howard knows all the tricks, and they manage, after much work and an accident that nearly costs Dobbs his life, to accumulate enough gold, which they divide in equal parts, as Dobbs demands. At this point, a rift begins to divide the small group, for a couple of reasons. One is the obvious distrust Dobbs has for the other two, despite the fact that Curtin risked his life to save him when he was trapped under the scaffolding of a mining hole (though Curtin did hesitate at the entrance of the hole before he decided to go to his partner's rescue; he had begun to distrust Dobbs as well). The other reason is the appearance of another drifter, who had followed Curtin when the latter visited Durango to get provisions. When the drifter appears at the camp, he demands that he get a share of the profits. Howard wants to have nothing to do with killing him, but the other two vote to do so; but before they can follow through, they are attacked by bandits, led by none other than Gold Hat (Bedoya), whose band had also attacked the group on the train. Of necessity, they give the drifter a gun and he joins them in the skirmish. But while the *federales* chase the bandits away, the trio discover that the drifter has been killed. His name is James Cody, as they find out in a letter he has received from his wife. She pleads with him to quit prospecting and come back to Texas, where she and their son are waiting, as the summer harvest is about to begin.

Another complication occurs when a tribe of Indians surround them, as they are sitting around the campsite fire. While Dobbs seems aggressive, Howard understands that they have someone sick, who needs care. It is a child who fell in the water and stopped breathing. Howard, whose practical resources seem inexhaustible, volunteers to go, and he applies some simple techniques, moving the child's hands up and down, in a scene that seems liturgical. The child recovers, but the tribe leaders demand that Howard stay with them, and as he joins them, the inevitable rift between Dobbs and Curtin begins. Dobbs becomes paranoid, and in a fight with Curtin, the latter disarms him, but Dobbs proves more durable, staying awake waiting for the other to fall asleep. When Curtin succumbs and dozes off, Dobbs takes his gun and shoots him, leaving him for dead at an isolated spot.

But Curtin survives and is somehow able to crawl up to the Indian camp, where he is found by some of the residents and brought to Howard, who takes care of his wounds, placing one of his arms in a sling. Howard recommends that he stay put, but Curtin is determined to catch up with Dobbs, so he rides off with a few tribesmen and Howard, who chooses to go along. Meanwhile, Dobbs, seeing in the coming daylight that the body of the supposedly dead Curtin has vanished, begins to have hallucinations, quickly descending into paranoia and despair. He drives his burros with the load of gold—one of them is seen left behind, dead—until he staggers, totally exhausted and thirsty, to a pool and starts drinking. As he does so, he sees the image of Gold Hat reflected in the water. Before he knows it he is surrounded by the three bandits, and Gold Hat recognizes him. When Dobbs attempts to shoot at them, he misfires, as the gun Curtin had left him is

The trio of Curtin (Tim Holt), Fred C. Dobbs (Bogart), and Howard (Walter Huston) eat dinner while camping in the Mexican mountains. *Warner Bros./Photofest © Warner Bros. Pictures, Photographer: Mac Julian*

empty of bullets. In a few moments he is overcome by the bandits, and out of the view of the camera, he is decapitated by Gold Hat with two quick swipes of his blade.

The bandits take his burros, not knowing the contents of the bags, and run away wearing his clothes, shoes, and hat. They throw away the bags, stepping on them in the sand scattering the gold nuggets, not realizing the wealth in them. Then, when they go back to the Mexican town and try to trade away the burros, a local boy recognizes the sign Ă, which has been branded on the burros; he tells the *presidente* (Santo Ragel), and the latter seizes the men. Quickly, they are led to the place of execution, forced to dig their graves before they are shot. Gold Hat is seen grabbing his hat from his grave before he is executed. Gunshots are heard, but the scene itself is not shown. The *federales* don't bother with lengthy trials, a commentator wryly observes.[2]

Curtin and Howard and their Indian companions arrive at the village only to learn what has transpired. They ask to be led to the place were Dobbs had been last seen, but when they arrive there, in a windstorm, they only find empty sacks, torn and stomped upon by the bandits who had no idea what they contained. The wind has blown the valuable gold dust away.

Howard breaks into a long riotous laughter, saying, "Back to nature where they came from!" He laughs and laughs and finally Curtin joins him, and still laughing, they retreat to a wall, sit down, and finally start wondering what they are going to do next. Howard knows. He has the Indian village to go back to, where he will have a good life as a *medico*—they are planning to make him head of their legislation, "whatever that means," the old man happily adds. His future assured, Howard looks at Curtin, who seems ready to resume his drifting, and suggests that Curtin use the money collected from the sale of his burros and the skins they carry (Howard even adds his own share to the bargain) and go to Texas, where Cody's wife is waiting for her husband, killed earlier. It's harvesttime, and a future is there for him, something better than the aimlessness of prospecting. Howard's theory that gold prospecting destroys men's souls proved true for both of them, and catastrophic for Fred C. Dobbs. Curtin seems attracted to the idea. Both men are honest and hardworking but have momentarily gone off the track. Both are to adjust to reality. The movie's last shot focuses on one of sacks that carried the gold dust hanging on a small cactus plant, emptied and blowing in the wind.

The Treasure of Sierra Madre has been categorized as a film noir and justly so, as it has one of the noir characteristics: it shows a character whose self-inflicted wounds bring him to his destruction. But, in contrast to the city noir, this is a film that takes the viewer to the outdoors, to a rugged terrain away from the enclosed spaces, asymmetrical compositions, and dark alleys, the habitat of urban crime. In the rocky terrain, dangers lurk everywhere: bandits, tigers, hostile tribes, and sandstorms. The three prospectors work hard through all of this and gather enough gold to ensure them good profits. Of the three, none of them is a hero. More than a touch of pessimism is introduced in Huston's film vocabulary—perhaps the result of the horrendous atrocities he experienced during his years at the war front. Two of his main characters are decent fellows, but one of them proves Howard's dictum that gold destroys a man's soul. The old man's prognostication also lends a touch of wisdom in the film. He has seen that in his years of prospecting. Curtin is an average, hardworking, and honest fellow. Howard is the man who lives every moment: he plays the harmonica and laughs in the face of disaster. Nothing will bring him down. He easily steals the show just by being a happy old goat, prancing and jesting, sipping a flavorful juice and munching delicacies as he is pampered by smiling young things at the tribe. His last laugh shows he is the only one undefeated by the three men's vain venture. Dobbs, on the other hand, is selfish, untrusting, devious, treacherous, torn apart by distrust and fear. With any other actor, these qualities would have looked repulsive and unredeemable. Yet Bogart makes his character a clinical dissection of meanness and paranoia. He does not believe that Curtin, the man who risked his life to save him from a collapsing mine, is to be trusted. Paranoia grows and grows to the point that a human cannot see at all beyond the self. It is like a spiritual blindness. Step by step, he grows more alone, until the moment he faces death. He does not even understand that he will die, as he clicks the trigger of an empty gun several times. His decapitation is mercifully not shown. But everything else is revealed, and only Bogart, who played Rick Blaine and Sam Spade and Harry Morgan and other brave-souled heroes, had the inner resources to show a man who loses his soul.

24

KEY LARGO

(Warner Bros./First National, 1948)

★ ★ ★

Director: John Huston
Screenplay: John Huston, Richard Brooks, based on a play by Maxwell
    Anderson
Producer: Jerry Wald. *Cinematographer:* Karl Freund. *Music:* Max Steiner
Cast: Humphrey Bogart (Major Frank McCloud), Lauren Bacall (Nora Temple),
    Edward G. Robinson (Johnny Rocco/Howard Brown), Lionel Barrymore
    (James Temple), Claire Trevor (Gaye Dawn), Thomas Gomez (Richard
    "Curly" Hoff), Dan Seymour (Angel Garcia), Marc Lawrence (Ziggy), John
    Rodney (Deputy Clyde Sawyer), Harry Lewis (Edward "Toots" Bass)
Release: July 16, 1948
Specs: 101 minutes; black and white
Availability: DVD (Warner Home Video); streaming (Ps3, Xbox, Kindle Fire,
    iPad, PC)

Reunited with John Huston after their two previous endeavors, *The Maltese Falcon* in 1941 and *The Treasure of Sierra Madre* in 1948, Bogart is also reunited with Lauren Bacall, in his fourth (and last) movie with her.[1] By this time Bogart and Bacall had been married for over two years, and their reunion in this picture is a far cry from the image she projected in her first two movies with Howard Hawks, *To Have and Have Not* and *The Big Sleep*, where she was a sexually aggressive and even a deceitful woman, though in both cases she and Bogart made friends in the end. In their third movie together, *Dark Passage* directed by Delmar Daves, she is a lover and mother figure, helping a persecuted man to find justice. In *Key Largo*, she appears as the compliant daughter of a paralyzed hotel owner, a nice and friendly woman who accepts the stranger who brings her news about her dead war-hero husband. They become friends but not before she has a chance to test his mettle as he confronts a gang of mobsters. It is also worth noting that in *Key Largo* Bogart reunites with Edward G. Robinson, who had killed him in several 1930s movies, dispatching him with five bullets in *Bullets or Ballots* (1936) and then again got rid of him in *Kid Galahad* (1937) and in *The Amazing Dr. Clitterhouse* (1938). Now that Bogart had risen to superstardom, he repaid the favor, as he and his friend Robinson met again as deadly adversaries.

Here Robinson plays a notorious mobster, Johnny Rocco, who has been deported to Cuba, and he and his gang reunite after eight years to transact some shady business with another mobster, holding the owners of Largo Hotel hostage until this is done. Coming off a bus, Frank McCloud (Bogart) stops at the Largo Hotel, Key Largo, Florida, to meet his dead friend's father and his widow, and then move on to Key West. Having served as a major in the campaign in Italy, decorated for valor, he is war weary, penniless, and homeless. We soon know that he was a newspaperman, but had also been a taxi driver, waiter, and other things before he joined the army and distinguished himself in battle.

McCloud looks resigned and unheroic, a man beaten by the ills of life, a common image in the later Bogart opus. In fact, he plans to stay at Key Largo only for a couple of hours, but as soon as they know who he is, James Temple (Lionel Barrymore), the owner, and his daughter Nora (Bacall), cordially invite him to stay the night, and stay on, if he wishes. McCloud accepts, and Nora hurries upstairs to make accommodations for him in her husband's, George's, room.

As he came in, McCloud had met some of Rocco's goons, who occupy the hotel on the pretense that they have come down from Milwaukee, Wisconsin, to go fishing. Rocco's lieutenant, the gum-chewing Curley Hoff (Thomas Gomez), sees McCloud as an intruder and possibly someone who might interfere with their plans. Hoff tells McCloud he is not welcome, but the gang let him stay after the owner himself has invited him, as they do not want to raise suspicions about why they are there. Rocco himself does not appear in the initial scenes, but former girlfriend Gaye Dawn (Claire Trevor, who had appeared with Bogart in *The Amazing Dr. Clitterhouse*) has arrived with one of the group to reunite with her ex-lover; Gaye shows up in a drunken state, out of control and an obvious annoyance to Rocco and his associates. She adds a special note to the mix of the drama, however, since she is Rocco's only contact with humanity; a wild "Irish kid" he once knew, as he describes her, but now a "lush,"[2] and no good to anybody. But he tolerates her presence, possibly to bolster his ego.

Tensions rise as a storm approaches, and Rocco is impatient to conduct his business and leave. But while there, he senses his antagonist, the decorated hero Frank McCloud, whom he provokes into a gunfight, giving him an empty gun and daring him to shoot. McCloud does not shoot, saying, "One more or less Rocco in this world would not make a difference," and tosses the gun aside. McCloud spitefully declares that he cares only for "what happens to me!" Gaye seconds him by stating, "A live coward is better off than a live hero," though she apologizes to McCloud immediately after that.

McCloud swallows the insult, which elicits a look of disapproval from Nora and a question from old Temple about whether McCloud knew the gun was empty. McCloud says he didn't know. While this can be regarded as a typical Bogart gambit, when he stays back in perilous situations before he becomes a hero, it is also possible that the Bogart character here is expressing real bitterness about war heroes who fought for the right causes only to come back and see honest citizens held at gunpoint by evildoers. Rocco, in a larger sense, symbolizes the postwar resurgence of repression, with the emergence of the House Un-American Activities Committee investigations, which threatened basic democratic rights, such as freedom of speech. In one instance, McCloud mouths the phrase Roosevelt had used during the war, "We are not making all the sacrifice of human effort and human lives to return to the kind of world we had after the last war."

Bogart had led the Committee for the First Amendment[3] and had marched to Washington with Bacall and many other Hollywood luminaries, only to be rebuffed and forced to recant his statements—saying he was not a communist.[4] This had left scars not only in him, but in John Huston, who had actually been in the war, seen its atrocities, and made three documentaries for the War Department, showing the hell of war as it is, not from the side of the victor. The most graphic of these documentaries, on the taking of San Pietro, was so disturbing that the War Department censored it heavily. In *Key Largo*, George, Nora's husband, had fought, had been killed, and was buried on a hillside near that location, as McCloud tells her and her father.

The scenario shows Rocco and his gang having come back to the States to sell his "merchandise" (counterfeit money) to his fellow mobster, Ziggy, and regain the prestige he once enjoyed among his fellow hoods. Rocco is a throwback to his first gangster character in *Little Caesar* (1930), Cesare Enrico Bandello, standing for Al Capone, considered the archetypal gangster hero who set off the gangster movie era that lasted through the 1930s. Even their names have similarities—Rico for Bandello; Rocco (albeit a

last name here) in *Key Largo*. A gangster-era nostalgia echoes through his
exchanges with his cronies—that Prohibition will come back, as Ziggy, the
mobster with whom he exchanges the counterfeit money, reassures him.
This time, they joke, the mobsters will unite to make it stick around. But, as
Andrew Sarris observes,[5] the gangster of the Prohibition era was regarded
as the hero of the story, albeit a dead one at the end, and was thus glorified,
as movies of the early thirties—*Little Caesar* (1930), *Public Enemy* (1931),
Scarface (1932)—demonstrate. Here, Rocco, strongly given by Robinson, is
the personification of evil, a despicable egomaniac with no care or concern
about anything or anyone but himself. He dies a coward, and that takes
away any heroic veneer.

It does not take long for McCloud to regain Nora's affections and the
audience's esteem. When Rocco forces his girlfriend to sing, "like in the
old days," in exchange for a drink and she does so, singing off-key and provoking headshakes from Rocco and his henchman Curly, Rocco sadistically
denies her that drink. McCloud gets up, pours a drink in a glass, and brings
it to her. She says, "Thank you" to him, while an enraged Rocco slaps Mc-
Cloud's face several times. Retaining his cool, McCloud shows no reaction

Johnny Rocco (Edward G. Robinson) pulls a gun on Frank McCloud (Bogart). *Warner Bros.
Pictures/Photofest* © *Warner Bros.*

to Rocco's insult, but says a simple, "You are welcome" to Gaye. A look from Nora tells him that she had misjudged him—and she later apologizes for her rudeness for having called him a coward. Aside from the developing romance, Nora becomes McCloud's moral judge, her approval becoming the means of shedding his apparent cynicism and regaining his status as a hero, the one she had come to admire from the descriptions of her husband.

As the storm passes, Sheriff Ben Wade (Monte Blue) comes in, responding to a call his deputy, Sawyer, had made at seven o'clock. Sawyer had been shot by Rocco, and old Temple keeps his silence, letting Wade assume that the deputy has left, but the sheriff discovers Sawyer's body, just outside the house, as the storm had blown it ashore. Brown privately tells him it was the Osceola brothers who had done it, and Wade finds them hiding and shoots both of them. Later, Wade apologizes to Temple for saving his life when Wade came in to inquire about his deputy's phone call. Had Temple said anything at that point, the gang would have killed him.

With the storm gone, Rocco recovers his nerve, and soon Ziggy, the man he is waiting for, arrives. The merchandise, a box full of counterfeit money, is exchanged for a bag of real money, which Rocco aims to take to Cuba, but his boat is gone, as apparently the captain preferred to steer it away than let it be sunk on the reefs. Rocco, however, is not without a resourceful mind. He chooses the "soldier" to drive the hotel's boat (named *Santana*, after Bogart's real boat), and under threat of torture, McCloud has no choice but to go. At the last minute, Gaye pretends to beg Rocco to take her with him, and while embracing him, she steals his gun from his pocket, which she soon passes on to McCloud.

The rest is pure action, in which the sagacity of the Bogart character comes into play. He is one against five, and his Odysseus-like mind tells him that he must do this cleverly to have a chance. The best way is to eliminate them one by one, as the odds in a shootout would not be in his favor. He steers the boat right on course, knowing that the gang will not touch him as long as he is needed. At a certain point he slows it down, asking Ralph, the big fellow at the back of the boat, to check if there is kelp that the rudder might have picked up. While the latter steps over to check, McCloud suddenly speeds the boat and Ralph is thrown into the water. Toots, seasick and nearly useless, is lying at the back of the boat and McCloud shoots him, but is in turn shot and wounded himself, but not badly. McCloud shoots Curly when he shows up at the door of the cabin, and then climbs at the top of it and looks down through the window. Curly falls backward and dies. Rocco orders Angel to go out and confront McCloud, but when he refuses, Rocco shoots him. He tries in vain to lure McCloud by offering him fifty–fifty of the money in the bag, and then all of it, affecting a businesslike transaction. But McCloud, though wounded, is a step ahead; he knows the gangster will eventually come out, so he waits, and when Rocco emerges, McCloud shoots him. It takes three shots to kill Rocco—a throwback to *Bullets or Ballots*, when it took Robinson's character several bullets to kill Bogart's. Finally, McCloud, though wounded, is able to transmit a message from the boat radio, and when a response comes, he tells of his situation, which requires "medical attention." He also asks for the Temple household in Largo Hotel to be notified.

This is a taut tale, told in the span of only twenty-four hours or so, during which a quick plot evolves, showing a gang of mobsters who have taken over the hotel, waiting for a deal to be concluded so they can run off to Cuba on a luxury boat waiting offshore. Aside from some opening shots of Key Largo and the Largo Hotel, which was a real establishment belonging to an Irishman, the rest of the movie was shot at the Warner Bros. Studios sets, confined in space, but appearing neither static nor claustrophobic due to Freund's fluent camera movements that follow the participants as they move around, both singly and in groups. With few exceptions, there is always space between them, which allows interaction, with quick dramatic climaxes, as when Rocco provokes McCloud to a fight or slaps him in the face for having offered Gaye a drink. The storm, of course, is also an element that keeps the tension mounting, as every moment seems to add to the expectations of impending doom, either from the weather or the impatient mobsters. None of the participants can predict what will happen next, and the audience shares their anxieties. Above all, Bogart again proves a hero, his reputation restored, and he gets the girl at the end, a prize justified on all counts.

25

KNOCK ON ANY DOOR

(Santana Productions, 1949)

★ ★ ★

> *Director:* Nicholas Ray
> *Screenplay:* Daniel Taradash, John Monks Jr., adapted from a novel by William
> Motley. *Producer:* Robert Lord. *Cinematography:* Burnett Guffey. *Music
> Score:* George Antheil. *Editor:* Viola Lawrence
> *Cast:* Humphrey Bogart (Andrew Morton), Susan Perry (Adele Morton), John
> Derek (Nick Romano), George Macready (District Attorney Kerman),
> Allene Roberts (Emma), Mickey Knox (Vito), Barry Kelley (Judge
> Drake)
> *Released:* February 22, 1949
> *Specs:* 100 minutes; black and white
> *Availability:* DVD (Sony Choice Collection; the Columbia Picture Collection[1])

Knock on Any Door proved to be a lesser Bogart vehicle, though it had a good cast and a dramatic story line. This one features Bogart as a defense lawyer, Andrew Morton, who undertakes, somewhat unwillingly at first, to defend a young man accused of murder. It was the first directorial effort by Nicholas Ray, who went on to distinguish himself with *In a Lonely Place* (1950), again with Bogart, and *Rebel without a Cause* (1955), with James Dean. Ray went on to champion social causes, especially disaffected youth wronged by an insensitive society.

The film was the first of the five to be produced by Santana Productions, an independent company started by Bogart, who was making an effort to break loose from Warner Bros. and Jack L. Warner, who had been his boss since 1936. Warner resented Bogart's independence of mind, and he was especially incensed by Bogart's creation of the Santana Productions, which led to the final rift between the two men.[2] Warner had also resented Bogart and Bacall leading the pack in the march to Washington a couple of years earlier as members of the Committee for the First Amendment, which Warners had considered a political embarrassment. Bogart's recantation in his ways back to Hollywood did not help, and Bogart, though still regarded as a high value commodity at Warners, saw his star status diminished. Santana produced four more movies—*Tokyo Joe* (1949), *Sirocco* (1951), *In Lonely Place* (1950), and *Beat the Devil* (1954)—and then faded away.

Knock on Any Door was by no means a failed film. Despite some mixed reviews, it was popular in its time, and it is a significant addition to the Bogart canon, for his persona is not that of a loner who fights a specific target, various villains, mobsters, or a national enemy, but as a goodwill representative of a social cause: the state of disaffected youth in the streets who fall easy victims to crime and criminals.

The film opens with the murder of a policeman by a man with a hat, so the audience does not see his face; two others escape, but he is caught and is seen in jail. He asks for a lawyer, named Andrew Morton (Bogart), who is shown on the screen playing a game of chess with his wife, Adele (Susan Perry), who urges him to take on the case of Nick Romano (John Derek). Morton seems quite reluctant to do so, but he gives in to his wife's pleas.

Next we see him at court, defending Romano, against Public Prosecutor Kerman, played by George Macready, whose scarred right cheek and patrician air had aided his career as a stylish villain in the 1940s and '50s. He is a tough opponent for Morton, who chooses to resort to two lines of defense: appealing to the jury's pity by presenting young Romano as a victim of circumstances and pleading not guilty, as the latter had told him. However, Morton changes the plea to guilty with extenuating circumstances when Romano confesses to the murder. He also counted on the young man's good looks and directed him to look directly to the jury, which included seven women—a trick that Kerman caught on to very quickly.

In a long speech, Morton tells the jury about Romano's life as he knew it, for the last six years, his narrative being interrupted by flashbacks that show several crucial episodes of Romano's life. Six years back, Morton had defended Romano's father, but not as effectively as he should have, being busy with another case. At that time, Morton was a small-time lawyer, just beginning his career, with a few partners. Now he is a corporate lawyer, having become established after serving in the army for three years during the war. Thus, as he explains to his wife, his reluctance to take up the case of a young man, whom he had tried to protect earlier.

In the first scene of the flashback, we see Morton visiting Mrs. Romano (Argentina Brunetti), whose husband was in jail ill with a heart ailment, who cannot speak English, and who complains to Morton—as does young Nick—that she had neglected her husband, and that is why he is in jail. As they talk, news is brought that Romano had died in jail of a heart attack.

Guilt ridden, Morton embarks on a mission to reform young Romano, keeping him out of trouble and steering him in the right path. But Romano soon mixes up with streets gangs and becomes a thief, stealing jewelry and carrying a knife. He is thrown in jail and serves time, but when he is out, Morton has already gone into the army and thus is unable to help the young man. Romano mixes with various characters, two of whom become his closest friends—Sunshine (Robert A. Davis) and Butch (Dewey Martin), and both of them are called at the trial and testify that he is innocent. Neither of them is effective.

During one of his attempts at robbery, Romano enters a small shop and, seeing nobody inside, intends to clean up the cash register while a friend of his keeps watch outside. A nice young woman comes in to inquire what he wants, and struck by her innocent looks and beauty, Romano decides not to rob the store. But he is seriously smitten and he asks her out, and soon they become close friends, both obviously in love. They soon marry, and Romano promises to keep out of trouble. But he keeps falling back on his old habits, and soon their marriage falls apart. When Romano tells his young wife that he is going away for a job, she tells him she is pregnant. Romano becomes furious and tells her that he does not want a child. When he goes, she turns on the gas oven and suffocates to death. After the job, Romano, on the run and wanting to take his wife along, returns and finds her dead. He is soon arrested for murder.

The trial does not go well. When pressed by Kerman on the stand, asking him if his wife committed suicide, Romano screams at him, breaks down, and confesses he is the murderer. Morton, entirely caught by surprise, delivers a fiery oration to the audience putting the blame on all present, including himself—and on society that has "killed" Romano.

The judge acknowledges that Morton's speech is moving and that he himself was moved, but he has no option but to send Romano to the chair. There is a final meeting between them, just before Romano is executed, and Morton promises that he will commit to saving other youths from taking the wrong path.

This change of pace seems to alter Bogart's image. Tough, yes, he still is, but his problems can no longer be resolved with a gun. As Pauline Kael aptly put it, he is orating, rather than using his "rod."[3] And on top of that, he loses the case. His final plea to the judge goes in vain.

But it could also be said that here Bogart sets in motion and projects an image markedly different from the tough heroes he had portrayed most of the time so far. He is the paternal figure to Nick Romano, and he tells Romano so many times what he must do in order to help him escape the social rut he has grown in. Morton had been like him in youth, but he made the extra effort to rise above his low status by hard work, dedication, and a clear goal. Romano is pulled in two directions: one is to see the light, get a job, and start a family; the other is to keep up his life of crime. His temper pulls him toward the latter. When readying himself for a job, he tells Emma, his wife, that he is the kind "who lives fast, dies young, and has a good-looking corpse."

Bogart's efforts, halfhearted as they seem at times—he acts after his wife prods him—show him in the light of a social reformer of disaffected youth, a theme yet to be explored fully in the movies. Bogart is quite capable of being an eloquent speaker, stirring up emotions in his audience and on the screen. "Knock on any door," the film's title, becomes a phrase on his lips not easily forgotten. The yarn may be a bit sentimental to some, a bit long-winded. But this makes for fine courtroom drama, especially with a villain-ous-looking public prosecutor, in the person of George Macready; a series of colorful witnesses on the stand; and, especially, John Derek's firebrand performance. Marlon Brando was the initial choice to play Romano, but he withdrew when Mark Hellinger, a producer and scriptwriter at Warners for many years, died of a heart attack.[4] Certainly Brando's presence would have made a difference. But this was Derek's first role—he was only twenty-two—and he definitely had an unforgettable screen image, but despite that, Derek never rose to the status of a big star. Perhaps his able competition of the times—Brando, Montgomery Clift, James Dean—outdistanced him and placed him in the rank of second-raters, or of actors with more glitter than glamor. In *The Ten Commandments* (1955), as Joshua, he looked just right, young, colorful, aggressive, and good-hearted, not to mention devout. But as movies go, these two films belong to two different universes.

As for Bogart, he was never as good a crusader as he had been in his "tough guy" (hero or villain) movies. Speak softly, or at any rate briefly, and carry a rod, to use Pauline Kael's expression. If anyone else played that zealous and garrulous lawyer, it might have been a disaster. The phrase "Knock on any door" becomes engraved in memory.

26

TOKYO JOE

(Santana Productions, 1949)

★ ★

Director: Stuart Heisler
Screenplay: Cyril Hume, Bertram Millhauser, adapted by Walter Doniger
    from a story by Steve Fisher
Producer: Robert Lord. *Cinematography:* Charles Lawton Jr. *Music Score:*
    George Antheil. *Editor:* Viola Lawrence
Cast: Humphrey Bogart (Joe Barrett), Alexander Knox (Mark Landis),
    Florence Marly (Trina Landis), Sessue Hayakawa (Baron Kimura),
    Jerome Courtland (Danny), Teru Shimada (Ito)
Released: October 26, 1949
Specs: 88 minutes; black and white
Availability: DVD (Sony Pictures)

Tokyo Joe was the second in a sequence of five movies[1] produced by the Bogart-owned Santana Productions and distributed by Columbia Pictures. It was filmed in the Hollywood Studios with footage of exteriors shot in Japan by a second unit. It is supposed to be another simulation of *Casablanca*, but it is a far cry from that classic movie. Any *Casablanca* imitation would involve a triangle: a rather average man who is in love with a high-class woman, who is married to, or friendly with, an upper-class gentleman. The woman is, of course, in love with Bogart's character, but she has undertaken moral or monetary obligations to her husband (or loyal friend), and eventually stays with him. The movie also figures a morally ambiguous pursuer, Bogart in his typical gambit, looking after himself at first, but in the end putting self-interest aside and rising to a heroic status.

Thus with Joe Barrett. He is an honorably discharged officer, who fought against Japan in the war and attained the rank of colonel, and a few years after the war he returns to Japan, still occupied by American forces, to resume a business he owned there before the war. He owned a gambling joint, called Tokyo Joe, and he assumes that he has the right to start his business as usual again in a defeated and crushed Japan. But he is viewed with suspicion by the occupying American forces there and is granted only a sixty-day visa. The military follow his steps, just in case he is involved in foul play. Japan is still rife with disgruntled ex-fighters, and Americans keep an eye on those who could help them foment an uprising.

But Joe has reasons for coming to Japan other than reestablishing his business. When he left, his wife, Trina (Florence Marly), stayed behind with a newborn child. Joe seeks her out and discovers soon enough that she is married to an influential civilian executive, with close ties to the military. Defiantly, Joe tells him that Trina is his wife, and they never had a divorce. Her current husband, Mark Landis (Alexander Knox), claims the opposite; that a divorce had been granted. A resentful Joe declares defiantly that he will have her back.

This turns out to be more difficult than he had imagined. His former partner, Ito (Teru Shimada), though friendly, is hesitant to renew relations but is convinced after he and Joe tackle in a friendly jujitsu bout, and together they visit Baron Kimura (Sessue Hayakawa), who agrees to come to terms with Joe to transport "merchandise"—frozen frogs—out of Japan, obviously a front for illegal trade. Having only sixty days and needing permission from the military to establish an airline for transporting freight to North and South America, Joe turns to Mark Landis, who graciously agrees to help him. The airline is just one rusty plane, and Joe hires two Americans to help him in the business.

But when Joe is asked to transport a cabal of three former insurrectionists from Korea to start an underground resistance movement in Japan, the military is informed. Kimura plots to abduct Landis's seven-year-old daughter. He agrees to let things alone and does not attempt to file for an annulment, or to reveal that, while imprisoned, Trina had collaborated with the Japanese, broadcasting enemy messages to save the child's life. Joe escapes from a burning plane, and during a dangerous scuffle in Kimura's hideout, Joe saves the child, Kimura dies in a gunfight, and the parents regain their child, Anya, who, it has been revealed in the meantime, is Joe's daughter. Seriously wounded and about to be taken out in a stretcher, Joe says goodbye to his daughter, selflessly withdrawing from any further claims. Though the movie remains relatively obscure, it offers, however, a first-rate performance by Bogart, whose character projects an intensity and decisiveness at a critical moment of his life and in the lives of those around him.

27

IN A LONELY PLACE

(Santana Productions, 1950)

★ ★ ★ ★

Director: Nicholas Ray
Screenplay: Andrew Solt, adapted by Edmund North from the novel by
    Dorothy Hughes
Producer: Humphrey Bogart. *Cinematographer:* Burnett Guffey. *Music Score:*
    George Antheil. *Editor:* Viola Lawrence
Cast: Humphrey Bogart (Dixon Steele), Gloria Grahame (Laurel Gray), Frank
    Lovejoy (Brub Nicolai), Carl Benton Reid (Captain Lochner), Art Smith
    (Mel Lippman), Jeff Donnell (Sylvia Nicolai), Martha Stewart (Mildred
    Atkinson), Robert Warwick (Charlie Waterman), Moris Ankrum (Lloyd
    Barnes), Jack Reynolds (Henry Kesler), Ruth Warren (Effie), Ruth
    Gillette (Martha), Steven Geray (Paul), Mike Romanoff (Himself)
Released: May 17, 1950
Specs: 94 minutes; black and white
Availability: DVD (Columbia Pictures); streaming (Amazon)

I was born when she killed me.
I died when she left me,
I lived a few weeks while she loved me.

In his tribute to Bogart,[1] Richard Schickel says that *Casablanca* made Bogart a big romantic star, but his individual preference for a Bogart movie remains *In a Lonely Place*. Produced by Bogart's own company, Santana Productions, and directed by Nicholas Ray, *In a Lonely Place* may not measure up to *Casablanca*'s mystique and aura, but it remains a solid, skillfully made film, and though not a big box office hit at the time, it has

grown in status among critics and Bogart followers in later years. Its theme
is dark, the tone somber, even gloomy, and the film has been categorized
as film noir.[2] As such it bears some similarities with *The Treasure of Sierra
Madre* and *The Caine Mutiny*, both showing the Bogart character as a man
disintegrating under mental or physical torment. But this one offers an
unparalleled portrait of Bogart as a man of two personalities—one who is
sympathetic and likable; the other, a man subject to violent fits of rage and
nearly homicidal. Bogart's abrupt changes from one side of his character to
the other show the depth of his skill as an actor, and have even inspired a
new version of the movie in modern times.[3]

Here Bogart plays a washed-up Hollywood writer, a role that differs
substantially from the image he had projected as Sam Spade or Philip
Marlowe, both of whom were men in control, sure of themselves, practically invulnerable and able to spar with friends and foes alike. In *In a
Lonely Place*, Bogart is a hardworking but disaffected Hollywood hack,
displeased with his job, as he is compelled to repeat himself script after
script and is a pawn in the hands of producers and directors. His Dixon
Steele is a man defeated by his own flaws—his inability to control his
temper that nearly turns him into a social pariah and a suspect for murder.
Here Bogart is visibly older and plays an unlikely romantic hero, although
he does attract the attention of several females. The movie is slickly made,
with a smooth plot and enough twists in it to hold the audience's attention, with an end that has a note of sadness in it. Socially, it can be seen as
a parable of Hollywood culture in decline, as the studios produced repeti-
tive scripts, routine crowd-pleasers rather than original works. Nicholas
Ray, known for socially oriented movies and his tortured heroes, has made
his case here, parodying Hollywood practices, but the center of attention
remains Bogart's odd behavior.

As Dixon Steele, Bogart is an instance of that decline, and his neurotic
personality may be seen as the outcome of the life of an artist in frustration.
In the opening scene at a restaurant where he is surrounded by his director,
Lloyd Barnes (Morris Ankrum), and his agent, Mel Lippman (Art Smith),
he complains to his friends about having written the same script twenty
times over. But as soon as his overbearing director insults Steele's friend
Charlie Waterman, a failed actor and a drunk who spouts Shakespearean
lines throughout the movie but a man Steele has taken under his wing,
Steele gets enraged and starts a brawl at the bar, hitting the director and
overturning some tables. His bad mood is also caused by the fact that his
next assignment is to turn into a script a novel he thinks is shallow and bor-
ing. As it is, he dislikes the novel so much that he hires a hat-check girl at

the restaurant, who has read the novel, to come to his house that night and talk to him about it, so he will not have to read it.

The girl's name is Mildred Atkinson (Martha Stewart), and she is so entranced with the idea that she would work with a famous screenwriter that she breaks her date to go with Steele. She proves rather inept, not even able to pronounce the name of the main character, saying "Alathea" instead of "Althea." When she suggests a flirtation, Steele pays her a generous twenty dollars and sends her off to get a cab. Next morning she is found murdered and mutilated, and Steele is asked to go to the police headquarters by his friend Sergeant Brub Nikolai (Frank Lovejoy), who pays him a visit at early hours. At the station, he is informed by Captain Lochner (Carl Bento Reid) that the young woman at his apartment has been murdered during the night, and Steele realizes he is under suspicion. His neighbor Laurel Gray (Gloria Grahame) comes in and, rather pertly, scoffs at Lochner's suggestion, saying she had seen the girl departing from Steele's apartment at 12:30, the time he had indicated. She also says that she finds Steele's face "interesting." Lochner lets Steele go, but makes sure he knows that he is the prime suspect.

Dixon Steele (Bogart) and Laurel Gray (Gloria Graham) in one of their happy moments. *Columbia Pictures/Photofest © Columbia Pictures*

Steele soon finds out that Laurel Gray is a failed actress who had managed to secure only minor parts in two movies. But he takes a liking to her and makes advances, and they soon develop a relationship. Steele begins to be inspired by the very book that Mildred had read to him and starts writing a first-rate script, to the delight of Mel (Art Smith), his longtime friend and agent. But suspicions grow in the mind of Laurel when, at the invitation of the relentless Lochner, she is shown newspaper clippings describing Steele's violent temper during several confrontations in the past. That and the babblings of her masseur, Martha, about Steele's violent temper plant the seeds of doubt in Laurel's mind.

And soon enough, Laurel has some proof of Steele's demonic side. During a beach party when Sylvia, Brub's wife, mentions that Laurel had visited Lochner and told him that she loves Steele and that he would get an invitation to their wedding, Steele gets enraged that all this took place behind his back. After shouting, "You are trying to pin a murder on me!" he goes off in a rage, with Laurel barely making it into the car. He drives at a high speed and nearly wrecks a man's car at a curve. When the man calls him a name, the enraged Steele gets out of the car and pummels him, then grabs a stone and seems about to crush the man's skull, when a scream from Laurel stops him.

Back in the car, he calms down and asks Laurel for a cigarette, and as he smokes, he speaks three lines, as if reciting verse: "I was born when she kissed me; I died when she left me; I lived a few weeks while she loved me." He asks Laurel to repeat them, and when she does and in turn asks him where they come from, he says he is looking for a place in the script to put them. He seems to have become conscious of his brutality, but by this time there is a road of no return. Laurel fears that the man is deranged and she is determined to flee. When Steele proposes marriage to her, making quick plans and forcing her to come with him to buy her a ring, she decides to fly to New York that same day. Steele learns of this, rushes into her bedroom where she is packing, and tries to choke her; a phone rings and stops Steele from committing a real murder. The phone call is from his friend Brub, who informs him that the real killer has confessed. He is Henry Kessler, Mildred's date the night she saw Steele, a character that makes a few appearances in the film; during one of these, Steele observes that he has a "strong grip" as they shake hands. Laurel picks up the phone and hears Captain Lochner apologizing to her for the ordeal he has put her through. Laurel's response is, "Yesterday this would have meant so much to us. Now it doesn't matter." As Steele is walking out of the building, she mutters, "I lived a few weeks while you loved me. Good-bye, Dix."

Where is this rage coming from? Bogart's performance is so convincing that one wonders whether the demons haunting him in real life had left their imprint in his impersonation of Dixon Steele. His encounters with the House Un-American Activities Committee had sullied his reputation and embittered him, the failure of his first three marriages were still raw wounds, and his foray into independence with Santana Productions was not yielding solid results. In fact, after Santana failed, Bogart ended his career as a hired hand at Warners and worked for several other producers,[4] still a well-paid and famous actor. It is also as possible—and more likely—that Bogart could, at this stage of his career, transform his inner turbulence into the performances of a virtuoso artist long attuned to his instrument.

Bogart's performance as a schizoid man is truly astonishing. Whatever his own inner turmoil may have been, he is secure in his knowledge that his audiences will find his performance convincing. His Dixon Steele can be good-natured, as when he is seen supporting the unemployed Charlie Waterman, victim of alcoholism and shunned by Steele's colleagues, making sure he has his tips when he visits him. Laurel understands that Steele has a decent side, and she herself tips the drunken friend when she sees him. Steele sent flowers to Mildred's address after he had heard the news of her death, and during his calm moments, he behaved like a perfect gentleman. His brief affair with Laurel had a beneficial effect on him, and he had started writing and producing fine work, a good omen that he had turned the corner. What sparks his rage seems to be the sense of betrayal by his close friends—as in the beach scene or when he learns Laurel is about to leave him—which turns him into a monster in minutes. At the moment he learns that Laurel had made a reservation to catch a plane for New York, his eyes gleam with the look of a madman. Laurel sees that and screams, "I can't be married to a maniac." After Brub's phone call that tells him that the murderer was caught, it is possible that Steele knows that his relationship with Laurel is finished, and he walks out of the house and out her life. His is a moment of self-knowledge. He may know that he is a sick man, not fit in society. This self-knowledge, cathartic to the audience, may ultimately save him. But for now the self is in an inferno.

SIROCCO

(Santana Productions, 1951)

★ ★ ★

Director: Curtis Bernhardt
Screenplay: A. I. Bezzerides, Hans Jacoby, adapted from the novel *Coup de Grâce* by Joseph Kessel
Producer: Robert Lord. *Cinematographer:* Burnett Guffrey. *Music Score:* George Antheil. *Editor:* Viola Lawrence
Cast: Humphrey Bogart (Harry Smith), Marta Toren (Violette), Lee J. Cobb (Colonel Feroud), Everett Sloane (General LeSalle), Onslow Stevens (Emir Hassan), Gerald Mohr (Major Leon), Zero Mostel (Balukjian), Nick Dennis (Nasir Aboud), Peter Ortiz (Major Robbinet)
Released: June 13, 1951
Specs: 698 minutes; black and white
Availability: DVD (*Humphrey Bogart: The Columbia Pictures Collection*); streaming (Amazon)

The last but one[1] of the Santana Productions, *Sirocco* is a movie that retains both the stamp of a Bogart hero who, as has been pointed out several times, is another version of the Rick Blaine follow-ups. In fact, it has been said that this is another remake of *Casablanca*—Bogart as one indifferent to any cause outside of his own who then changes into somebody who sacrifices both girl and self-interest to a cause.

Outside of this oft-repeated, commonplace observation, *Sirocco* has a contemporary ring to it that makes it historically relevant to our times, though less famous by far than *Casablanca*. It takes place in Syria, in Damascus to be specific, after the French occupation of Syria following World War I, in the year 1925. The French had a mandate from the League of Nations to take over in Syria to protect it from anarchists and Syrian underground fighters who threated its unity. A sacred obligation at that, as General LaSalle (Everett Sloane) explains to Colonel Feroud (Lee J. Cobb, in one of his off-beat roles playing a foreigner with a Brooklyn accent), who doubts the effectiveness of the general's harsh oppressive measures. The Syrian resistance forces are underground, hiding inside tunnels of ancient Roman catacombs, where any stranger allowed to enter is led there blindfolded. Very few have access, and those who are allowed are gunrunners or profiteers, the kind who take advantage of similar situations to exploit the more needy side.

One of those is Bogart, this time called Harry Smith, an undistinguished name, as the man who bears it initially seems to be. He is under scrutiny by authorities, specifically by Colonel Feroud, who is jealous because his girlfriend, the exotic-looking Violette (Marta Toren), finds Smith's face both "ugly" and "handsome," a dubious compliment, since Bogart in this one is nowhere near looking like the Rick Blaine of some years back. Smith passes her a sparkling golden bracelet, but she says no! A bit later, when she gets a beating from Feroud, she comes back to Smith, asking him if he can get her a pass for Cairo.

Things get complicated at this point, as five of the known profiteers, among them a youngish and plumb Zero Mostel, in a prelude to his later glories as zany and absurd as any comic genius that ever graced the screen, are arrested for running guns illegally. Smith, too, is seized and about to go before a firing squad, but Feroud proposes a compromise, in exchange for visas for him and Violette. Feroud has expressed a wish to obtain a twenty-four-hour truce with Emir Hassan, who rules the resistance forces, and he trusts that Smith, who has his connections, can obtain entrance to the underground headquarters of the movement to propose the truce. Smith does not have to go, as General LaSalle has already granted him two visas—one for him and one for Violette—honoring the promise that Feroud had made. But Smith volunteers to go, out of moral obligation, showing a sudden change of heart and reverting to the man he had been during the war, a decorated hero. Here is, of course, the opportunity for Smith to repair his image and turn a cynical opportunist and profiteer into a champ. Feroud and Smith go inside the catacomb headquarters, and Emir Hassan gives his word that the truce will be held. He dismisses Feroud, but holds back Smith, releasing him after a short chat, and as Smith is about to climb the stairs of the underground haunt, he sees an oversized guard and knows his destiny. He goes to it without hesitation, and shortly after he has entered the exit tunnel, a hand-grenade explosion kills him. He is seen dead among the ruble.

Not quite a *Casablanca* ending, but it will do. Smith had been regen-
erated and dies honorably, as Violette has her exit visa and Feroud his
truce. There is an ironic twist to all of this, if one looks at this patched-up
melodrama from a strictly contemporary point of view. It all happens in
Damascus (albeit in a studio lot), as a ramrod-back general, conscious of the
savagery of his occupation forces, has scruples about the legitimacy of his
troops occupying a foreign land that wants independence. The French had
bombed Damascus before they went in, and the French occupation was the
result of the Picot-Sykes agreement that had been signed during the Arab
Revolt in 1917, which had already decided the fragmentation of Arabia
that continues today. It might be presumptuous to say that one might have
been the result of the other, but one cannot help but notice the ironies
generated, perhaps unintentionally, by the actions in this film. This picture
deserves some historical footnote, not so much for the image of Bogart it
presents but for the chord it strikes about the causes of a troubled part of
the world that does not seem to have been freed from either internal dis-
cord or foreign intervention. As for Bogart, he certainly had the know-how
and talent, at this stage of his career, to turn from a profiteer to a man of
principle dying for a cause, and, incidentally, for the freedom of a woman
he loved.

29

THE AFRICAN QUEEN

(Horizon-Romulus Productions, 1951)

★ ★ ★ ★ ★

Director: John Huston
Screenplay: James Agee, John Huston, based on the novel by C. S. Forester
Producer: S. P. Eagle (Sam Spiegel). *Assistant Director:* Guy Hamilton.
   Cinematographer: Jack Cardiff. *Music Score:* Allan Gray. *Editor:* Ralph
   Kemplen. *Art Direction:* Wilfred Singleton. *Special Effects:* Cliff
   Richardson
Cast: Humphrey Bogart (Charlie Allnut), Katharine Hepburn (Rose Sayer),
   Robert Morley (Reverend Samuel Sayer), Peter Bull (Captain of
   Louisa), Theodor Bikel (First Officer of *Louisa*)
Release: December 23, 1951
Specs: 105 minutes; color
Availability: DVD (Warner Bros.); Blu-ray (Paramount Home Entertainment;
   Special Feature: Embracing Chaos: Making *The African Queen*);
   streaming (Amazon)

*By the authority vested in me by Kaiser Wilhelm II, I pronounce you
man and wife. Proceed with the execution!*

—Captain of the *Louisa*

The African Queen is a perennial crowd-pleaser, and with good cause.
To begin with, it presents Humphrey Bogart and Katharine Hepburn, an
unparalleled pair of Hollywood stars at the peak of their careers, teaming
up for the first time on the screen and delivering the goods. Masterfully
directed by John Huston and stunningly photographed in Technicolor by
Jack Cardiff, the movie looks as fresh today as at the time it was made. It

combines adventure, romance, an exotic locale, and the unique opportunity for Bogart to appear side by side with one of the great actresses of his day. It also netted him the only Oscar of his career—and a well-deserved one.

The African Queen was based on a C. S. Forester novel that lay dormant since its publication in 1935, as studios were unwilling to invest in a movie featuring two aging protagonists. It was Sam Spiegel (appearing as S. P. Eagle in the credits), responsible in later years for producing such megahits as *On the Waterfront* (1954) and *Lawrence of Arabia* (1962), who undertook to film the novel, acquiring the rights of the book and securing the financing with Horizon-Romulus Productions. Spiegel was also able to round up the services of a powerful cinematic trio—John Huston, Humphrey Bogart, and Katharine Hepburn—who accepted to undertake the arduous trip to Africa, where the movie was to be made. Most of the actual shooting took place on the Ruiki River, a narrow stream of black water that is a tributary of the Congo River in the then Belgian Congo. John Huston, who coauthored the screenplay with James Agee, chose the Belgian Congo, as he found the initial locations in Nairobi, Kenya, not to his liking—too pretty, he said, and much like the English countryside. The shooting in Africa was done under extreme conditions—heat, tropical diseases, polluted waters, inadequate facilities—lasted for four months,[1] and was completed at the Isleworth Studios in England. The movie earned an Oscar nomination for Best Screenplay (John Huston–James Agee), Best Actress for Ms. Hepburn, and Best Actor for Humphrey Bogart, who was pitted against Marlon Brando for *A Streetcar Named Desire*.[2] This was the sixth collaboration between Bogart and Huston (with one to follow[3]), and by this time the two men had become good friends and trusting collaborators.

The tale starts on a tragic note. A preacher and his sister run a Methodist church in a jungle village, unaware of what goes on in the rest of the world, their only connection with it being a river boatman, Charlie Allnut, who brings them news and supplies at various intervals. The peaceful life of the two missionaries is shattered by marauding German troops, aided by sympathizer locals, who burn the village and cause the brother (Robert Morley) to die of distress. This is during the First World War, and the Germans have occupied a large part of northeastern Africa under Keiser Wilhelm II. The news that the boatman has brought is that Europe was aflame with war, the main rivals being the English and the Germans, with lots of other countries taking sides. He can't quite remember which—"Oh, the French, too!" he mutters, pausing after a gurgle coming from his stomach.

The boatman is seen coming back, after the village is destroyed, approaching Miss Sayer, who is sitting despondent in her porch, pretending to be occupied with something. Her brother had died that morning, and the boatman respectfully suggests that they bury him and hurry away, as the Germans are likely to return soon. His boat carries explosives and various other items the Germans would like to get their hands on. It also has enough water and "grub" to last them for a while. She complies and follows him to his boat, and they start their trip down the river.

The occupants of the boat could not have been more dissimilar characters. He, a downtrodden, scrawny little man running an antiquated riverboat named *African Queen* and content to be soaked with the gin he carries aboard in a case full of bottles. She, a bony spinster, prim, dignified, proud, willful, and disdainful of the company that circumstances have thrust her into. At first, she is appreciative of his good nature and follows his advice to bury her brother, take shelter in his boat, and move somewhere else. But as soon as they are together in the confined space of the boat, their differences in class and disposition become strikingly evident. He is content to call it a day while it's still daylight, imbibe a generous dose of gin, and dose off. She, on the other hand, sorrow and all, becomes increasingly bossy—and curious. What are the contents of those boxes out there in the boat? Blasting gelatin, he explains. And what about these tubes? Oxygen tanks, he responds. Can't you put the explosives in the tubes, turn them into torpedoes, go down the river, reach the lake where the German gunboat the *Louisa* is, and torpedo it? When she sees that he looks at her aghast, she asks him whether he is patriotic. Doesn't he want to help his country in an hour of need? (He is a Canadian, she from the Midlands in England.)

What Allnut does not suspect at this moment is that Miss Sayer will eventually win her argument. What she also suggests is that since they still have two hours of daylight left, why not take advantage of it and go farther down the river? He complies. He knows that from now on the leadership belongs to the lady, and he gives in. After all, he has his cases of gin to console himself with. But that does not last long. As Allnut wakes up from his moments of stupor, he sees her busy emptying the contents of the bottles, one by one, into the river, mercilessly, until the last one is gone. A shot shows us the empty bottles floating away and out sight. When he complains that it is human nature to find consolation in drink, she responds archly that we have been placed here on this earth "to rise above nature."

At this point, the battle of the sexes is in full swing. For the first time in his cinematic career, Bogart loses a verbal skirmish with a lady. Miss Sayer stubbornly reads her Bible and refuses to speak to him until he complies with her wishes. She is determined to go down the Ulanga River, get to the lake, and torpedo the German ship. He desperately tries to remind her how crazy this idea is. To do so, he explains, means they have to sail past the German fortress Shona, where their boat will be blown to pieces, and then go down the rapids, where the boat will be smashed on the rocks. She reminds him that Spengler, the famous mapmaker, had navigated the same rapids, and if he did it, they can. Unable to stand her disdainful silence, Allnut gives in. They sail past Shona, under heavy fire; Allnut displays some daring when he fixes a pipe severed by a bullet and starts the engine again. A moment later, they get into the rapids and, as if by a miracle, the boat, which should have been shattered to bits, gets through and they survive. Ecstatic with joy they embrace and kiss, and before he knows it, Allnut kisses her on the mouth.

Both are shocked, embarrassed, but blissful as they discover their developing feelings for each other. They start to chatter to hide their embarrassment, she asking for the name of the flowers around them, he answering that he does not know, but they are beautiful anyway. Miss Sayer's face glows at the discovery that a man can be attracted to her, especially one who had, not long ago, called her "a skinny old maid." He throws her hat away, and her rich hair flows down her shoulders, and she suddenly looks much younger and actually beautiful. Shyly, she asks to know his first name—she had called him "dear" after their kiss. He tells her, "Charlie." "Charlie! What a lovely name!" she responds, delighted.

From now on it is Charlie and Rosie, and they are lovers—in the purest sense, it seems. The river tramp is a hero—in her eyes only, but that is good enough for him. Suddenly, the old spinster becomes a woman, loved and desired, even if by such a lowly fellow. And he becomes a hero, even if he needs her persistent prodding to be so. To transform an ordinary man into a hero is something that no one can do better than Bogart. But in this case the transformation is done simply and naturally. Both Charlie and Rosie were deprived of sex, she because of her primness and religious beliefs; he out of necessity. His drunkenness and homeliness had doomed him to sexual deprivation. It's a sexual renaissance of sorts, for both of them.

Now, they are united in their will to go out into the lake and sink the German ship. But the river adventure is not yet over. A waterfall interrupts a tranquil interval, and the *African Queen* plunges into it and is tossed about and nearly wrecked. The shaft holding the propeller is twisted, and one of the blades of the propeller is broken. Can't be fixed, he says. Slyly, she suggests that they take the things out themselves and fix them—"weld"

the blade on. "Is that the right word, dear?" she asks. Being now her hero, Allnut cannot refuse. He dives underwater,[4] and she with him, and they remove the damaged shaft, build a fire, and improvise a sort of bellows; the shaft is straightened, the propeller blade parts (if it broke, where did they find the other half of it?) welded together, and the *African Queen* sails on.

They now have reached the part of the river called Bora, which means they are near the lake. But the waterways are clogged by masses of papyrus reeds. He pulls the boat with a rope through the thickets, wading into water. She helps as much she can, like him getting into the water and pulling the boat, until they get stuck in the mud. They lie down to die, and she utters a prayer, asking the Lord to welcome her and Charlie to heaven. But a rainstorm at night raises the water level, and in the morning Charlie wakes to find out the boat is moving. They are in the lake!

At once, their plans to torpedo the *Louisa* are revived, as the *Louisa* appears to be coming toward them. They hide behind an inlet and fix the oxygen tubes, filling them with explosives, and he constructs the detonators with the ease of a master. At night, they go out to sink the *Louisa*, but a storm sinks the *Queen*. After a fade-out, we see Charlie standing in front

Charlie Allnut (Bogart) and Rose Sayer (Katharine Hepburn) contemplate their future on the *African Queen*. *United Artists/Photofest © United Artists*

of the captain (Peter Bull) of the *Louisa*, flanked by two of his officers, questioning him about his whereabouts. He says he was fishing. The captain condemns him to death by hanging, "The sentence to be carried out immediately." But a boat approaching brings a female: "Rosie!" a joyous Charlie cries out. When she is in and knows that Charlie is about to be hanged, she tosses her head back defiantly and says to the captain that they were there to sink the ship—with torpedoes. "Torpedoes!" cries the astounded captain. Yes, she says, and to his question where they have come from, she answers that they sailed the Ulanga River, or Bora as they call it here. "Impossible!" he cries. "That river is unnavigable!" "Nevertheless, we did it!" she replies smugly. Charlie then explains, modestly, how he turned the oxygen tubes into deadly war weapons.

When they are led to the hanging spot, he pleads with the captain for a "last request." Would he marry them? "What kind of craziness is this?" the amazed captain says. "It would only take a minute," Charlie begs, "and it would mean so much to the lady." It does, for Rosie bursts out with, "What a lovely idea!"

The captain proceeds with a brief ceremony and then gives the order (quoted at the beginning of the chapter). But with the newlyweds' heads already in the nooses, two explosions shatter the *Louisa*, and her crew, mostly black natives, are seen jumping into the water. Swimming in the water, the captain's first officer (Theodore Bikel) is seen saluting his superior, while a short distance off Charlie and Rosie are swimming blissfully toward the shore. He still doesn't know what happened, and she points to a piece of wood from the boat with the inscription, *African Queen*. Even upside-down, the *Queen* had done her job. Fate had lent a hand (or Hollywood did, which is the same thing).

"Which way is the east shore?" Rosie asks, now with the familiarity of a wife. "The way we are swimming, Mrs. Allnut," he answers. Charlie calls himself "an old married man." The irony is that the captain had delayed the execution in order to marry them for just enough minutes to save them from hanging while the old *African Queen* was doing its part: not only are they are alive, but married as well.

A comedy? At the end, most definitely. The captain and his officers are shown as buffoons, reminding one of the Nazis in *Hogan's Heroes*,[5] if anything. In post–World War II America, in the era of the House Un-American Activities Committee investigations, the victory of an errant couple sinking a German gunboat was seen as a big plus for both Bogart and Hepburn, who had been perceived as leftists, as many in Hollywood had been, and their reputations smeared. But the movie is much more than a pitch to patriotic sentiment. It has the pathos of an extraordinary romance and one that involves middle-aged people, who were also big stars in their own distinct ways. The mix, the direction, the first-rate script, the ambiance of the jungle, the Technicolor (rare in those days), and above all, Bogie and Katharine at their best made the picture a loveable yarn, for all tastes. Is this Bogie's most romantic movie ever? Shot for shot, Bogie and Hepburn had more screen time together here—in fact they *are* the movie—than any lovers' duo in any other Bogart movie. Perhaps one can say yes, if one concedes that the gap between youth and old age can be bridged by a blossoming middle age—or that opposites attract.

THE ENFORCER

(United States Pictures/Warner Bros., 1951)

★ ★ ★ ★

Director: Bretaigne Windust (and Raoul Walsh, uncredited)
Screenplay: Martin Rackin
Producer: Milton Sperling. *Cinematography:* Robert Burks. *Music Score:* David
    Buttolph. *Editor:* Fred Allen
Cast: Humphrey Bogart (Martin Ferguson), Ted De Corsia (Joseph Rico),
    Everett Sloane (Albert Mendoza), Roy Roberts (Captain Frank
    Nelson), Zero Mostel (Big Babe Lazick), Lawrence Tolan (Duke
    Malloy), Bob Steele (Herman), Harry Wilson (BJ), John Kellogg (Vince),
    Adelaire Klein (Olga Kirshen), Tito Vuolo (Tony Vetto), Jack Lambert
    (Philadelphia Tom Zaca), Patricia Joiner (Teresa Davis/Angela Vetto),
    Susan Cabot (Nina Lombardo), Mario Siletti (Louis, the Barber), Greta
    Granstedt (Mrs. Lazick), Karen Kester (Angela as child)
Released: February 14, 1951
Specs: 97 minutes; black and white
Availability: DVD (Olive Films)

The Enforcer is the last film Bogart made for Warners, terminating his
relations with the studio that had made him a superstar and after he had
signed a fifteen-year multimillion-dollar contract with them three years
earlier. Bogart, who had craved independence since his fortunes rose after
The Maltese Falcon and *Casablanca* and several other hits, had already
ventured into film production with his own Santana Productions, which up
to this point (1951) had turned out four films—*Knock on Any Door* (1949),
Tokyo Joe (1949), *In a Lonely Place* (1950), and *Sirocco* (1951)—and was
yet to produce one more, *Beat the Devil* (1954). *Chain Lighting* (1950), his

previous film with Warners, had been "routine and un-inspired," according to a Bogart historian,[1] while *The Enforcer*, first titled *Murder, Inc.*, "looked backward, not forward, with a formula that dated from the Depression."[2] For this or any other reason, *The Enforcer* lay in the shadows for a long time, lacking media exposure, not being issued on DVD until 2013.

The movie explores a new concept in the crime zone, at least as far as the gangster-era movies of the thirties and forties were concerned, when crime was set in the streets and gangsters were busy killing each other, rather than seemingly innocent civilians. In *The Enforcer*, a clever man cashes in on the concept that any criminal—or any other murderer, for that matter—becomes a suspect when his motive is discovered. So it occurs to him to commit the crime without a motive, killing a total stranger, so long as he is well paid by the one who has the motive. The actual killer has a "contract," and his victim is a "hit," in the parlance of the business. A crime syndicate is built on that basis. First, a "troop" is assembled of persons who undertake a contract for high wages (and bonuses), execute their hit, and remain available for new contracts at any time or place. There is a middle man, the only one who knows the top person and who runs the troop with an iron hand, making the payoffs and meting out punishment to the ones who fail or stray. The killers are killed mercilessly if they go to the police, become witnesses against anyone in the organization, or try to skip town. It's a well-oiled machine that has thrived for years. The police have, of course, compiled a large file on the activities of the group, and know who the top man is, but they have difficulty lining up witnesses to testify against him, as the troop includes a small squad of expert killers who terrorize potential witnesses. The idea about committing a crime without a motive is introduced by a high-caliber mobster, Albert Mendoza (Everett Sloane), who has built the organization on that principle. Bogart plays Martin Ferguson, a zealous district attorney who has a steely determination to catch and convict the murderer, and not let him slip through his fingers. The movie is a classic film noir, mostly photographed at night, with narrow alleys, dark passages, asymmetrical compositions, and a rapidly paced plot so as to create a high level of suspense from start to finish.

When the movie starts, Mendoza is in prison, his trial pending, but the one witness to testify against him, Joseph Rico (Ted De Corsia), the next-to-the-top member of Mendoza's gang, is nervous, fearing that if he does testify, Mendoza's goons will kill him. Ferguson knows that he has one night to quiet Rico's anxiety and reassures Rico that he will be perfectly safe after he takes the stand in the morning against his former boss. But Rico tries to get out of his room. He reaches for the fire escape, and despite Ferguson's efforts to save him by holding on to his hand, Rico falls to his death.

Ferguson, with the assistance of Captain Frank Nelson (Roy Roberts) is busy through the night trying to come up with another witness, and the rest of the movie is a search shown in a series of flashbacks that gradually reveal the depth and complexity of the Mendoza organization. As Ferguson and Captain Nelson go through a row of folders that fills an entire shelf, the first flashback shows a young man, later identified as James "Duke" Malloy (Michael Tolan), bursting into a police station and telling the officer behind the desk that he has murdered his girlfriend. Soon Ferguson is brought in, and Malloy takes them to the spot where the killing occurred. He had buried her body in a nearby place, but now the grave is empty. Under pressure, he confesses that three men had taken her in a station wagon, naming the three: Philadelphia Tom Zaca, Smiley Schultz, and Big Babe Lazick. The police hold Malloy, but when they try to see him again in his cell, Malloy has hanged himself.

The police search for Philadelphia and find him in an insane asylum. He looks wild, and the doctors there certify that he is an insane person. They look for Smiley, but soon find out that he was burned in a fire. When they

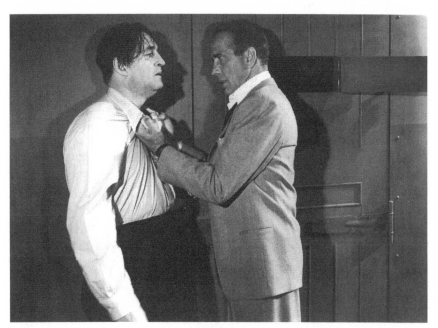

DA Martin Ferguson (Bogart) grabs a shaken-up Joseph Rico (Ted de Corsia), trying to convince him to testify. *Warner Bros./Photofest © Warner Bros.*

search for the third person, Big Babe Lazick (Zero Mostel), a neighbor, reveals where he lives, adding that Lazick had taken off in his car, going to a
church. They drag Lazick from the church, kicking and screaming and claim-
ing he knows nothing. But when Ferguson threatens to put his wife in jail for
complicity, Lazick's tongue loosens. He describes how he was lured into the
organization by Malloy, who brought him to a place at the back of a lunch
stand belonging to Olga Kirshen (Adelaide Klein), where he learns how the
"group" works (the viewer learns more than him). Rico is the power man,
assigning contracts and rewarding hits, the coded terms used throughout the
movie to describe assignments for murder and the actual murder. If someone is caught, smart lawyers will get him out for lack of evidence or motive.
If he is jailed or killed, his "pension" continues to be handed to his family.
But anyone who loses nerve or comes back from a hit looking panicky is soon
eliminated. Rico is the boss at the meeting, but a phone call indicates he is
following orders about contracts and hits from someone higher up.

Big Babe's collaboration produces some results. He takes Ferguson and
his men to a marsh, where they haul a station wagon out of the mire. In it
there is a dead young woman of medium size, black hair and brown eyes.
She is identified as Nina Lombardo (Susan Cabot), the one murdered by
Duke Malloy. The police find out where she lived and talk to her roommate, who goes under the name of Teresa Davis, a pretty blond with blue
eyes. She says that she had met Nina in the place they worked together,
that they liked each other and shared a room. Ferguson asks her for more
details but the only thing she can add, after some nervous hesitation, is that
Nina had changed her name from Angela Vetto to Nina Lombardo. That's
a detail that Ferguson keeps in mind, but at the time it leads nowhere.

Meanwhile Philadelphia was released from the mental institution, for
he was only pretending he was insane and hiding out. From him Ferguson
learns the address of the Undertaker, or "Sad Eyes" (Edwin Max), who is
shortly arrested and reveals the place where the victims are buried—in the
same marsh where the body of Nina Lombardo had been found. Ferguson
orders a search, and countless bodies, or parts of bodies are found. Only a
few can be identified, but Ferguson orders that their names be broadcast,
along with the details of the findings. This sends ripples of fear through the
organization and many of them try to skip town. One of those is Rico, who
is hiding out at a country house, where two assassins are sent to kill him
along with his two associates. Rico slips away and makes a phone call to
Ferguson, asking to see him, alone and with no weapon, at a pier near the
harbor. Ferguson goes, and Rico is now ready to tell his entire story and he
does, in a long confession that is taped.

From him Ferguson learns the extraordinary story of Rico's first encounter with Mendoza. They had met ten years earlier, when Rico was manhandling him outside a café belonging to a man called John Webb. Mendoza told Rico that as the old ways of doing business as a racketeer had declined, he had come up with a new concept: kill a person entirely unconnected to you on a contract. You are doing it for somebody else who wants another person out of the way. This is the contract. The hit is the actual killing. No one will suspect you, and the person who gave you the money and the commission remains silent, for he is himself subject to persecution if he speaks. To demonstrate his point, Mendoza takes a carving knife out of a knife holder, goes over to the café owner, and stabs him to death. A cabdriver and his young daughter who happen to be entering the place see Mendoza, and the young girl starts screaming. Rico wants to run, but Mendoza displays his extraordinary ability to stay cool under pressure: walk, don't run. Mendoza collected $500 for this hit, and that seals the deal between him and Rico, who becomes the leader of the "troop," taking orders from his boss, who stays out of sight and direct action. In ten years, the organization has prospered; the idea worked, and dozens of people, whether innocent or not, have been killed.

We are now back to the present; morning is approaching and the trial is only a few hours away. As he and Captain Nelson are playing and replaying Rico's tape, Ferguson takes some photographs of the victims and goes to Mendoza's cell, telling him to look at his victims and have nightmares for the rest of his life. When back at his office, Captain Nelson is still playing the tape. Ferguson listens and is struck by one detail: the girl who had witnessed John Webb's murder had "big blue eyes." In the photograph Ferguson had just given to Mendoza, Nina Lombardo had black hair and brown eyes. Mendoza makes the same discovery by looking at the photograph of the dark-haired girl. His man, Malloy, had killed the wrong girl. He rushes to the window and asks the guard to let him call his lawyer. A big-jawed man, BJ (Harry Wilson), answers the phone and tells Herman (Bob Steele) that they have a job to do right away.

Ferguson and Captain Nelson rush to the place of Teresa Davis, for she is the blue-eyed girl, the real Angela Vetto. A woman there tells them that she's gone out, but two men were just there asking for her. One of the most intense scenes in film follows. It is one of Hitchcockian suspense: an innocent woman, ignorant of the danger she is in, is being pursued by two killers and also by the police, who are trying to save her life. Ferguson has an additional motive: she is the material witness he needs to nail Mendoza. The killers spot Angela walking down the street and try to take aim, but a truck blocks their view. Ferguson and Captain Nelson stand before a music store that has two big loudspeakers outside playing music. Ferguson rushes into the store, grabs the microphone, and uses the loudspeakers to warn Angela that she is in danger and to get off the street. He gives her the telephone number of the store he is in, and tells her to call. To be sure, the alarmed but quick-thinking young woman rushes into a shop gets into a telephone booth, calls, and tells Ferguson where she is. He asks her to stay there and orders the policemen to go around the block from the other side while he goes directly to where she is. Captain Nelson tells Ferguson to take a "friend" with him, and hands him a gun.

Ferguson goes into the store where she is; Herman sees him and follows him. Ferguson finds the frightened girl inside a booth, tells her to stay there, then tilts the booth door to see in the reflection the entering man through the revolving door. As soon as Herman is within a shooting distance, Ferguson turns around and shoots him several times, knowing that tough guys shoot back. It takes several shots to get Herman stumbling backward through the door and falling down on the street. (Incidentally, Herman is played by Bob Steele, who was Canino in *The Big Sleep*, and it took Bogart's character three bullets to down him there.) Ferguson, who was never shown carrying a gun as a DA in this movie, knows how to handle one, being a Bogart character.

A viewer may have missed a crucial clue in this plot. Why was Nina Lombardo taken as the hit, and killed, instead of her roommate, Teresa Davis, the real Angela Vetto? Without this mistake, which only becomes apparent at the very end of the story, there would have been no witness to testify against Mendoza once Rico was killed. The answer is given in a small detail right after the discovery of Nina's body in the marsh, inside the station wagon. It was a tiny piece of paper left on the wheel with a name and address, sixty miles away. The man's name was Thomas O'Hara (Don Beddoe). Ferguson and Nelson rush there only to find out that the man was shot and is near death at the local hospital. They just have time to question him, and his story (in another flashback) clicks with the rest. He was the man to identify the hit, and he had pointed at the wrong girl, Nina Lombardo, when O'Hara and Malloy were sitting in a car outside the two girls' apartment. Malloy had fallen in love with Nina and intended to run off and marry her. He paid O'Hara $1,000 to call Rico and tell him that the hit had been successful. But Malloy's flight was blocked, as we have seen, and he was forced to kill Nina. The irony is that no one had suspected that the wrong girl was implicated and shot, and this whole episode adds a touch of tragedy to the story. Angela Vetto's father, Tony Vetto, is the only other person who could implicate Mendoza in his first killing of John Webb, the café owner. Unfortunately for Vetto, he recognized Mendoza in his taxicab, and Mendoza knew immediately that he had been recognized. The hit on Vetto, who was killed at Louis's barbershop while being shaved, was executed by Rico and several of his goons, one being Duke Malloy. The death of her father is what prompted Angela Vetto, now a grown woman, to change her name, perhaps not entirely understanding why she was in danger, other than she had witnessed a murder when she was very young.

In this maze, Bogart as Ferguson gets high marks. When the story begins and his main witness has fallen to his death, he has seven hours to stop Mendoza from walking out free. In these few hours, his search through flashbacks gradually reveals the truth, to him and to the audience, in the manner of a jigsaw puzzle, where all the pieces have been put together. The plot is not burdened with a love interest or other diversions, as Ferguson has no ties of family or friends to sidetrack him from his mission. As a DA, he wears a bow tie and looks a gentleman of manners, but in the final few minutes he shows that he can handle a gun. His persona as a tough guy surfaces, but it is his quick thinking that points to the final clue. The final moments, as the audience sees Angela Vetto (Patricia Jones) striding confidently through a crowded street, when a killer is aiming a gun at her, add the final touches to this intense thriller. Bogart has his witness, has saved a lady in distress, but that is all we know, and need to know.

31

BATTLE CIRCUS

(MGM, 1953)

★ ★ ★

Director: Richards Brooks
Screenplay: Richard Brooks, adapted from a story by Allen Rivkin and Laura Kerr
Producer: Pandro S. Berman. Cinematography: John Alton. Music Score: Lennie Hayton. Editor: George Boemler
Cast: Humphrey Bogart (Major Jed Webbe), June Allyson (Lieutenant Ruth McGara), Keenan Wynn (Sergeant Orvil Statt), Robert Keith (Lieutenant Colonel Hillary Whalters), William Campbell (Captain John Rustford), Perry Sheehan (Lieutenant Lawrence), Patricia Tiernan (Lieutenant Rose Ashland), Jonathan Cott (Adjutant)
Released: March 6, 1953
Specs: 90 minutes; black and white
Availability: DVD (Warner Archive Collection)

Battle Circus is one of the two movies Bogart made for MGM,[1] and this was at a time when he had broken all ties with Warners and was working either independently for studios like 20th Century Fox, Paramount, Stanley Kramer Productions, or Columbia. The movie exteriors were shot in Fort Pickett Army Base, Virginia, which provided helicopters, army materiel, and other services. Bogart had worked with Richard Brooks before (he was a coauthor with John Huston of the screenplay of *Key Largo*), and Brooks had become a good friend and lifelong admirer of Bogart. *Battle Circus* was neither a top-tier Bogart movie nor a great popular success, but it was timely, as the Korean War was about to come to its conclusion, and notable, because it presents another facet of Bogart's screen personality, which aside from his early gangster roles had figured him as a detective, lover, adventurer, soldier, naval officer, gold prospector, writer, jet test pilot, and lawyer.

Here Bogart is a top-notch surgeon during the Korean War, at a Mobile Army Surgical Hospital (MASH8666[2]), a unit close to the front lines, jammed with incoming injured soldiers brought by an incoming helicopter, which also had to fly in supplies to keep up with the frantic pace of medical emergencies. The unit was often under fire, and had to change places, taking down its tents, packing them into trucks, and shoving them off to a new location, then speedily putting them up again. Given the period it was made, the movie is realistic, showing the conditions under which trauma patients were treated, as well as the lives of those who were involved in the hard-fought bloody conflict in the Korean Peninsula. Hollywood always thrived on war conflicts during the twentieth century, with actors eager to participate, studios to finance, and audiences to swarm theaters for entertainment, and, potentially, instruction. The producers of this movie dedicated it to the "indomitable human spirit."

Bogart, as is well known, made several war movies during World War II (the most famous being *Casablanca*), but very few afterward; *Battle Circus* is one example. His performance as a doctor at close proximity to the battlefield is convincing, as by this time he had honed his skills as an actor and was ready to play nearly anyone. His persona, however, is wavering on one front: his romantic presence is not what one would expect from the image Bogart had scrupulously maintained with women—a cool attitude, often of a gallant gentleman who let the ladies come to him, rather than one who makes a rude pass, embarrassing a lady, and provoking an audience's dislike. Doctor (Major) Jed Webbe loses no time in singling out a newly arrived nurse, Lieutenant Ruth McGara (June Allyson), a likable and somewhat naive young woman who joins the small band of nurses who service the hospital. Their cheerful group pass on jokes during slow intervals between action, mostly about Doctor Webbe, whose overactive libido seems to be a form of relaxation after a tense surgical procedure. Some of the ladies seem to have obliged, though nothing improper is shown on the screen, these being super-conservative times. The unique mixture of war, sex, and bedlam was left for the 1970s decade, for the rambunctious *M*A*S*H* movie and its long-running TV sequel.

As Ruth McGara, June Allyson stands her ground opposite Bogart's aggressive Dr. Webbe. Allyson, a singer and dancer for MGM for years, was known for her endearing looks, cheery disposition, husky-toned singing voice, and dancing skills. As a newly arrived nurse, she beams at the idea that she is actually at the war scene and stands under the revolving blade of a helicopter; it takes a nod and finger-pointing by Sergeant Orvil Statt (Keenan Wynn) for her to understand that she could be decapitated any moment. As two Korean planes fly overhead, strafing the camp, she stands up, lost, in the middle of everything, until Dr. Webbe dashes forward, lifts her off her feet, and carries her a few steps, pushing her under a truck. She keeps saluting him, every time he speaks, until he tells her to stop doing that. An incredibly lovable novice, she quickly becomes acclimatized and rushes to offer help and cheer wounded soldiers just arrived in the helicopter. She knows a thing or two also, when pushy men try something on her. When Webbe puts his hand over her shoulder during a night as the unit had hastily decamped and moved to another direction, she knows very well what a pass is. Webbe is no man to accept defeat from a young[3] and attractive nurse—or any woman for that matter. She tells him she wants one man in her life—to love and to marry and to stay with. None of that matters to Webbe, who presses on, and soon the two are seen kissing during a torrential rain, in a deliciously photographed mud bath.

The two lovers are swept along by rapid action sequences, both in the air, showing a brave Captain John Rustford (William Campbell) carrying injured men and supplies, and inside the surgical quarters, with intense sequences. Webbe, Ruth learns, is not just a pushy lover, but a dedicated and able surgeon. When a Korean boy is brought in with several chest wounds, everybody gives up except Webbe, who undertakes to operate. As Ruth looks on, along with the incredulous Lieutenant Colonel Whalters, Webbe first extracts the pieces of shrapnel, then persistently massages the heart after the boy's pulse stops and orders oxygen and adrenalin to be given, and soon the boy revives. Ruth nearly faints, and Colonel Whalters shakes his head, saying he still doesn't believe what he saw. But all is not all right with the brave and daring doctor. He likes his cups, and when he directs the landing of the unit's helicopter carrying blood supplies during a storm, Rustford, who had flown the helicopter, gives Webbe a bottle of whiskey, as a gift for saving his life. Webbe steps inside his tent, and when Colonel Whalters looks for him early in the morning, he finds him smashed. No two ways about it, says the colonel. Either the worthy doctor decides to abstain entirely from the stuff, or out he goes, to court-martial and life-long expulsion from medical practice. The intrepid colonel, played ably by Robert Keith, also knows something about women's psychology, at least as far as those women having to deal with Webbe, so he gives Ruth some expert advice. Go after him, he says, show him what you can do. Translation: Don't be passive, take initiatives. She does, and her attitude toward Webbe

and others becomes more positive. Bogie occasionally yields to assertive
women, as he has done so many times with Bacall, admiring courage and
self-assurance. But that policy works on another front: when a North Korean captive is brought in, he holds an undetected grenade inside his belt,
and then he pulls it out and threatens to blow up the surgical unit. Ruth
approaches the half-crazed man, and with soothing words, she manages to
calm him down and give up the grenade.

There is more action, as the unit has to split in order to reach safety.
The nurses with the injured proceed on a truck that the ingenious Sergeant
Statt—a loyal, patriotic, and sensitive character (an image of Keenan Wynn,
whom Stanley Kubrick destroyed in his *Dr. Strangelove* a decade later)—
has placed on a rail platform that replaces the ruined train. The other unit,
led by the brave Jud Webbe, is the entire convoy of trucks driving through
muddy tracks and side roads to a safe destination. There is action and suspense in this part of the movie, but finally all is accomplished and the two
units and the two lovers reunite, and all is well, Hollywood fashion. This is
not a great movie, and Bogart and Allyson are not a perfect fit. But both are
professionals, both likable, and besides, they worked for a common cause.
Audiences liked the movie enough to give it a thumbs-up, doubling its cost,
about $1,200,000, at the box office. For the modern viewer, the movie offers
a dose of detoxification after the convulsive spasms of laughter in the now
mythical 1970s *M*A*S*H** movie and TV show. By the way, "Circus" of the
title is attributed to Allyson, as she repeats the word describing the camp,
first spoken by Sergeant Statt. For trivia seekers, the canteen restaurant of
the camp bears the inscription, "THIS MESS IS RECOMMENDED BY
ROMANOFF." Mike Romanoff was a famous restaurant owner in Hollywood,[4] a friend of Bogart, who liked to have dinner at Romanoff's with his
friends, followed by nights of carousing.

32

BEAT THE DEVIL

(Santana-Romulus Productions, 1954)

★ ★ ★

Director: John Huston
Screenplay: John Huston, Truman Capote, based on the novel *Beat the Devil*
   by James Helvick
Producers: John Huston (Humphrey Bogart, uncredited). *Cinematographer:*
   Oswald Morris. *Music Score:* Franco Mannino. *Editor:* Ralph Kemplen
Cast: Humphrey Bogart (Billy Dannreuther), Jennifer Jones (Gwendolen
   Chelm), Gina Lollobrigida (Maria Dannreuther), Robert Morley
   (Peterson), Edward Underdown (Harry Chelm), Ivor Barnard (Major
   Jack Ross), Marco Tulli (Ravello), Peter Lorre (Julius O'Hara), Bernard
   Lee (Inspector Jack Clayton), Saro Urzi (Captain of SS *Nyanga*), Juan
   de Landa (Hispano-Swiza Driver)
Released: December 17, 1954
Specs: 89 minutes; black and white
Availability: DVD (Echo Bridge Home Entertainment, Collector's Edition);
   streaming (Amazon)

Beat the Devil was the final film produced by Santana Productions, Bogart's own film company, in collaboration with Horizon-Romulus, which was based in England. It was directed by John Huston, the last film in the long association between Huston and Bogart. After the initial authors, Peter Viertel and Anthony Veiller, had failed to give the script enough luster, Truman Capote was brought in, and he and Huston rewrote it. The story was based on a novel by Claud Cockburn (a.k.a. James Helvick), but the scenario never took a definite form as it was written on a day-to-day basis by the various authors already mentioned. It was supposed to be a comedy/thriller, where a group of swindlers attempt to hunt for an elusive treasure, a uranium mine in Kenya, but things do not go well for the swindlers or the producers, who lost money in the process. As a Bogart vehicle, it was one of the messiest affairs of his life, stranding him in Ravello, a small Italian town, for months, aside from costing him over half a million dollars of his own money. The project also necessitated a separation from his wife, who had accompanied him in all his previous projects, because Bacall was doing *How to Marry a Millionaire* at the time.[1] The movie was shot in black and white (color had been considered), and delays were caused by a change of crew and the fact that the ship they were supposed to embark on had mechanical problems.[2] The movie is still worth watching, as it is sporadically (and sometimes unintentionally) funny.

The story begins with four swindlers shown coming back from their failed enterprise in handcuffs. Bogart's voice intones that they deserve what they got, and then, going back six months, it starts the rueful tale that brought them to this predicament. Bogart's connection with these men remains vague for a while, but we eventually learn that he has promised to bring them into contact with a man essential for their venture in Africa. He is himself part of two couples, also waiting for the same ship: Bogart, with one of the most unappealing names he ever took on a character—Billy Dannreuther—is married to Maria (Gina Lollobrigida), an Italian woman who wishes to be English. And Jennifer Jones, affecting a British accent and sporting a blond wig, plays the wife of Harry Chelm (Edward Underdown), who claims to be going to Africa to start a coffee plantation. Chelm begins to like Maria, while his wife, Gwendolen, starts a flirtation—and a rather too obvious one—with Dannreuther. While Dannreuther is an associate of a bunch of crooks, he pretends to be a man of means, while Harry Chelm, who adopts the airs of English gentry—tall, imposing, a bit aloof—proves to be the son of innkeepers. He is as money hungry as anyone else around him.

Peterson, played by a jowly Robert Morley, is the leader of a group of nondescripts that seem unfit for any enterprise, even cheating: Mario Tulli plays Ravello, a bony, hapless good-for-nothing, while Peter Lorre, gray-haired and overweight (though as short as ever), answers to the weird appellation of Julius O'Hara, pronounced "Ohora" by Ravello. Their fourth member, Major Jack Ross, is a diminutive and belligerent fellow who arrives from London after a suspicious murder of an important colonial official, Paul Vanmeer, in Soho, is reported. Maria notices that piece of news while reading a newspaper, and she tells her husband, who seems to know or suspect who the murderer is. Aside from Peterson, who is the leader, and Major Ross, who is the assassin, the other two members of the gang are useless weight just being dragged along.

The story line is a succession of comic episodes, rather than a coherent plot. The two groups are stuck in the small Italian town (just as the producers were), as the ship that is supposed to take them to Africa is being repaired. The naughtiness between the two couples continues, as Gwendolyn flirts openly with Dannreuther, who, to show his largesse, invites them to his restaurant/villa up in the hills. Their means of transportation is a vehicle that used to belong to a famous toreador, allowing passengers enough room to stand up and driven by a corpulent Hispano-Swiss driver, who has inherited the vehicle from Dannreuther. The restaurant has been closed for months; yet, despite that, Gwendolyn meets openly with Dannreuther at a nearby villa, telling him that she likes men of distinction, above the madding crowd, men like Byron, for instance. Her husband attributes her chatty frivolities to her hopeless romanticism, while he himself is nursed by Maria, as he has caught a chill (she pronounces it "cheel"), an accommodation that seems to suit both couples. The delay has obliged Peterson and Dannreuther to drive to another town to catch a plane to Africa, but their vehicle stalls, is pushed by the two men and the Spanish chauffer, and runs downhill on its own, until it collides with an oncoming bus and ends at the bottom of the Adriatic Sea. Maria swoons as she hears the news of her husband's presumed demise.

But the lost duo reappear soon, and, finally, the ship is repaired and they sail, as a new set of misadventures awaits them. Chelm has a new story now; he is not going to Africa to start a plantation, but to save the natives from sin. "Sin?" an incredulous Peterson asks. The tangled tale of the six adventurers, with their two female companions, eventually unravels. All this happens on a ship with an inept crew and a drunken captain who bears an uncanny resemblance to tenor Luciano Pavarotti and who screams as much, but without the latter's musicality. Some details come to the surface during the trip. Chelm gets a cable from London and learns that the man who was murdered at Soho, a colonial official, was on the track of the Peterson bunch, and that the murderer was none other than the pugnacious Major Ross. Soon after, Chelm is attacked by the major but is saved by the quick-thinking Dannreuther—his only brave act in a movie of nonheroes. But Chelm is subject to abuse by his own wife, Gwendolyn, who tells the captain that he suffers from paranoia; as a result, Chelm is chained to a pole in his cabin. Gwendolyn then tells everyone that her husband is out to make a buck—or pound—going to Africa for the same reasons as the others, taking hold of the uranium field. Maria swoons, the ship is sinking,

Chelm disappears, and the rest of the group leave on the ship's rescue boat. The captain screams.

The boat lands on an African coast, and all but the vanished Chelm are soon captured by armed horsemen, who bring them to the Arab officer of the region (Manuel Serano), who questions them. Peterson undertakes to explain their situation, and assuming the sheik doesn't know English, he attempts to persuade him in sign language (of his own invention) that they are victims of a shipwreck. The sheik answers in perfect English, while sucking at his gurgling hookah, and asks for their passports. The gang fail to produce these documents (Peterson had buried his in the sand), and all remain in detention. Only Dannreuther tries to escape by jumping out of a window with the agility of a panther, but he is quickly grabbed by the sheik's hordes. We next see him, his head full of bumps and bruises, sitting next to the sheik, who is reposing on a recliner, serenely sipping at his hookah, a pinup photo of Rita Hayworth on his wall. That was the time (1949–1951) when Hayworth had married and divorced Prince Aly Khan, a rich playboy living in Paris, sending ripples of condemnation through the gossip columns of Hollywood. The scene, one of the truly funny ones in the movie, parodies dreamy men of wealth in Europe or Africa pursuing Hollywood goddesses. A barefaced liar, Dannreuther is trying to convince the sheik that he has connections with Rita in Paris and that he could bring the sheik in touch with her, if he lets them go! Rita serves as the deus ex machina.

In no time, we see the group on a yawl, sailing back to Italy. When they arrive at the harbor, the SS *Nyanga* is also there, and its excitable captain standing on the prow is screaming that they stole his boat. When they are on shore, a Scotland Yard inspector, Jack Clayton (played by Bernard Lee, who later appeared in many James Bond movies), is there, investigating the murder of the man at Soho. Gwendolyn is in a black scarf, mourning the demise of her husband. When she learns what the inspector is investigating, she reveals that Major Jack Ross had stabbed her husband with a stiletto hidden in the swagger stick he always carried with him, and that he had just arrived from London when the news of Vanmeer's murder was announced. Peterson was the leader of the group, and the major his executioner. The four are led away in handcuffs—the same scene was shown when the story began—and the rest are free. But the mourning Gwendolyn is handed a telegram from . . . Chelm, who is alive and well and has taken ownership of the uranium mine; he says that all is forgiven and she can go back to him anytime. Maria swoons—she always wanted an estate in England.

Call this a farce, a parody or comedy, even a spoof of adventure stories. The picture lacks focus and purpose. It was made for the sake of making

Concerned captives in a North African sheikdom, Billy Dannreuther (Bogart), Gwendolen Chelm (Jennifer Jones), and Maria Dannreuther (Gina Lollobrigida). *United Artists/Photofest* © *United Artists, Photographer: Robert Capa*

it, perhaps to signal the end of Santana Productions, which had pioneered independent productions in Hollywood and had managed to produce several good movies. But this was the last and least of Bogart's efforts to be a producer. Nathaniel Benchley reports that when Bogart was leaving Italy, a customs official remarked, "If you make one more picture like that, we won't let you back."[3] Bogart left Italy—Bacall had joined him in the meantime—licking his wounds, having lost money in the venture. His parting shot was that only "phony intellectuals" liked a movie like that, and he committed it to oblivion. Over the years, viewers have revisited it, and a few have assigned it to the status of a "cult classic." For sheer fun, it is worth watching Hollywood megastars—Bogart, Morley, Lorre, Lollobrigida, Jones—making asses of themselves, on occasion saved by Truman Capote's clever quips.

33

THE CAINE MUTINY

(Stanley Kramer Productions, 1954)

★ ★ ★ ★

Director: Edward Dmytryk

Screenplay: Stanley Roberts, based on the Pulitzer Prize–winning novel by
Herman Wouk

Producer: Stanley Kramer. *Cinematographer:* Franz Planer. *Music Score:* Max
Steiner. *Editors:* William Lyon, Henry Batista. *Art Design:* Gary Odell

Cast: Humphrey Bogart (Captain Philip Francis Queeg), Van Johnson (Lieutenant
Steve Maryk), Fred MacMurray (Lieutenant Tom Keefer), José Ferrer
(Lieutenant Barney Greenwald), Robert Francis (Ensign Willie Keith),
Tom Tully (Captain DeVriess), E. G. Marshall (Commander Chalee),
Katharine Warren (Mrs. Keith), May Wynn (May Wynn), Lee Marvin
(Meatball), Claude Akins (Horrible), Jerry Paris (Ensign Harding)

Released: June 24, 1954

Specs: 121 minutes; color

Availability: DVD (Sony Pictures Home Entertainment)

The Caine Mutiny was made at a time when Bogart had broken his ties
with Warner Bros. and had already produced several movies himself as an
independent producer of his own Santana Productions, established in 1949.
Like many other major stars, he had chosen to work with independent
producers to allow him flexibility in the parts he played. So when Bogart
was offered the role of Captain Philip Francis Queeg by Stanley Kramer
Productions, a role he actually pursued, he worked hard to bring to life a
mentally disturbed man, and he was rewarded with another Oscar nomination.[1] Bogart was joined by a first-rate ensemble cast, but by the end of
the film there was no doubt in anyone's mind that Bogart had delivered

one of his finest performances. As Kramer himself put it, "It was his own character. He wasn't like Queeg, but he had Queeg-like qualities, like his violence, which I was never a party to, but which must have been intense."[2] Directed by Edward Dmytryk, a controversial figure at the time,[3] the movie was a smashing success at the box office and won seven Oscar nominations, though winning none. For Bogart it was another triumph, consolidating his position as one of the leading superstars of all time.

The movie opens with a disclaimer that there has never been a mutiny in the US Navy,[4] as an indication that the story is fictional—as indeed it was—based on the Pulitzer Prize–winning novel by Herman Wouk, which had also been turned into a successful stage play.[5] It begins innocently as a love story, that of Ensign Willie Keith, fresh from the Naval Academy at Princeton and ready to embark on the destroyer *Caine*, saying good-bye to his obsessive mother, while his girlfriend, May, played by May Wynn (retaining her actual name), stays on the sidelines. May is a nightclub singer, and Keith does not feel it appropriate to introduce her to his mother. The movie begins with Keith and ends with him, as most of the action is seen through his eyes, his story forming a framing device, establishing a point of view.

The ship Keith embarks at Pearl Harbor is a dilapidated war tub that has seen better days, run by crusty, war-weary Captain DeVriess (Tom Tully), and an odd collection of a crew that look more like street vagrants than a disciplined navy unit. The officers on ship are another odd group that cause Keith's exalted notion of a warship at wartime to vanish quickly. He is puzzled by the behavior of some, particularly Lieutenant Tom Keefer, the communications officer, whose cutting remarks about the ship and crew make him wonder what these people would do in an emergency. Keith also meets executive officer Lieutenant Steve Maryk (Van Johnson), whose actions later become the focus of the story.

The major player, of course, is Captain Queeg, who does not appear until twenty-five minutes into the movie. Bogart as Queeg looks his age, at fifty-four, and right at the outset he gives the impression of an insecure man. By that time, three years before his death, Bogart appeared fragile and smaller than all the rest of the officers, but right away he makes the impression of a man determined to run a tight ship, as a navy vessel during wartime should be. At the first meeting with his officers, as he talks to them with affected authority, Queeg takes several metal balls out of his pocket and begins to roll them between his fingers, perhaps the sign of a man who tries to ease his tensions. This detail does not escape the notice of Keefer, who glances at him with a knowing smile, as if he has just spotted an oddity. When a sailor interrupts the meeting, bringing the captain a message, Queeg reprimands him for letting his shirt hang out and readily assigns Keith, whose fresh face and demeanor attract him, as the "morale officer." Keith, who had bitterly complained to Captain DeVriess that the shipmen looked like a street gang, is pleased to receive this commission, seeing in Queeg a man who means business. But at the conclusion of the meeting, Keefer drily observes, "Here comes Captain Bligh."

Queeg readily gives orders to Keith that every man on board have his shirt tucked in, shave, and look presentable at all times. He demands that Keefer, who has been seen hitting the keys of his typewriter, stop writing his novel. But with discipline also come signs of erratic behavior. While reprimanding a sailor for some infraction during an exercise, the captain fails to notice that the ship is going around in a circle, towing a shooting target, and cutting its own towline, despite protests from the crew. A bit later he gives orders to abandon a group of boats carrying marines after a Japanese attack, hurrying away to San Francisco, an order interpreted by the officers and crew as an act of cowardice. He turns the ship upside down to find a quart of missing strawberries, eaten by the crew, and embarks on the search of an imaginary key to find them. Queeg is told by Ensign Harding, as the latter leaves the ship to attend to his sick wife, that some of the mess crew ate the strawberries and that a key does not exist. When Queeg makes an effort to elicit sympathy from his officers, telling them that he too is human and that he has a wife, a son, and dog, his effort fails, as the officers remain distant.

Keith, who initially had admired the eccentric captain, sees that Queeg is not only an authoritarian but that he shows signs of being unbalanced. Keefer starts talking of paranoia to Lieutenant Maryk, posing as a psychologist who knows human nature, since he is an author of a novel. He also, and rather slyly, refers to the United States Navy Manual, Article 184, which describes conditions under which an officer can take over the command of a ship. Maryk, though disturbed by Keefer's insinuations that the captain may be sick, is an experienced and brave naval officer unlikely to follow the path of disobedience. But Keefer keeps needling him, and when a storm breaks out and the ship seems about to founder, Maryk is forced to act. Queeg stubbornly refuses to change course as the ship is tossed about by the violent typhoon, and Maryk tells the helmsman that he is taking over, but not before he orders all the officers to be present on the bridge to witness his decision. The helmsman obeys and the ship is saved, but Maryk, and with him Keith, who went along with his orders, are charged with mutiny.

In the ensuing trial, the fourth major star of the movie appears, José Ferrer, who plays Lieutenant Barney Greenwald, the lawyer who undertakes

Captain Philip Queeg (Bogart) is investigating the "stolen" strawberries, as members of the crew witness the proceedings. Among the officers are Lieutenant Steve Maryk (Van Johnson), to the right, and Lieutenant Tom Keefer (Fred MacMurray) standing. *Warner Bros./Photofest © Warner Bros.*

to defend Maryk, against his own judgment and after numerous other legal officers have declined to do so. Ferrer, who was one of the most dynamic actors in Hollywood at the time, plays his cards right. The trial is, indeed, the major event of the movie and had been the basis of the highly successful stage play, based on the Wouk novel.

The trial is given, with only a few minor cuts, as a straightforward episode, building tension and filled with swift twists and turns, and not without a few ironies. First, Ensign Keith is called to the stand, and under the relentless questioning by Prosecutor Commander Chalee (in a virtuoso performance by E. G. Marshall), he admits that he knows little about mental illness when he states that Maryk took over because Captain Queeg was a sick man—the central point of the defense. Two seamen succeed him on the stand—one being the helmsman (an early role for Lee Marvin), nicknamed "Meatball"—but neither is able to offer useful testimony in favor of Maryk. Keefer, called to the stand, denies that he advised Maryk to commit mutiny; he only says they had "discussed" the matter with him. Asked whether he believes the captain was mentally ill, he says "No," to the dismay and shock of Maryk, who jots down a note to his lawyer, saying, "He's lying." Greenwald does not cross-examine him, saying to Maryk that he wants a hero not two mutineers.

That concluded, a navy psychiatrist is called to the stand, but he does not help matters when he attests that a board of psychiatrists had examined Queeg and found no traces of mental illness in him; even a paranoid man is by definition not unable to function normally. Called on the stand, and stunned by Keefer's cowardly evasions, Maryk defends himself poorly by stating that he took over command because he thought the captain was a sick man, and therefore he thought the ship was in immediately danger of foundering. When questioned about psychiatric terms like *paranoia* and *paranoid*, he confesses that he has no knowledge of these or any other medical terms, but he stands by his decision, saying that if he had to do it again, he would. Asked whether he should be found guilty under those terms, he answers, "I guess maybe so."

Maryk's case seems lost at this point. But Greenwald tells him not to worry, because, as he puts it, "This is only the first act." Queeg himself is called next. Bogart is seen striding in, his head looking bigger than ever, his shoulders humped, his body shrunk, but wearing a smile of self-assurance when greeting a group of concerned officers outside the courtroom. When he is on the stand, he first appears to be under control, but he becomes agitated when Greenwald asks him about errors he committed while captaining the *Caine*, like cutting his own towline. Greenwald keeps prodding him, asking him if he conducted a search for missing strawberries and ordered his crew to find an imaginary key when the strawberries were hidden. Queeg suddenly erupts and starts pounding the arm of his chair, stating, "There was definitely a key!" A surprised prosecutor asks for a recess, as his client is evidently agitated. But Queeg shouts that he does not want a recess. He starts ranting, saying that he thought the matter over, "with geometric logic," adding that every officer besides him was lying. In a series of close-ups, director Dmytryk shows Bogart's face, the two little lined scars[6] quite visible and adding to the effect of mental disorder. These are stunning shots, as the mask drops, revealing a man's raw mental lesions under the scrutiny of a relentless camera. When he reaches into his pocket and brings out the metal balls, rolling them over in his fingers, the clashing balls break the silence, as the naval officers in the court look on in astonishment. Sight and sound (and silence) combine to create an electric moment, one of those rarest ones in the history of cinema.

Momentarily, Queeg regains his senses, looks apologetic, and says that recounting events from memory does not help him, and that he is ready to answer all questions one by one. The camera cuts to the faces of those in the room: Maryk's stunned and pitying glance, the presiding judge's shock, Greenwald's sorrowful and even guilty face, as he knows he has raked up a disturbed man's psyche in public; even Prosecutor Chalee looks on in disbelief. "No more questions," says Greenwald, and the court judge intones, "The case is closed."

Bogart's performance shows an intriguing fine line between his acting and reenacting of his own inner turbulence. Like Queeg, Bogart had undergone years of the intense pressure on his way to the top. One recalls the demeaning roles imposed on him at Warners for many years, three painful divorces, personal tragedies, and political persecution—the accumulated anger that had a chance to surface in some of his screen performances. There were times when Bogart the actor and Bogart the man became identical. This performance also makes Queeg an ambiguous figure at a time when movies wanted clean lines drawn between good and evil, heroes and villains. Though evidently paranoid, Queeg was not a coward, as Greenwald explains to the court: "A man who rose to be a captain in the US Navy cannot possibly *be* a coward!" Yet, under pressure, when chased by the enemy, he abandons boats with marines and speeds away. Mockingly (and bitterly) the crew names him "Old Yellowstain," the name for a coward. At his prime, Queeg may not have lacked courage, but worn out by a lifetime of trials, he finally falls apart under extreme stress.

It does not help matters that Queeg knows that he is being ridiculed by his own crew and is making a spectacle of himself. By this time, Bogart had developed a skill of showing ambiguity in his characters, playing men disintegrating under pressure—witness his collapse in *The Treasure of Sierra Madre* (1948) and *In a Lonely Place* (1950), as noted already in previous chapters.

The scene following, while the officers implicated celebrate their "victory," a drunken Greenwald barges in and begins fuming about how Queeg was railroaded by those in the court, including himself. In a show of utter disgust, Greenwald tosses his drink in the face of Keefer, the man who had goaded Maryk to mutiny, but did not tell the whole truth to the court. At this point, Keefer was the villain Greenwald would rather have prosecuted. This scene is high theatrics, and José Ferrer, a distinguished actor, who had played Cyrano de Bergerac (*Cyrano de Bergerac*, 1950) and Toulouse-Lautrec (*Moulin Rouge*, 1952), had the powerful presence to make it a devastating indictment of the real culprits. The scene, however, seems to blur the difference between mutiny and the action of Maryk, which under the circumstances was fully justified. Perhaps, as two commentators seem to imply,[7] the scene was to compensate for dumping a man who had been a war hero and longtime loyal navy officer. Greenwald shows his guilt in a manner that seems appropriate in that he goes into his ranting while drunk.

The last scene of the movie Ensign Keith, now married to May, says good-bye to his mother, who waves to him from a cab; kisses his new bride passionately; and once more embarks on the same ship for his second naval duty. And, surprise! The same Captain DeVriess is his new commander. After the usual salutes and knowing smile from DeVriess, Keith is told to "take her out!" Things have come full circle. The naive young ensign has now returned a full-grown man. In this turnaround in tone—from the tragic to normal—the filmmakers have restored the reputation of the navy. Yes, and in the process they have asserted that, in spite of a few bad apples here and there, the navy—and by implication, the country—can forgive and forget that the few don't make up a whole, and even those scarred by misfortune can be honorably discharged and then forgiven. We never really know what happens to Queeg—or any of the others. As usual, Bogart came and went, taking over a slice of the movie, the most dramatic, and then vanishing, not to be heard of again. But when the camera closes in, fully capturing his face, in pain, loss, joy, or sadness, we know he has hit one out of the park.

SABRINA

(Paramount Pictures, 1954)

★ ★ ★ ★

Director: Billy Wilder
Screenplay: Billy Wilder, Samuel Taylor, Ernest Lehman, based on the play
　　Sabrina Fair by Samuel Taylor
Producer: Billy Wilder. *Cinematographer:* Charles Lang Jr. *Music Score:*
　　Frederick Hollander. *Editor:* Arthur Schmidt
Cast: Humphrey Bogart (Linus Larrabee), Audrey Hepburn (Sabrina
　　Fairchild), William Holden (David Larrabee), Walter Hampden (Walter
　　Larrabee), John Williams (Thomas Fairchild), Martha Hyer (Elizabeth
　　Tyson)
Released: October 15, 1954
Specs: 113 minutes; color
Availability: DVD and Blu-ray (Warner Home Video); streaming (Amazon)

Playing Linus Larrabee in *Sabrina* was an oddity for Bogart in any number
of ways. For one thing, he is an unlikely romantic hero, far removed from
those he played earlier—the likes of Rick Blaine, Harry Morgan, Philip
Marlowe, and several other tough guys in risky situations, who won (or lost)
the lady of their choice in gunfights after villains were removed from their
path. He is not a war hero, in army or naval battles, roles he undertook during and after the war ended. And he is not a troubled man, as he is in *In a
Lonely Place* (1950), or a spy or a pilot or a deranged man and vicious killer,
roles with which he was familiar throughout his career. And though in a
comedy, he is not truly comic, though funny at times. The movie was shot in
the Glen Cove neighborhood at Long Island, the place Victorian-era man-
sions were built by the great tycoons of the early twentieth century, men

like J. P. Morgan, the Rockefellers, and many others of similar ilk, and perhaps it could be interpreted as a satire of high society of a bygone era, with all its frivolities and follies, while their hirelings live in separate quarters serving the whims of their masters. It seems like something of a prelude to the decades-later BBC show *Upstairs Downstairs* (and today's *Downton Abbey*), such dramas created when the two classes mingle. However, the movie, produced and directed by Billy Wilder, entranced audiences of its time and continues to do so today.

Here Bogart plays Linus, the middle-aged, multimillionaire chief executive of the Larrabee Company that produces among other things unbreakable glass made from sugarcane. Linus is the serious side of a duo of brothers; the younger, David, embodied by William Holden, is a playboy busier with marriages and divorces than with taking part in the onerous task of running a large conglomerate. But the oddest of all other oddities is that at his age (now nearing fifty-five) Bogart as Linus falls in love with the much younger— Sabrina, at twenty-two—daughter of the stolid, dignified chauffeur of the estate, Thomas Fairchild, played with sangfroid by John Williams, who had appeared as the unflappable detective in Hitchcock's *Dial M for Murder* (1954) and a blundering insurance agent in *To Catch a Thief* (1955). He is troubled by the impulsive behavior of his young daughter, a gawky young woman who hides in a tree and peeps at the high-class socialites who mix in the Larrabee parties with a sense of inferiority and jealousy. She is secretly in love with David, but he is already divorced and engaged again, and Sabrina is stuck in reverse, as her dreams of nebulous romance are not likely to be realized. Desperate, she attempts suicide, turning on the engines of eight cars at the spacious garage of the Larrabee residence. She would have been dead in a very short time if Linus had not passed by and smelled the exhaust; he entered the garage and brought back to life the impulsive young woman. Creaking with age and all, Bogart loads her on his shoulders and carries her upstairs and delivers her to her father. Nothing comes out of this as far as he is concerned, but events unfold that will allow him to notice her.

As Linus Larrabee, Bogart looks levelheaded, in a soft felt homburg, twirling an umbrella as he walks past the lawn to be driven to his office and tending to his duties, giving the impression of a man in complete control of himself amid his environment of tycoons and blasé aristocrats. He is used to his brother's fripperies and his octogenarian father's oddball ineptitudes (the old man fails to get an olive out of a bottle for his martini), though he is rather unhappy that his brother's impending marriage to a rich heiress (Martha Hyer), and the prospect of a big merger, may be imperiled.

Bogart holds on to his starchy image until something unexpected happens. Sabrina, the gawky young girl he had saved from suicide, returns from France, now an elegant debutante who immediately catches the eye of David, who drives her home from the train without realizing who she is. From that point on, the movie becomes a full-blown screwball comedy, and in the hands of Billy Wilder, a slightly frenzied one. David falls madly in love with her, without first realizing who she is. Wild scenes ensue; at a party, he sits on a pair of champagne glasses, something that puts him out of action, so Linus, who has also fallen for Sabrina, can make his move. But Sabrina, now confused by her own feelings for David, suddenly finds herself conscious of the mess she has created in the family, not to mention the distress to her father. She and Linus are seen taking a boat ride, and in any boat, Bogart, the proud owner of the luxury yawl *Santana*, is in his element. Sabrina is delighted with the ride, and her influence on him begins to show. She straightens the rim of his homburg, pulling the front down, so Bogart looks like his old self, a tough guy with a fedora aslant on his head, his rim lowered to look like Sam Spade or other hatted Bogart incarnations. In fact, there is something of old Bogie resurfacing here. He proposes a bold scheme: leaving the business to his younger brother, who seems to have come to his senses, and taking a boat trip to Paris with Sabrina. He knows she belongs there. But in the end he wavers. He changes his mind, leaves her to take the boat by herself, and goes back to the office for a crucial conference on the merger. But this time David is ahead of him. He has taken over the business and has decided to marry his fiancée, Elizabeth Tyson, so the merge of the two companies will be assured. He also has a speedboat ready to take Linus to the steamer, which is just at that point leaving the port. Linus goes, finds Sabrina sitting dejectedly on the deck, sticks his umbrella on the back of the belt of a passenger, lowers the rim of his homburg—and lo! The real Bogie stands up!

It seems odd indeed that all these things are happening in a movie, which can't really decide what it is: a screwball comedy, a hilarious farce, and, for what's worth, a romance between creaky middle-age and fresh-faced elegance. By all accounts this shouldn't work. Billy Wilder and Bogart were not getting along, there were scuffles on the set, Bogart was sore that he had been a second choice to Cary Grant, and he and the "golden boy" Holden, then at the peak of his career, weren't exactly sociable to one another. Bogart was also disgruntled that, he, a big star, for the first time in his career was without a long-term contract, as he had long ago detached himself from Warners, while his Santana Productions had failed (this movie was made by Paramount). The fact that he was also in ill health did not help his mood, although such worries did not seem to affect his screen presence.

No one on the set, including the director, believed that Bogart could supplant Cary Grant, for whom the role was created, in charm and elegance.

Sabrina (Audrey Hepburn) looks at Linus Larrabee (Bogart) as David Larrabee (William Holden) kisses her on the cheek. *Paramount Pictures/Photofest © Paramount Pictures*

But Bogart had been born into privilege, and his instincts could tell him what to do when a role demanded that he play a mannered gentleman. Bogart thrives on transformation, when the role he plays demands it. He can do excellently as an upper-crust wimpy boss who turns into a romantic lover. Never mind the dissimilarities in age. If Audrey Hepburn didn't object, why should we? In the end, the fedora did it. By turning the rim of his bowler hat down—a very consciously made minor detail—Sabrina had turned her man into the Bogart audiences knew. Bogart's face was long, and it grew longer as he aged. The fedora (with the rim down) changed the symmetry; it hid the long forehead, and let his intense black eyes shine more. Cary Grant's face, round to begin with, would have been turned into a caricature (it occasionally did), something like Red Skelton's. Not so flattering an image for the screen's king of charm.

Bogart was once described as a limited actor.[1] Maybe he is; there is no one who doesn't have limitations. But Bogart is unique in being Bogart, no matter where the winds (and whims) of moviemaking blow him. His formula for success, he once said, was, "Keep working." He did that, to the day he died. He schooled himself to be a man of many seasons.

35

THE BAREFOOT CONTESSA

(United Artists, 1954)

★ ★ ★

Director: Joseph L. Mankiewicz
Screenplay: Joseph L. Mankiewicz
Producer: Joseph L. Mankiewicz. *Cinematography:* Jack Cardiff. *Music Score:*
   Mario Nascimbene. *Editor:* William Hornbeck
Cast: Humphrey Bogart (Harry Dawes), Ava Gardner (Maria Vargas/Contessa
   Torlato-Favrini), Edmond O'Brien (Oscar Muldoon), Marius Goring
   (Alberto Bravano), Valentina Cortesa (Eleanor Torlato-Favrini),
   Rossano Brazzi (Vincenzo Torlato-Favrini), Elizabeth Sellars (Jerry),
   Warren Stevens (Kirk Edwards), Haria Zanoli (Maria's Mother),
   Renato Chiantoni (Maria's Father)
Released: September 29, 1954
Specs: 128 minutes; Technicolor
Availability: DVD (MGM Home Entertainment); streaming (Amazon)

The is one of the weaker vehicles for Humphrey Bogart, despite direction
by Joseph L. Mankiewicz and a star-studded cast, including Ava Gardner,
Marius Goring, Edmond O' Brian (in an Oscar-winning performance), and
Italian luminaries like Rossano Brazzi and Valentina Cortesa. The story is
about Hollywood manipulative practices, in a way attempting to replicate
the success Mankiewicz had achieved in *All about Eve* (1950). But this does
not come close to that famous masterpiece, and the possible reason is not
lack of good performances—with a few exceptions—but lack of unity in
the plot, which is fragmented and told in flashbacks, uneven in visual value
and dramatic intensity. The main reason for this, however, seems to be the
lackluster performance by Gardner, who seems to have no chemistry with

Bogart, and at least one historian[1] opines that her recent divorce with Frank Sinatra had affected her performance. Despite all of that, the movie has enough dramatic moments to be revisited.

Bogart is relegated to a narrator, commenting on the fortunes of the protagonist Gardner as Maria Vargas, a young Spanish flamenco dancer, whom he practically adopted and tried to lure to Hollywood, acting on orders by his boorish producer, Kirk Edwards (Warren Stevens), who decides to make a new star out of an unknown dancer in a Spanish village. Edwards is also aided by the fawning and sweaty Oscar Muldoon (Edmund O'Brien), who will stoop to anything to carry out orders from his domineering boss.

The story, told from the point of view of several individuals, begins with a scene in a cemetery, in the rain, where a funeral service is held, with the late contessa's marble statue literally dominating the scene, dwarfing the participants, as if to remind them they are still under her dazing spell.

We don't have a clue as to who she is at this point and why she died, yet soon enough Bogart—as Harry Dawes, a Hollywood writer and director—begins a woeful tale of one young Spanish woman who caught the eye of Hollywood executives and became a great star before her career took unexpected turns, including her premature death.

A scene or two later, we see a compliant Bogart—an image alien to his tough character we are used to—who is told in no uncertain terms by his ill-mannered boss that he either gets her or he is fired. Bogart plays godfather, taking the young Maria Vargas under his wing (resembling a Pygmalion without authority), and bringing her along, not without some difficulty, for the young woman has a recalcitrant and shrewish mother who doesn't want her to be an actress. Maria becomes his Cinderella, a term that flies through the dialogue often—even in Spanish, "La Generentola," also the name of an opera by Gioacchino Rossini. Along with the Italian phrase *Che sara sara* ("What will be will be"), the Cinderella theme is followed throughout, as Maria Vargas remains chaste until the prince comes to sweep her off her feet.

There are moments in this tardy, slow-rolling drama when sparks fly, as for instance when Maria, now in Hollywood, after her first film had drawn rave reviews from an adoring public, learns that her father had killed her mother. She is told that if she goes to his defense, her budding career will be in jeopardy. But she does go to the trial, where in defense of her father, she testifies that her mother was a monstrous woman and that her father had acted in self-defense. That result is an acquittal for her father, but instead of the disaster expected by her supporters, her fame doubles and she becomes a world-known celebrity. After fame and two more movies, she attracts the attentions of South American multimillionaire and notorious playboy Alberto Bravano (Marius Goring), an arrogant, immoral man, who flaunts his wealth as a shield from numerous scandals. He virtually steals her from Edwards, her producer, as Oscar, emboldened by Bravano's challenge and in his only act that shows spine, deserts his boss and goes off with Maria and her new protector. This part of the story is narrated by O'Brien, who is also one of those who attend her funeral, reminiscing. The oily press agent revolts against his revolting boss—and O'Brien wins an Oscar for his labors. Bogart's Harry Dawes stays off the screen for a while, but he picks up the thread not too long afterward. Has his Cinderella found her prince?

Not quite, it seems, for Maria has a yearning to find "her" people, so she joins a band of gypsies and dances—one moment Gardner truly comes alive. An Italian aristocrat, who sees her dance, picks up the thread of the story after she and Goring part. Up to this point, the movie's hypnotic pace generates little interest. Enter Rossano Brazzi, an Italian heartthrob of the times, as Count Vincenzo Torlato-Favrini, handsome, elegant, and wealthy, who falls madly in love with Maria and proposes marriage to her. His sister, Eleanor Favrini, played by a young-looking and elegant Valentina Cortesa, objects to the impulsive decision of her brother, but Maria, dazzled by the wealth of Vincenzo and falling for his good looks, accepts, and a luxurious wedding takes place.

On the wedding night, Maria waits in her nightgown, looking ravishing and expecting Vincenzo to come in and perform his nuptial obligations—but something entirely unexpected happens. Vincenzo does come in, does kiss her, and then steps back and begins his doleful tale. During the war, in 1942, to be specific, at Benghazi, he was "blown apart," and it was after much effort doctors were able to put him together again—except that he had lost his manhood.

An amazing scene, this is, in some ways, remindful of a Jake Barnes in Hemingway's *The Sun Also Rises*, which incidentally had been made into a movie about the same time, with the same Ava Gardner (as Lady Brett Ashley) and Tyrone Power (as Barnes). It is not known whether Mankiewicz had Hemingway's novel in mind, but the coincidence cries loud and clear. Many people had suffered that fate during the war. But what seems incongruous here is that Vincenzo had assumed that a woman of Maria's background would accept his condition just to become a countess. Neither of them was prepared for the shock of recognition: he for having wrongly assumed that she would accept him as he was; she at his presumption that a woman of her status and beauty would go along with his preposterous plan.

As Bogart tells his part of the tale, he mentions that the Maria/Contessa had visited him in his place and told him what had happened, and also that she was pregnant with another man's child. She was going to tell that to her husband. But when Maria faces Vincenzo with her truth, he shoots her twice. Bogart happened to be in the neighborhood and held the dead woman in his arms. He concludes his tale at the cemetery, as the rain finally stops, and we see Vincenzo in handcuffs taken away by the police.

That is the story of Cinderella, La Generentola, but with an unusual and shocking—and tragic—twist. Bogart cannot remember the Spanish word for it. In the end, it is a sad, tragic story, with sparks to evoke some pity and wonder, but not enough to make a masterpiece or even a near one. Bogart here looks old, bent, and out of step, and is too often absent from the screen. Age, cancer, and some fatigue were taking their toll. Still, he delivers his lines with the fortitude of a man who saw his dream of making up a queen out of a peasant girl crumble, while the commanding statue of hers reminds him (and us) of a line he had delivered earlier: "What dreams are made of."[2]

36

THE LEFT HAND OF GOD

(20th Century Fox, 1955)

★ ★ ★

Director: Edward Dmytryk
Screenplay: Alfred Hayes, adapted from the novel by William E. Barrett
Producer: Buddy Adler. *Cinematographer:* Franz Planter. *Music Score:* Victor
   Young. *Editor:* Dorothy Spencer
Cast: Humphrey Bogart (James Carmody, alias Father O'Shea), Gene Tierney
   (Anne Scott), Lee J. Cobb (Mieh Yang), Agnes Moorehead (Beryl
   Sigman), E. G. Marshall (Dr. David Sigman), Carl Benton Reid (Father
   Cornelius), Don Forbes (Father Keller), Victor Sen Ung (John Wong),
   Robert Morton (Reverend Martin)
Released: November 14, 1955
Specs: 87 minutes; color (CinemaScope)
Availability: DVD (20th Century Fox, the Limited Edition Series); streaming
   (Amazon)

Bogart biographer Nathaniel Benchley said that Bogart was a "man of many
sides,"[1] and as a biographer, he meant that Bogart, the person, could be a
man of contradictions, that people's memories had him as loving, loyal, and
warmhearted—but also as "a sadistic bastard." That view of many sides,
however, could be applied to Bogart the actor. He had played thugs, killers
of all sorts, gangsters and traitors (especially in his early days), tramps and
panhandlers, but he also could rise to heroics, playing clever sleuths, great
patriots, lovers, soldiers, navy captains, writers, spies (for a good cause), and
what have you. But playing a priest—and a fake one at that? After *The Left
Hand of God* was shown to audiences, as Benchley reports, someone asked

him, "Mr. Bogart, how does it feel to be a priest?" "How would *I* know?" was Bogart's response.[2]

Bogart was indeed a man of many parts, as Benchley said, controlled and gentlemanly, but also subject to fits of rage and drunkenness, and prone to teasing and needling those he thought pompous or ill-mannered. Bogart's secret of his chameleonic persona has not been completely fathomed by his biographers, though Lauren Bacall, his wife of eleven years, comes close to it: "He stood behind his choices," she explains. Further, "That intractable sense of self was Bogie's greatest strength."[3] That sense of self was indeed Bogart's strength and it is from that inexhaustible inner flow that he drew his ability—especially on the screen—to sketch the unparalleled variety in his roles. On the screen, he appeared assimilated by the context—and assimilating the parts he played. A priest, fake or not, was a variation on a theme by Humphrey Bogart, and *The Left Hand of God*, a movie that has become a cult classic to many, is a proof of that.

Directed by Edward Dmytryk, who had also directed Bogart in *The Caine Mutiny* two years earlier, *The Left Hand of God* was filmed in CinemaScope, a medium that requires filling up space around the actors, longer takes, and crowd scenes, in which the screen image of Bogart seems diminished. Even so, there is no doubt in the audience's mind who commands the scene. Most of the action, photographed in medium or long shots, deprived the viewer of the usual close-ups that probe Bogart's lined face. (When shooting *The African Queen*, Bogart told cinematographer Jack Cardiff that it took him years to grow his face and he had no use for any makeup.) But on the whole, the movie gains by the new medium, for, although it was only eighty-seven minutes, it had an epic sweep to it. Photographed in California—the Malibu Ranch belonging to 20th Century Fox[4] subbing for the Chinese mountains—the film has the glamor of adventure and romance, while the impassionate music score by Victor Young adds to the allure of the story.

The main plotline is about an American pilot, James Carmody, shot down and captured by a Chinese warlord, Mieh Yang, who forces Carmody into servitude, making him second in command, in name only, with orders to protect his territories. China at that time, 1947, was torn by civil war, and the numerous mission centers, both Catholic and Protestant, remained exposed to the whims of Yang. For the most part they were poor villages with minimal medical care and volunteer priests, doctors and nurses risking their lives to keep schools and churches open. Entirely by accident, Carmody runs into one of them, when, after two years in captivity, he finds a way to escape. Yang, who had been educated in an American university, is played by Lee J. Cobb, whose size, bald head, and Bronx accent make him an unlikely Chinese warlord, but Cobb seems to relish the part and to have fun exchanging verbal barbs with Bogart as Carmody. When pay time comes, Yang holds up a wooden cup, shakes it, and tosses dice from it, asking Carmody to do the same. If Yang wins, he keeps the money. Carmody gets tired of this life and asks to be released, but Yang refuses. But chance plays a part when the priest of a nearby mission, Father Peter O'Shea, is killed by one of Yang's bandits, and Carmody takes up the suggestion of a friendly servant, dons the priestly vestments of Father O'Shea, and slips away.

The film begins at this point, with him riding a donkey with his possessions, but during a storm a bridge collapses, the beast carrying his belongings falls into the gorge, and Carmody walks to a nearby mission, presenting himself as Father O'Shea. At first he feels uncomfortable with performing priestly duties, confining himself to giving sermons and blessing the sick and those dying. Soon he meets the resident doctor and his wife, Dr. David and Mrs. Beryl Sigman (E. G. Marshall and Agnes Moorehead), as well as the head nurse, Anne Scott (Gene Tierney). Dr. Sigman wants to close the mission, as life in a mountain outpost in the middle of the civil war seems unsustainable to him. But he gradually changes his mind, especially after Carmody seems to adjust to a priest's duties to the amazement of everyone around him, especially the young boys in the school; his personal servant, John Wong (Victor Sen Yung); and many of the villagers, who begin to worship their new priest, attributing his extraordinary abilities to "miracles." Part of his allure comes from that fact that he delivers some of his sermons in Chinese, which he had mastered during the years of his captivity.

But there are also signs of trouble. Anne Scott is attracted to Carmody, and as a devout Catholic, she becomes unsettled. This attraction, despite Carmody's efforts to ignore it, does not escape the attention of Beryl Sigman, who tells her husband about it. When the doctor finds it to be impossible, Beryl states that this is to be attributed to the priest's "magnetism," which everybody is talking about, and to the fact, as she calls it, that women's "biological structures" make it difficult for their minds to control their actions. Beryl also tells Carmody what she suspects, something that unsettles him, too, mostly because he himself has felt attracted to the beautiful young nurse. Beryl suggests that he visit Reverend Martin (Robert Morton), who is the minister of a nearby Protestant mission, for advice.

Carmody decides to visit Reverend Martin, telling the reverend who he really is and the story of his enslavement to Yang, in a flashback. A stunned Martin hears Carmody's extraordinary tale and his reasons for leaving the mission community. Carmody takes his collar off, determined not to wear

James Carmody, masquerading as Father O'Shea, ponders his role. *20th Century Fox Film Corporation/Photofest © 20th Century Fox Film Corporation*

it again, and then news arrives that Yang is bearing down with his army on the mission and the surrounding villages. Carmody puts on the collar again and returns to the village, where Dr. Sigman and his wife try to decide what to do. They think that the best solution is to resist, as the peasants who are capable of fighting in the surrounding villages outnumber Yang's forces. But Carmody knows from experience that this is folly. Yang would simply destroy everything in his path. What is the solution then? He tells the doctor and his wife that they cannot fight and they cannot run. Carmody then suggests his meeting Yang face-to-face. "It is me he wants," he says to the doctor.

Though the Sigmans think it a slim chance, they take it. Yang knows Carmody's abilities well and is willing to take him back for five years of servitude in exchange for the freedom of the mission. Carmody proposes that they play a game of dice—winner take all. They play a first round and Carmody wins. In the second round, wagering the freedom of a neighboring Protestant mission, Carmody draws only two 3s but still wins, as Yang throws the dice and comes up with two 2s. Careful not to gloat over his victory, knowing how capricious Yang can be, he waits a moment, adding suspense. Taking it as a joke, to save face, Yang disdainfully says the villages are not even worth the trouble destroying—and he departs. But before he does, Yang informs Carmody that two priests are coming to replace him, though he does not know that this was the result of a letter Carmody had sent to the bishop.

The two new priests soon arrive to replace Carmody, Father Cornelius (Carl Benton) and Father Keller (Don Forbes), both of whom know that Carmody is not a priest. Carmody tells them that no one knows; the previous night, however, he had told Anne Scott the truth. Father Cornelius requests that Carmody not tell the villagers who he is, since they believe that his turning back Yang was the result of a miracle. The bishop will decide what to do with Carmody. As he is departing, accompanied by the cheers of the innocent villagers and a song he has taught the children, the two priests watch the scene in amazement. Anne Scott, standing next to Father Cornelius, says, "I don't even know his name." "James Carmody," says Father Cornelius, as the latter climbs on his horse and rides off. Before he left, Carmody had told Father Cornelius and Father Keller how he had stopped Yang from destroying the village. The two priests attribute this to a miracle. Carmody says no; it was just the luck of the draw. Yet winning two times against Yang had the ring of something mystical. After all, nobody has ever explained what a miracle is.

When he came into the mission, Carmody had only one purpose: figuring out how to save himself from the wrath of Yang. His motives were self-preservation and nothing else. Yet the survivalist is seen praying before he goes out to meet Yang, though not kneeling, and does so despite the fact he is a nonbeliever. Yet he prays to save the village and possibly to get rid of his illicit passion for the beautiful Anne Scott. Whether his prayers were answered is not the point. What matters is that, once more, we see an indifferent-to-a-cause Bogart character entering the scene and exiting by achieving something extraordinary. He has saved a parish from destruction after serving it loyally, and perhaps divested himself of a carnal feeling that would have probably ended in disaster. As usual, what happens before and after does not matter. Carmody's visit to the village had transformed him— he did as well, or better, than any real priest would have done.

THE DESPERATE HOURS

(Paramount Pictures, 1955)

★ ★ ★

Director: William Wyler
Screenplay: Joseph Hayes, adapted from his novel and play
Producer: William Wyler. *Cinematographer:* Lee Garmes. *Music Score:* Gail
    Kubrik. *Editor:* Robert Swink
Cast: Humphrey Bogart (Glenn Griffin), Fredric March (Dan Hilliard), Martha
    Scott (Eleanor Hilliard), Gig Young (Chuck), Mary Murphy (Cindy
    Hilliard), Richard Eyer (Ralphie Hilliard), Arthur Kennedy (Jesse Bard),
    Dewey Martin (Hal Griffin), Robert Middleton (Sam Kobish)
Released: October 5, 1955
Specs: 122 minutes; black and white
Availability: DVD (Warner Home Video)

Twenty years after *The Petrified Forest*, Bogart reverted to Duke Mantee, the image of a born killer that many had thought had been eradicated from his mind for good. At least his wife, Lauren, thought so when she saw him leaning over their young baby boy, Stephen, whispering tender words to him.[1] As it happens, that image would be resurrected twice, once on live TV about that time (1955), when he reprised the Mantee role with Henry Fonda as Alan Squier and Lauren Bacall as Gabby Maple. The other instance was in *The Desperate Hours*, a film that revived a Mantee image that was even more vicious and unattractive than the earlier one, an image that one might have wished had been purged from his consciousness. The film, the last but one of Bogart's, was an intense thriller, and though it failed to attract wide audiences in its time, it still holds up as first-rate entertainment, still keeping a modern audience captive till the last minute.

In *The Desperate Hours*, Bogart is a criminal hunted down after a prison escape, and taking a group of innocent people hostage until he gets his way. As Glenn Griffin, Bogart looks aged, worn-out, tough as always, but reconciled to the prospect that this might be his last stand. He is also crafty, quick on his feet, unbending in his demands, and holding on to the bitter end. His face shows wear and tear, as, at the age of fifty-five, he was already showing signs of advanced cancer that was to take his life less than two years later. Director William Wyler transformed an average melodrama about an innocent family taken hostage by a gang of hoods to a first-rate thriller, with unexpected twists, a mood of despair (as the title suggests), and unrelieved suspense. Fredric March, paired with Bogart for the first time (originally the role was going to be given to Spencer Tracy, who backed off at the last hour), delivers a convincing performance as Dan Hilliard, an average parent of a suburban family who takes matters into his own hands when all else fails. Martha Scott plays Eleanor Hilliard, the distressed mother of two children who endures the ordeal and holds the family together at a moment of crisis. Mary Murphy plays Martha's young daughter Cindy, who shares her family's distress, and Richard Eyer is Ralphie—the impulsive boy who likes to be called the Ralph.

As Glenn Griffin, Bogart is an escaped convict who grouped with his much younger brother, Hal, and the beastly Sam Kobish, played by Robert Middleton, a known heavy (he is truly so, at six foot three and nearly three hundred pounds) to form a trio that invaded the Hilliard house and terrorized the family for nearly thirty-six hours before the drama is resolved. Griffin's left jaw had been broken by police chief Jessy Bard (Arthur Kennedy), who is now in charge of the pursuit of the convicts. There is a full police alert, and Bard knows that Griffin will stay in town until a connection from Pittsburgh arrives at Indianapolis to bring Griffin money and means to escape. That scheme fails, as the person driving to meet the convicts has been arrested, and now the money must be mailed to Hilliard's office. Of necessity, Griffin has to let the family go pick it up. Cindy goes with her dad, and he advises her to stay away and go to a friend's at night, but she doesn't. When Cindy's boyfriend, Chuck (Gig Young), sees her outside the house looking tense, he begins to suspect something but he still seems slow to catch up with what is going on—an improbability in the plot. Young, nearing middle age, also seems an unlikely suitor of the teenaged Cindy. He does become more energetic in the last part of the movie, when, after he knows what is going, he acts decisively to rescue Cindy from her captors.

The action is tense from the get-go. The treatment of the hostages is brutal, but Griffin knows that to win he must keep them alive and functioning. Hilliard, as previously said, is allowed to go to his office the next morning to pick up the money, but he finds no mail addressed to him with the money. He gives instructions that he be told immediately when any mail arrives. But an unexpected event brings another twist to the plot. A garbage collector, Mr. Paterson (Walter Baldwin), stops at the house to collect garbage and old newspapers, and Griffin forces Eleanor Hilliard to write him a check, as it was his payday. But when Paterson enters the garage to pick up old newspapers, he discovers the getaway car of the fugitives and reads the tag number. Kobish jumps on the old man's truck as he leaves, forces him to an isolated spot, and shoots him as he tries to escape. Kobish uses three bullets of the only gun the gang possess, and that proves critical later.

The most dramatic part of the plot comes when Griffin's younger brother, Hal, fed up with his brother's and Kobish's cruelty to the family, decides to go away on his own and escape. Griffin cannot stop him, as Hal has the gun he took from Mrs. Hilliard, but gives him some money, wishing him the best of luck. Hal is probably the only person Griffin cares for. Hal stops at a diner to call to his brother, but there are police cars surrounding the area and one of them recognizes him. As Hal tries to shoot his way out, he is wounded by firing policemen, falls to the ground, and is unable to avoid an oncoming truck that crushes him to death. When he is identified as a Griffin after he is shot, Bard knows he has his man. He gives orders to have the Hilliard house surrounded by police cars, and his men stop Hilliard, who had gone out to collect the money mailed to Griffin at the Special Delivery Post Office. Bard and the local sheriff debate their approach, but an FBI man gives the go-ahead to allow Hilliard to go in and deliver the money to Griffin. Bard persuades Hilliard to take a gun with him, but the latter empties the gun of bullets before he goes in.

This trick saves the day. Griffin searches him, takes the money and the gun, not knowing that it is empty of bullets. Hilliard, his indignation now turned to fury, knows now that he will be the winner, as Kobish, having received his share of the money, becomes careless. When Kobish opens the door to see what is going on outside, Hilliard shuts the door on him and the latter's gun falls inside during the scuffle. Kobish rushes out screaming in pain as a hail of bullets from the police razes him to the ground. Hilliard picks up the gun, and he is now the possessor of the only a serviceable gun in the house. When Griffin tries to force him to go out first while holding the empty gun against his son's head, Hilliard calls to the boy to run away. Griffin's gun, of course, misfires, and now it is Hilliard's turn to play avenger. As Griffin pleads to be killed, here and now, Hilliard refuses, and then reveals to Griffin that his brother is dead. He has his satisfaction as the avenger, then and there, with a modicum of justified cruelty in his voice.

The approaching end seems tragic. Bogart's Griffin is as bad as any hood he had played in the past Bogart's face is lined, his shoulders hunched, his movements showing wear, and his speech a bit slurred. He is authoritative and the unquestioned leader of the gang, but his brother's leaving the group hurts him, and he shows some humanity, giving Hal part of the money that had reached him in the meantime. But he waits for the big pay to arrive, having no alternative. These are desperate hours too, as the title suggests. And when he finally loses the battle, he implores Hilliard to kill him, after the latter tells him his brother is dead. But Bogart has long practiced playing losers. When Bard, having caged his beast, commands that he come out, his hands behind his head, Griffin does so and walks toward the police. But he suddenly tosses his empty gun against the flashlight blinding him, smashing it, a suicidal move of defiance. As bullets pepper him, he crawls forward with incredible dying energy, yard for yard, until he is finally stilled. His face is up, one of his glazed eyes vacantly looking at the camera, until a blanket covers it.

No joy is derived from this end, no catharsis, just a bit of pity and fear for the human condition. The released family is rejoined by Chuck, happy enough, but not rejoicing. The family has gone through gruesome hours but comes out intact in the end. Maybe the ethos of Hollywood requires this. But Bogart's presence has driven a wedge in what might be called the shiny mirror of happy suburban coexistence. A bit like Hitchcock's *Shadow of a Doubt*, *Desperate Hours* is a movie that unveils, perhaps without Hitchcock's slickness, disturbing undercurrents of danger lurking beneath the shining surface of daily routine. A mealy-mouthed head of a family, mockingly called "Pop" by the sardonic gangster, is challenged by a young boy's daring acts of disobedience, thus awakening the father's slumbering rage, when his nest of siblings is menaced. After such heroism, after justice is done, will the family settle to its earlier serene suburban routine and happiness? Perhaps there is shadow of a doubt here too, as the blood of corpses is seeping down into the front-yard lawn.

38

THE HARDER THEY FALL

(Columbia Pictures, 1956)

★ ★ ★ ★

Director: Mark Robson
Screenplay: Philip Yordan, adapted from the novel by Budd Schulberg
Producer: Philip Yordan. *Cinematography:* Burnett Guffey. *Music Score:* Hugo
    Friedhofer. *Editor:* Jerome Thomas
Cast: Humphrey Bogart (Eddie Willis), Rod Steiger (Nick Benko), Ian Sterling
    (Beth Willis), Mike Lane (Toro Moreno), Max Baer (Buddy Brannen),
    Carlos Montalban (Louis Agrandi), Nehemiah Persoff (Leo), Harold J.
    Stone (Art Leavitt), Pat Comiskey (Gus Dundee)
Released: May 9, 1956
Specs: 109 minutes; black and white
Availability: DVD (TCM Vault: *Humphrey Bogart: The Columbia Pictures
    Collection*)

This was Bogart's last film, and for all intents and purposes, it demonstrates how well he had mastered his acting skills just before his untimely death. Pitted against one of the powerhouses of method acting, Rod Steiger, whose explosive energies seem to blow up the screen, Bogart stands his ground and shows that it does not take a high-pitched voice and crunching gestures to dominate a scene. This all comes with a moral attached. Two men, one a well-known sports writer, the other a boxing racketeer, try to promote a dim-witted Goliath as a would-be boxing champion on entirely false grounds. Both men are wrongdoers, but only one ends up knowing his wrongdoing. This is melodrama of high order, a scathing indictment of the boxing business of the times, and a gem of a movie that should not be missed. It is also one of Bogart's best performances.

The movie is known for its harsh realism, gory ring sequences, and sharp verbal exchanges (in today's cinema it would mean an expletive every three or four words). Eddie Willis (Bogart) has been writing sports columns for many years, but now that his newspaper has gone out of business, he is unemployed, with no savings, and strapped for cash. For years, Nick Benko—a name that implies ethnicity but without pressing the point—is a boxing racketeer whose business thrives on promoting new talent by any means, fair or foul, getting unknowns and raising them to be contenders the easiest way possible: fixing fights. This time around he has brought a giant from Argentina, Toro Moreno (Mike Lane), who has arrived escorted by his manager, Louis Agrandi (Carlos Montalban). Mike Lane, who plays Moreno, was a six-foot-eight, 275-pound giant (his weight is given as 278 in the movie), making his debut as an actor; he continued to play supersized heroes, including Hercules. The movie includes real pro fighters, including Max Baer (1909–1959), who had actually defeated Primo Carnera, a boxer comparable in size to Lane, for the World Championship in 1934. Baer appears as Buddy Brannen in the film, the heavyweight champion against whom Moreno fights. Pat Comiskey is Gus Dundee, another of Toro's opponents, and Jersey Jo Wolcott, is George, Toro's trainer.

It is George, one of Benko's hirelings, who gives Toro his first test in the ring. The giant quickly shows that he has clay feet, and his future seems bleak to Eddie Willis. When pressed by Benko to find a solution, Willis proposes that they move to California, where "freak shows" are popular, and the whole entourage moves there, except for Benko, who stays behind to take care of other business. The first fixed fight is a disaster, as Toro floors an opponent who is reluctant to go down with a vertical hit on the head, which causes boos from the crowd and a gasp of astonishment from a former friend of Willis, Art Leavitt (Harold J. Stone), a radio announcer, who has a hard time believing that his friend would go along with this fraudulent scheme. It takes all of Eddie's powers of persuasion to convince Art not to expose the fake fight by broadcasting the lie it was, let alone report the fake fight to the Boxing Commission.

As things get tougher, Eddie asserts himself, taking over the management from Leo (Nehemiah Persoff), Nick's lieutenant and the manager of the operation, who is as corrupt and unscrupulous as his boss. Things get worse, though, as the helpless giant does not seem to realize that his "victories" are faked and that he is being used by Benko, who bets large odds against him. When Toro's friend and manager, Louis, is dismissed rudely and sent back to Argentina, Eddie undertakes to convince Toro to stay on. But Eddie still lies to Toro about his potential and the fact that he is a hopeless amateur. Eddie finally decides to demonstrate this point to Toro by having George, the old veteran and member of Nick's retinue, hit him with a right, for real. Toro tumbles to the ground, stunned to know that his run for the championship is a travesty. Eddie still convinces him to stay and take on the champion of the world, Brannen, because then he could return to his native country with money—as even a fake championship, or a well-paid loss, is better than nothing.

The story is complicated by Eddie's own struggles to get rid of his self-loathing for having compromised his self-respect (and principles) for the sake of his bank account. One thing that compels him to stay is his wife, the charming Ian Sterling playing Beth Willis: Eddie wants to provide her with the lifestyle she deserves, after his failure to build an economic basis, having lived from paycheck to paycheck for years writing a column. Beth senses his struggle and proposes to come out west to find him, but Nick is enraged (he is nothing but throughout the movie), knowing that if Beth comes to Eddie, the latter would be influenced by her, perhaps his conscience awakened, which is the last thing Benko wants, that is, people with a conscience.

But as the entourage moves east, Toro gets more and more chances to demonstrate his boxing "talents," or at least take on opponents of Benko's choice, always with the help of the compromiser Eddie. He takes on a washed-up boxer and former champion, Gus Dundee (Pat Comiskey), who had suffered a serious head injury after a fifteen-round match with Buddy Brannen (Max Baer). Both Eddie and Benko know of this injury, but for the sake of promoting a "big victory" for young Toro, they sign him up for the match. The result is devastating. After a few blows, even from a hapless amateur like Toro, Dundee staggers and falls on his face, goes into a coma, and dies a few days later. Brannen laughs at the idea that Toro was really the one who had caused a head injury to Dundee, as he knows that he had caused that injury himself. But he takes on the amateurish Toro because the gate is expected to clear over $1 million.

Action and moral dilemmas converge at this point. After another shouting scuffle with Benko (most of the shouting done by the latter), Willis fires back by saying that Toro has been fed lies so far, so why not try the truth? When Toro knows who he really is after a right from an aging George floors him, he still decides to take on the challenger for the sake of making enough money to return to his native Argentina. George, not without some affection for the helpless amateur and knowing what Toro can suffer from Brannen, advises him to defend himself by using his reach and by staying close during exchanges. But that does not prevent Brannen from tearing Toro's face to pieces on the ring, breaking his jaw. Toro had made a choice to get the beating for the sake of the payment, but after the books are fixed by Leo, the amazed Eddie finds out that Toro is getting, "after expenses," only forty-nine dollars. On top of that, Benko plans to arrange more matches for Toro, counting on the fact that his protégée now has a name, having fought the heavyweight champion of the world. Eddie rushes to get Toro to the airport, and on the way there, he gives Toro his share of the deal, the $26,000 he had in an envelope, saying that money was his. Toro whispers, "That's a lot of money in my country." Eddie counters, "That's a lot of money in any country."

The story has an epilogue. Benko with two of his men storms into Eddie's apartment, where his wife is present, and demands that he get his money back—the $26,000 Eddie gave to Toro, and other moneys, up to $75,000, total. After a shouting match—most of the shouting done by the excited Benko—Eddie promises Benko that he will get his money back, in time. He plans to write again. "I wouldn't give twenty-six cents for your future," Benko snarls, before exiting the door with his goons.

The camera shows Beth, his wife, with a smile on her face. As Eddie sits before his typewriter and starts hitting the keys, she goes over to the kitchen, pours a cup of coffee and brings it to him. She reads the title of the book and the first sentence:

The Harder They Fall
   The boxing business must rid itself of the evil influences of racketeers and crooked managers even if it takes an Act of Congress to do it.

These are Bogart's final words on the screen—albeit written, not spoken. They might as well have been his epitaph. Bogart had an image that he had labored for nearly three decades to hone and to perfect—the man who rises from the ashes by pulling himself together after a moral crisis, straightening the ship just before it capsizes. Even Duke Mantee had a glance of admiration for the man who was giving his life to ensure a girl he loved would have a future. Sam Spade recounts his code of honor that demands that "a man must do something about it when his partner is killed." The list goes on with Rick Blaine, head and shoulders above the others when he bids farewell to Ilsa. Then there is Harry Morgan in *To Have and Have Not*, Philip Marlowe of *The Big Sleep*, Vincent Parry of *The Dark Passage*, Frank McCloud of *Key Largo*, Joe Barrett in *Tokyo Joe*, Harry Smith of *Sirocco*, Charlie Allnut of *The African Queen*, Jim Carmody of *The Left Hand of God*, and Eddie Willis in this movie. Only Bogart could do this metamorphosis with class and sincerity, without much ado or the onus of sentimentality, which he hated. Although he sprinkles Edward G. Robinson with bullets in *Key Largo*, most of this transformation occurs without excessive violence or a show of hatred. There is a delicate balance in Bogart's persona, which, when at his best roles, shows him viewing the world around him as a sympathetic observer, one who takes the blows fate has dealt him without rancor. His screen image is that of a hard-bitten man, one who has seen it all but decides to stay in the arena, for he believes the world around him has meaning.

As Benko exits in *The Harder They Fall*, tossing his contempt for the people he cheats and describing them as "sitting in front of their TVs, with their bellies full of beer," Eddie starts hitting the keys of his typewriter. He will tell the people that Benko despises the truth, even if he only gets twenty-six cents for it.

FILMOGRAPHY

This complete filmography includes star ratings as found in the key at the beginning of this book. Each film's director is indicated in parentheses.

Broadway's Like That (Murray Roth), Vitaphone, 1930. ★

A Devil with Women (Irving Cummings), Fox, 1930. ★ ★

Up the River (John Ford), Fox, 1930. ★

Body and Soul (Alfred Santell), Fox, 1931. ★

Bad Sister (Hobart Henley), Universal, 1931. ★

Women of All Nations (Raoul Walsh), Fox, 1931. ★

A Holy Terror (Irving Cummings), Fox, 1931. ★

Love Affair (Thornton Freeland), Columbia, 1932. ★ ★

Big City Blues (Mervyn LeRoy), Warner Bros., 1932. ★ ★

Three on a Match (Mervyn LeRoy), Warner Bros., 1932. ★ ★

Midnight (Chester Erskine), All-Star Productions, 1934. ★

The Petrified Forest (Archie Mayo), Warner Bros., 1936. DVD: Warner Home Video, 2005. Blu-ray: Warner Bros., 2013. ★ ★ ★ ★

Bullets or Ballots (William Keighley), First National/Warner Bros., 1936. DVD: Warner Home Video, 2006. ★ ★ ★

Two against the World (William McGann), First National/Warner Bros., 1936. ★ ★

China Clipper (Ray Enright), First National/Warner Bros., 1936. ★ ★

Isle of Fury (Frank McDonald), Warner Bros., 1936. ★ ★

Black Legion (Archie Mayo), Warner Bros., 1937. DVD: Warner Home Video, 2006. ★ ★ ★

The Great O'Malley (William Dieterle), Warner Bros., 1937. ★ ★

Marked Woman (Lloyd Bacon), First National/Warner Bros., 1937. DVD: Warner Home Video, 2006. ★ ★ ★

Kid Galahad (Michael Curtiz), Warner Bros., 1937. DVD, Warner Home Video, 2012. ★ ★ ★

San Quentin (Lloyd Bacon), First National/Warner Bros., 1937. ★ ★

Dead End (William Wyler), United Artists/Samuel Goldwyn, 1937. DVD: HBO Home Video, 2014. ★ ★ ★

Stand-In (Tay Garnett), United Artists, 1937. ★ ★

Swing Your Lady (Ray Enright), Warner Bros., 1938. ★ ★

Crime School (Lewis Seiler), First National/Warner Bros., 1938. ★ ★

Men Are Such Fools (Busby Berkley), Warner Bros., 1938. ★ ★

The Amazing Dr. Clitterhouse (Anatole Litvak), First National/Warner Bros., 1938. DVD: Warner Home Video, 2012. ★ ★ ★

Racket Busters (Lloyd Bacon), Warner Bros./Cosmopolitan, 1938. ★ ★

Angels with Dirty Faces (Michael Curtiz), First National/Warner Bros., 1938. ★ ★ ★

King of the Underworld (Lewis Seiler), Warner Bros., 1939. ★ ★

The Oklahoma Kid (Lloyd Bacon), Warner Bros., 1939. ★ ★

Dark Victory (Edmund Goulding), First National/Warner Bros., 1939. ★ ★ ★

You Can't Get Away with Murder (Lewis Seiler), First National/Warner Bros., 1939. ★ ★

The Roaring Twenties (Raoul Walsh), Warner Bros., 1939. DVD: Warner Home Video, 2005. ★ ★ ★

The Return of Dr. X (Vincent Sherman), First National/Warner Bros., 1939. ★

Virginia City (Michael Curtiz), First National/Warner Bros., 1940. ★ ★

It All Came True (Lewis Seiler), First National/Warner Bros., 1940. DVD: Warner Home Video, 2012. ★ ★ ★

Brother Orchid (Lloyd Bacon), Warner Bros./First National, 1940. ★ ★

They Drive by Night (Raoul Walsh), Warner Bros./First National, 1940. DVD: Warner Home Video, 2003. ★ ★ ★

High Sierra (Raoul Walsh), Warner Bros./First National, 1941. DVD: Warner Home Video, 2006. ★ ★ ★ ★

The Wagons Roll at Night (Roy Enright), Warner Bros./First National, 1941. ★ ★ ★

The Maltese Falcon (John Huston), Warner Bros./First National, 1941. DVD: Warner Home Video, 2006. Blu-ray, 2012. ★ ★ ★ ★ ★

All Through the Night (Vincent Sherman), Warner Bros./First National, 1942. DVD: Warner Home Video, 2012. ★ ★ ★

The Big Shot (Lewis Seiler), Warner Bros./First National, 1942. ★ ★

Across the Pacific, (John Huston), Warner Bros./First National, 1942. DVD: Turner Classic Movies, 2012. ★ ★ ★

Casablanca (Michael Curtiz), Warner Bros./First National, 1942. DVD: Warner Home Video Two-Disc Special Edition, 2003. Blu-ray: Warner Home Video 2012. Blu-ray: Three-Disc Ultimate Collection, 2012. ★ ★ ★ ★ ★

Action in the North Atlantic (Lloyd Bacon), Warner Bros./First National, 1943. DVD: Turner Classic Movies, 2012. ★ ★ ★

Thank Your Lucky Stars (David Butler), Warner Bros./First National, 1943. ★ ★

Sahara (Zoltan Korda), Columbia Pictures, 1943. DVD: Sony Pictures, 2001. ★ ★ ★ ★

Passage to Marseille (Michael Curtiz), Warner Bros./First National, 1944. DVD: Turner Classic Movies, *Humphrey Bogart: The Signature Collection, Volume 2*, 2012. ★ ★ ★

To Have and Have Not (Howard Hawks), Warner Bros./First National, 1944. DVD: Warner Home Video, 2003. Blu-ray: *Best of Bogart Collection*, 2014. ★ ★ ★ ★

Conflict (Curtis Bernhardt), Warner Bros./First National, 1945. ★ ★

Two Guys from Milwaukee (David Butler), Warner Bros./First National, 1946. ★ ★

The Big Sleep (Howard Hawks), Warner Bros./First National, 1946. DVD: Warner Home Video, 2000. Blu-ray: *Best of Bogart Collection*, 2014. ★ ★ ★ ★

Dead Reckoning (John Cromwell), Columbia Pictures, 1947. DVD: Warner Home Video, 2006. ★ ★ ★

The Two Mrs. Carrolls, Cir. (Peter Godfrey), Warner Bros./First National, 1947. ★ ★

Dark Passage (Delmar Daves), Warner Bros./First National, 1947. DVD: DVD, Warner Home Video, 2006. ★ ★ ★

Always Together (Frederick De Cordova), Warner Bros./First National, 1948. ★ ★

The Treasure of Sierra Madre (John Huston), Warner Bros./First National, 1948. DVD: Warner Home Video, 2010. ★ ★ ★ ★ ★

Key Largo (John Huston), Warner Bros./First National, 1948. DVD: Warner Home Video, 2006. ★ ★ ★

Knock on Any Door (Nicholas Ray), Santana Productions, 1949. DVD: DVD: Columbia Pictures Collection, 2014. ★ ★ ★

Tokyo Joe (Stuart Heisler), Santana Productions, 1949. DVD: Sony Pictures, 2004. ★ ★

Chain Lightning (Stuart Heisler), Warner Bros./First National, 1950. ★ ★

In a Lonely Place (Nicholas Ray), Santana Productions, 1950. DVD: Columbia Pictures Collection, 2013. ★ ★ ★ ★

Sirocco (Curtis Bernhardt), Santana Productions, 1951. DVD: Columbia Pictures, 2014. ★ ★ ★

The African Queen (John Huston), Horizon-Romulus Productions, 1951. DVD: Warner Home Video, 2010. Blu-ray: Paramount Home Entertainment, 2010. ★ ★ ★ ★ ★

The Enforcer (Bretaigne Windust; Raoul Walsh, uncredited), Warner Bros., 1951. DVD: Olive Films, 2013. ★ ★ ★ ★

Deadline—U.S.A. (Richard Brooks), 20th Century Fox, 1951. ★ ★

Battle Circus (Richard Brooks), MGM, 1953. DVD: Warner Home Video, 2013. ★ ★

Beat the Devil (John Huston), Santana-Romulus Productions, 1954. DVD: Echo Bridge, 2003. ★ ★ ★

The Caine Mutiny (Edward Dmytryk), Stanley Kramer Productions, 1954. DVD: Sony Pictures, 2010. ★ ★ ★ ★

Sabrina (Billy Wilder), Paramount Pictures. 1954. DVD: Warner Home Video, 2001. Blu-ray: Warner Home Video, 2014. ★ ★ ★ ★

The Barefoot Contessa (Joseph L. Mankiewicz), United Artists, 1954. DVD: MGM, 2001. ★ ★ ★

We're No Angels (Michael Curtiz), Paramount Pictures, 1955. ★ ★

The Left Hand of God (Edward Dmytryk), 20th Century Fox. 1955. DVD: 20th Century Fox, Limited Edition, 2011. ★ ★ ★

The Desperate Hours (William Wyler), Paramount Pictures, 1955. DVD: Warner Home Video, 2003. ★ ★ ★

The Harder They Fall (Mark Robson), Columbia Pictures, 1956. DVD: Turner Classic Movies, Columbia Pictures, 2014. ★ ★ ★ ★

NOTES

INTRODUCTION

1. A. M. Sperber and Eric Lax, *Bogart* (New York: William Morrow and Company, 1997), 221.

2. David Thomson, *A Biographical Dictionary of Film*, 3rd ed. (New York: Alfred A. Knopf, 1996), 71.

3. Sperber and Lax, *Bogart*, 151.

4. Sperber and Lax, *Bogart*.

5. Nathaniel Benchley, *Humphrey Bogart* (Boston: Little, Brown and Company, 1975), 45.

CHAPTER I

1. Nathaniel Benchley, *Humphrey Bogart* (Boston: Little, Brown and Company, 1975), 57; italics are in the original.

2. Benchley, *Humphrey Bogart*, 57.

CHAPTER 2

1. The Eighteenth Amendment, known as the Volstead Act, was ratified by Congress in 1919, and was repealed by Congress with the Twenty-First Amendment in 1933.

2. Robinson was awarded a posthumous Honorary Oscar shortly after his death in 1973.

CHAPTER 3

1. Quoted in A. M. Sperber and Eric Lax, *Bogart* (New York: William Morrow and Company, 1997), 79.
2. Sperber and Lax, *Bogart*, 79.
3. Leonard Maltin, *Movie Guide* (New York: A Signet Book, 2011), 137.

CHAPTER 4

1. The woes of the Bogart-Methot marriage are described by many, but perhaps the most interesting are to be found in several places in Stephen Bogart's, *Bogart: In Search of My Father* (New York: Dutton Books, 1995), 214–28.

CHAPTER 6

1. They reappeared in *Angels with Dirty Faces* (1938), playing basically the same roles, alongside James Cagney and Humphrey Bogart.

CHAPTER 10

1. The father of Alan Hale Jr., who played the Skipper in *Gilligan's Island*, a popular TV show in the 1960s. Father and son look (and behave) amazingly alike.
2. In a featurette included in the DVD extras called "Divided Highway: The Story of *They Drive by Night*," Leonard Maltin explains that the story was recycled from an earlier version, as Warners used the A. I. Bezzerides novel, adding the tale of the truckers in the movie.

CHAPTER 11

1. A. M. Sperber and Eric Lax, *Bogart* (New York: William Morrow and Company), 116.

CHAPTER 12

1. A. M. Sperber and Eric Lax, *Bogart* (New York: William Morrow and Company, 1997), 148.

2. In his running commentary on *Casablanca*, Warner Bros. DVD (2003) and in the "Special Features" of the 2012 Blu-ray edition.

3. Foster Hirsch, *Film Noir: The Dark Side of the Screen* (New York: A De Capo Paperback, 1981), 13.

4. The word *gunsel* or *gosling* means gunman, but is also a slang derivative of catamite, a homosexual. The word was so rarely used that it escaped the attention of the Breen Office.

5. The full quotation is from Shakespeare's *The Tempest*, spoken by Prospero (act III, scene i, lines 41–42).

CHAPTER 13

1. Sherman, at an advanced age, shares a DVD commentary with Eric Lax, Bogart biographer, and most of his observations relate to his handling of the group scenes.

CHAPTER 14

1. Huston actually was called up before the movie ended, and the direction was assigned to Vincent Sherman, who finished the movie uncredited. See A. M. Sperber and Eric Lax, *Bogart* (New York: William Morrow and Company, 1997), 631.

CHAPTER 15

1. Nathaniel Benchley, *Humphrey Bogart* (Boston: Little, Brown and Company, 1975), 100.

2. Leonard Maltin, *Leonard Maltin's 2011 Movie Guide* (New York: A Signet Book, 2011), 218.

3. David Thomson, *Biographical Dictionary of Film*, 3rd ed. (New York: Alfred A. Knopf, 1996). Thomson debunks *Casablanca* in several entries in his book, but gives some credit to director Michael Curtiz for transforming "soppiness to such an extent that reason and taste began to waver" (p. 165).

4. Raft had signed with Warners in 1940 and had already costarred with Bogart in *They Drive by Night* (1940), where he played the lead.

5. Michael B. Druxman, author and screenwriter, in a DVD documentary: *"The Maltese Falcon": One Magnificent Bird*, Warner Bros., 2006.

6. See *Bogart*, A.M Sperber and Eric Lax (New York: William Morrow and Company, 1997), 190.

7. Richard Schickel, "'The Genuine Article,' Appreciation by Richard Schickel," in *Bogie: A Celebration of the Life and Films of Humphrey Bogart* (New York: St. Martin's Press, 2006), 15.

8. Ann Sheridan, who had worked with Bogart in *It All Came True* (1940) and *They Drive by Night* (1940), was allegedly dropped because of her American presence—and accent; a European actress would fill the role better.

9. See Sperber and Lax, *Bogart*, 191.

10. Sperber and Lax, in *Bogart*, state that the coauthors Julius and Philip Epstein visited Selznick in his office and said that *Casablanca* wasn't much of a movie, just "another shit like *Algiers*" (1928). Selznick immediately said yes.

11. See Sperber and Lax, *Bogart*, 199.

12. He had already played Hal Ebbing, a Nazi agent organizing a plot inside the United States, in Warners' *All Through the Night* (1942), in which Bogart is his pursuer.

13. Roger Ebert, in his commentary to *Casablanca* on the DVD and Blu-ray versions says that the letters function like Hitchcock's McGuffin, an object that everybody wants, and for that reason they control the plot.

14. See Sperber and Lax, *Bogart*, 199.

15. Elliot Carpenter played the piano behind the scenes.

16. In Murray Burnett and Joan Alison's play, he was a lawyer, married with children, but this detail was dropped from the script, and his past was left vague. See Druxman in the 2003 DVD commentary.

17. *Casablanca* won two other Oscars, for Best Picture and Best Screenwriting, out of a total seven nominations. The other nominations were for Best Actor (Bogart), Best Supporting Actor (Claude Rains), Best Cinematography, Best Film Editing, and Best Music Score.

CHAPTER 16

1. A. M. Sperber and Eric Lax report that President Roosevelt praised the movie, as he knew that it would be impossible to defeat Hitler's Germany without the help of the USSR. See *Bogart* (New York: William Morrow and Company, 1997), 195.

2. This line is a paraphrase of what is said to Odysseus by Teiresias in *The Odyssey*, when he sees him in Hades, there implying that Odysseus will be an explorer on land. Here, O'Hara means that he's had enough of being a sailor and sea life with its constant perils.

3. For photo and other information, refer to Nathaniel Benchley's, *Humphrey Bogart* (Boston: Little, Brown and Company, 1975), 18.

4. Benchley, *Humphrey Bogart*, 178. Benchley, in the same passage, explains that the name *Santana* is derivative of *Santa Ana*, the name of the wind that blows from the desert in Southern California.

CHAPTER 17

1. Kenneth Koyen, "War in the Sahara, Bogart Style," *Eve's Magazine*, 2001, www.evesmag.com/bogart.htm. Retrieved December 17, 2014.

CHAPTER 19

1. The US government was uncomfortable with an American associating himself with Cuban hooligans, as Cuba was then under the dictatorship of Batista.
2. This was Carmichael's first screen appearance, but Hawks chose him for his spirited performances in nightclubs and because he was a friend both of Hawks and Bacall.
3. Initially spelled *Bacal*. It was changed to Bacall after Charles Feldman, Howard Hawks's agent, misspelled it when he traveled to New York to escort her to Hollywood. A. M. Sperger and Eric Lax, *Bogart* (New York: William Morrow and Company, 1997), 239.
4. Lauren Bacall, *Lauren Bacall by Myself* (New York: Alfred A. Knopf, 1979), 93.
5. Sperber and Lax, *Bogart*, 247.
6. Bacall, *Lauren Bacall by Myself*, 94.
7. Bacall, *Lauren Bacall by Myself*, 98.
8. Bacall, *Lauren Bacall by Myself*, 96.
9. A hypnotist in the novel *Trilby* (1984) by George du Maurier. This was usually a man of power or influence who manipulated persons (usually female) under his control.
10. A Cypriot sculptor who created a statue of a woman that was so beautiful he fell in love with it (her). Pygmalion implored Aphrodite to bring her to life; the goddess granted his wish, and Pygmalion married her. George Bernard Shaw based his play, *Pygmalion*, on this myth, teaching Eliza Doolittle, a flower girl, to speak correct English.

CHAPTER 20

1. In the novel, the glass scene and the erotic overtones do not exist. Marlowe simply walks out after the saleswoman gives him a description of Geiger. Andrew Sarris calls the taking off of her glasses by Malone one of the "erotic epiphanies" of

American cinema. See *"You Ain't Heard Nothing Yet": The American Talking Film, History & Memory, 1927–1949* (New York: Oxford University Press, 1998), 404.

2. For more on this point, see Foster Hirsch, *Film Noir: The Dark Side of the Screen* (New York: Da Capo Press, 1981), 75.

3. See Lauren Bacall, *Lauren Bacall by Myself* (New York: Alfred A. Knopf, 1979), 121.

4. Raymond Chandler, *The Big Sleep* (Rockville, MD: Serenity Publishers, 2013), 30.

5. One of the most famed scenes in the 1946 version of the film. Bacall pays Marlowe and then starts a conversation about race horses, stating that she likes to be rated as a horse rider, "depending who is in the saddle."

6. Dick Powell in *Murder, My Sweet*, 1944; Elliott Gould in Robert Altman's *The Long Goodbye*, 1973; and by Robert Mitchum in the British film *The Big Sleep*, in 1978.

CHAPTER 21

1. Gulf City is a ghost town, completely abandoned in 1920, forty miles from Tampa, Florida.

CHAPTER 22

1. Lauren Bacall, *Lauren Bacall by Myself* (New York: Alfred A. Knopf, 1979), 152.

CHAPTER 23

1. Bogart was wearing a wig, as he had lost almost all of his hair by that time, and this first one is replaced in the film twice later, as his hairpiece was adjusted to his appearance in the dusty desert. See Eric Lax's commentary on the DVD.

2. Eric Lax, in his DVD commentary.

CHAPTER 24

1. Lauren Bacall, as is well known, outlived Bogart by several decades and died in August 2014. In her book, *Lauren Bacall by Myself* (New York: Alfred A. Knopf, 1979), she describes in detail her first meeting with Bogart and their first pairing in *To Have and Have Not*, and subsequently the eleven-plus years they lived together as a married couple.

2. A vulgar term for a drunk, disrespectful woman.

3. A. M. Sperber and Eric Lax, *Bogart* (New York: William Morrow and Company, 1997), 370–72.

4. Sperber and Lax, *Bogart*, 397–403.

5. Andrew Sarris, *"You Ain't Heard Nothing Yet": The American Talking Film History & Memory, 1927–1949* (New York: Oxford University Press, 1998), 73–74.

CHAPTER 25

1. This collector's box contains five Bogart movies: *Love Affair* (1932), one of the first he ever made; *Tokyo Joe* (1949); *Knock on Any Doo*r (1949); *Sirocco* (1951); and *The Harder They Fall* (1956), Bogart's last movie. All but the first of these are included in this book.

2. For an account of Bogart's Santana Productions, see A. M. Sperber and Eric Lax, *Bogart* (New York: William Morrow and Company, 1997), 423–24.

3. Sperber and Lax, *Bogart*, 424.

4. Sperber and Lax, *Bogart*, 423.

CHAPTER 26

1. The five movies were *Knock on Any Door* (1949), *Tokyo Joe* (1949), *In a Lonely Place* (1950), *Sirocco* (1951), and *Beat the Devil* (1954).

CHAPTER 27

1. Richard Schickel, *Bogie: A Celebration of the Life and Films of Humphrey Bogart* (New York: St. Martin's Press, 2006), 15.

2. Foster Hirsch, *The Dark Side of the Screen: Film Noir* (New York: Da Capo Press, 1981), 194–95.

3. The modern Santana Films was initiated by Stephen Humphrey Bogart, son of Humphrey Bogart and Lauren Bacall, comanager of the company created in 2013, which is supported by the Humphrey Bogart Estate. Writer/Producer/Director Steve Anderson has directed the company's first film, *This Last Lonely Place* (2014), an updated film noir, which has already won acclaim as the winner of the Special Jury Prize for Cinematography at the Newport Film Festival.

4. Horizon-Romulus, Stanley Kramer Company, Paramount, Figaro Incorporated, 20th Century Fox, Columbia Pictures, from 1951 to 1956.

CHAPTER 28

1. For the record, the four Santana Productions were *Knock on Any Door* (1949), *Tokyo Joe* (1949), *In a Lonely Place* (1950), and *Sirocco* (1951), and all four were distributed by Columbia Pictures. One more, and the last one, was *Beat the Devil* (1954), made with Romulus Productions and distributed by United Artists. Nathaniel Benchley, *Humphrey Bogart* (Boston: Little, Brown and Company, 1975), 239. All five are included in this book.

CHAPTER 29

1. For a colorful account of the shooting in Africa, see Lauren Bacall's memoirs, *Lauren Bacall by Myself* (New York: Alfred A. Knopf, 1979), 182–201. Also, of great interest is the memoir of Katharine Hepburn, titled *The Making of* The African Queen (New York: Alfred A. Knopf, 1987). This is an altogether engaging and candid description of the adventure in the African jungles, but told as Hepburn's personal impressions of all involved and is not a critique of the movie.

2. *The African Queen* also won a nomination for Best Director (John Huston). The film was registered in the National Film Preservation Board, USA, in 1994.

3. If one counts *High Sierra* (1941), the screenplay of which was written by Huston, adapted from the novel by W. R. Burnett (who also coauthored the script). The others were *The Maltese Falcon* (1941), *Across the Pacific* (1942), *Key Largo* (1948), *The Treasure of Sierra Madre* (1948), and *Beat the Devil* (1954).

4. All the underwater scenes were at the studios in England, as the waters of the river were polluted and full of diseases, and the actors could not be exposed to these dangers. Blu-ray Special Features, "Embracing Chaos: Making *The African Queen*." The commentators on the Blu-ray feature include Richard Schickel; Martin Scorsese; Richard Brooks, the cinematographer; Jack Cardiff; John Huston; and Katharine Hepburn, among others.

5. A television show (1966–1971) that ridiculed the Germans during World War II.

CHAPTER 30

1. A. M. Sperber and Eric Lax, *Bogart* (New York: William Morrow and Company, 1997), 431.

2. Sperber and Lax, *Bogart*, 431.

CHAPTER 31

1. The other was a short, *U.S. Savings Bonds Trailer*. Nathaniel Benchley, *Humphrey Bogart* (Boston: Little, Brown and Company, 1975), 239.

2. Some consider *Battle Circus* a prelude of sorts to the famous and Oscar-winning *M°A°S°H°* of 1970, directed by Robert Altman and written by Ring Lardner Jr. And, of course, to the long-running and popular TV show of that name.

3. Allyson, born in 1917, was thirty-six at the time, eighteen years Bogart's junior.

4. The relationship of Bogart and Romanoff was described in some detail and much color by Nathaniel Benchley in his book *Humphrey Bogart* (Boston: Little, Brown and Company, 1975), 202–17.

CHAPTER 32

1. Lauren Bacall, *Lauren Bacall by Myself* (New York: Alfred A. Knopf, 1979), 205.

2. Nathaniel Benchley, *Humphrey Bogart* (Boston: Little, Brown and Company, 1975), 219.

3. Benchley, *Humphrey Bogart*, 220–21.

CHAPTER 33

1. The winner for Best Actor in 1954 was Marlon Brando for *On the Waterfront*. The nominations were for Best Picture, Best Actor (Bogart), Best Supporting Actor (Tom Tully), Best Screenplay, Best Sound (John P. Livadary), Best Editing, and Best Music Score.

2. A. M. Sperber and Eric Lax, *Bogart* (New York: William Morrow and Company, 1997), 480.

3. Dmytryk was one of the original Hollywood Ten, who had served a year in prison, and then resumed his career after recanting and naming names. Sperber and Lax, *Bogart*, 481.

4. This fact is disputed by film historians Richard Piña and Ken Bowser in their DVD commentary on *The Caine Mutiny* (Columbia, 2010).

5. The play concentrates only on the trial and altogether omits the love story. See the DVD commentary mentioned in note 4.

6. There are several explanations of how this happened, but the one most commonly believed is that while in the navy someone hit him with a chain. The badly mauled upper lip suffered a severe wound and the navy doctors botched the attempt to repair it. Subsequent face-lifts did not quite succeed in eliminating it. For a full account of the incident, see Nathaniel Benchley, *Humphrey Bogart* (Boston: Little, Brown and Company, 1975), 19. Also Stephen Humphrey Bogart's, *Bogart: In Search of My Father* (New York: Dutton Books, 1995), 137–38. Stephen Bogart, son of the actor, has some doubts about the veracity of Benchley's account. See Bogart, *Bogart*, 136–37.

7. See footnote 4.

CHAPTER 34

1. David Thompson, *A Biographical Dictionary of Film*, 3rd ed. (New York: Alfred A. Knopf, 1996), 71.

CHAPTER 35

1. A. M. Sperber and Eric Lax, *Bogart* (New York: William Morrow and Company, 1997), 496.
2. The last line he delivers in *The Maltese Falcon*.

CHAPTER 36

1. Nathaniel Benchley, *Humphrey Bogart* (Boston: Little, Brown and Company, 1975), 5.
2. Benchley, *Humphrey Bogart*, 224.
3. Lauren Bacall, *Lauren Bacall by Myself* (New York: Alfred A. Knopf, 1979), 226.
4. See the introductory essay "The Left Hand of God," by Julie Kirgo, in the Limited Edition Series booklet, 20th Century Fox DVD (2011).

CHAPTER 37

1. The story is told by Bogart's biographer Nathaniel Benchley, *Humphrey Bogart* (Boston: Little, Brown and Company), 166.

BIBLIOGRAPHY

Bacall, Lauren. *Lauren Bacall by Myself*. New York: Alfred A. Knopf, 1979.
———. *Lauren Bacall Now*. New York: Alfred A. Knopf, 1994.
Balfour, Alan G. *Humphrey Bogart: Pyramid Illustrated History of the Movies*. New York: Pyramid Communications, 1973.
Benchley, Nathaniel. *Humphrey Bogart*. Boston: Little, Brown and Company, 1975.
Bogart, Stephen Humphrey. *Bogart: In Search of My Father*. New York: Dutton Books, 1995.
Chandler, Raymond. *The Big Sleep*. Rockville, MD: Serenity Publishers, 2013.
Coe, Jonathan. *Humphrey Bogart: Take It and Like It*. London: Bloomsbury, 1991.
Early, Steven. *An Introduction to American Movies*. New York: A Mentor Book, 1979.
Ebert, Roger. *The Great Movies*. New York: Broadway Books, 2002.
Eisenschitz, Bernard. *Humphry Bogart*. Paris: Le Terrain Vague, 1967.
Gehman, Richard. *Bogart: An Intimate Biography*. New York: Faucet-Gold Medal, 1965.
Harmetz, Aljean. *The Making of Casablanca: Bogart, Bergman, and World War II*. New York: Hyperion Books, 2002.
Hepburn, Katharine. *The Making of* The African Queen: *Or How I Went to Africa with Bogart, Bacall and Huston and Almost Lost My Mind*. New York: Alfred A. Knopf, 1987.
Hirsch, Foster. *The Dark Side of the Screen: Film Noir*. New York: Da Capo Press, 1981.
Hyams, Joe. *Bogie: the Biography of Humphrey Bogart*. New York: New American Library, 1966.
Koyen, Kenneth. "War in the Sahara, Bogart Style." *Eve's Magazine*. Retrieved December 17, 2014, from www.evesmagazine/bogart.htm.

Leamer, Lawrence. *As Time Goes By: The Life of Ingrid Bergman*. New York: Harper and Row, 1986.

Lebo, Harlan. Casablanca*: Behind the Scenes*. New York: Fireside, 1992.

Maltin, Leonard. *Leonard Martin's 2011 Movie Guide*. New York: A Signet Book, 2011.

Miller, Frank. Casablanca*, as Time Goes By: 50th Anniversary Commemorative*. Atlanta, GA: Turner Publishing, 1992.

Norman, Barry. *The 100 Best Films of the Century*. New York: A Citadel Press Book, 1993.

Pettigrew, Terrence. *The Definitive Study of His Film Career*. New York: Proteus, 1981.

Sarris, Andrew, *"You Ain't Heard Nothing Yet": The American Talking Film History & Memory, 1927–1929*. New York: Oxford University Press, 1998.

Schickel, Richard. New York: St. Martin's Press, 2006.

———. *Keepers: the Greatest Films—and Personal Favorites—of a Movie-Going Lifetime*. New York: Alfred A. Knopf, 2015.

Sperber, A. M. and Eric Lax. *Bogart*. New York: William Morrow and Company, 1997.

Thomson, David. *Biographical Dictionary of Film*, 3rd ed. New York: Alfred A. Knopf, 1996.

———. *Humphrey Bogart*. New York: Faber and Faber, 2010.

INDEX

ABOUT THE AUTHOR

Constantine Santas received his BA at Knox College, his MA at the University of Illinois at Urbana, and his PhD in American Literature at Northwestern University. He taught at Milwaukee Downer College (1962–1964) and University of Illinois at Chicago (1964–1971) and served as chairman of the English Department at Flagler College from 1971 to 2002, when he retired as Professor Emeritus. At Flagler College he initiated a program of Film Studies in 1987, which continues today. His publications include *Aristotelis Valaoritis* (1976), *Responding to Film* (2002), *The Epic in Film* (2007), and *The Epic Films of David Lean* (2011); he is a coauthor of *The Encyclopedia of Epic Films* (2014). Santas has published literary and film articles and has authored translations of three ancient Greek plays, performed at the Flagler College Auditorium. He was a recipient of a Danforth Foundation Teacher Grant (1967–1969) and was included in *Choice* as an Outstanding National Teacher in 1983, in *American Hellenic Who's Who* in 1990, and in *Who's Who among American Teachers* in 2002. Currently, he is working on a translation of Homer's *The Odyssey*.